GOODBYE GLUTEN

HAPPY HEALTHY DELICIOUS EATING WITH A TEXAS TWIST

KIM STANFORD

BILL BACKHAUS

Number 4 in the Great American Cooking Series

University of North Texas Press • Denton, Texas

10 9 8 7 6 5 4 3 2 1

Permissions:
University of North Texas Press
1155 Union Circle #311336
Denton, TX 76203-5017

The paper used in this book meets the minimum requirements of the American National Standard for
Permanence of Paper for Printed Library Materials, z39.48.1984. Binding materials have been chosen
for durability.

Library of Congress Cataloging-in-Publication Data

Stanford, Kim, 1957- author.
  Goodbye gluten : happy healthy delicious eating with a Texas twist / by Kim Stanford and Bill
Backhaus. -- First edition.
     pages cm. -- (Number 4 in the Great American cooking series)
  Includes index.
  Summary: Book is a collection of gluten-free recipes with an emphasis on Southwestern and Texas
flavors.
   ISBN 978-1-57441-578-0 (pbk. : alk. paper) -- ISBN 978-1-57441-588-9 (ebook)
1. Gluten-free diet. 2. Gluten-free diet--Recipes. 3. Cooking--Texas. 4. Cooking, American--
Southwestern style. I. Backhaus, Bill, 1958- author. II. Title. III. Series: Great American cooking
series ; no. 4.
  RM237.86.S74 2014
  641.5'638--dc23
                        2014021208

Goodbye Gluten: Happy Healthy Delicious Eating with a Texas Twist is Number 4 in the Great American
Cooking Series
The electronic edition of this book was made possible by the support of the Vick Family Foundation.

Designed by Mark Lerner

DISCLAIMER: Nothing in this book should be construed as a substitute for medical care or advice.
This information is provided for education only.

I dedicate this book to my mother, Irene. She taught
me to cook the way her mother taught her to cook. My
favorite line from my mother is, "Honey, I didn't teach
you to ride in the backseat. . . ."
—Kim Stanford

I dedicate this cookbook to my family and all the great
cooks who have taught me so much. Thank you.
—Bill Backhaus

CONTENTS

ACKNOWLEDGMENTS

My sweet husband, Mike Wolf for his amazing support!

Many thanks to Kathleen Davis Neindorff, our publishing consultant and literary agent for her expertise, patience and dedication. What an antonishing talent in the literary world!

We would like to thank Matt Bowman, our photographer, for his incredible work. His expertise and creativity take "food photography" to a whole new level. We thank you, Matt, for your support and for your outstanding work on this cookbook. Without you, this would not have been possible.

And thanks to Kim Pierce, our editor. She completely understood and resonated with our passion for this book and applied her expertise to make this into a book we love. We love your passion, Kim. We also want to thank Tiffany Yates Martin, for her endless hours of editing and helping us with every detail. Her creative support and ideas were endless, as well as her dynamic energy. She is also the most generous person we know when it comes to love and time. We would also like to thank her husband, Joel Martin, for being so incredibly wonderful. What a sweet team they make.

We would to thank David Kimmel for his encouragement and his vast wealth of information, which he so generously shared.

We would also like to thank the following for their support: Zita Raymond, for her continuous encouragement, Jamie Barshop, Debbie Dehaas, Narda and John Hurt, Caroline and John Trube, Jan and Mitchell Davis, Tina Amberboy, Hollis Amberboy, Mimi Hinton, Kent and Lisa Thomas, Maggie and Joe Longley, Patrick and Tracy Parker, Patti Halliday, Katheryn Lott, Retta Kelley, Gloria Smejakl, Celia Bunt, Rene Harbison, Robert Ondash, Radhia Gleis, Kowecha Street, Trish Bales, Caren Coe, Whitney Morrison, David Garrido, Richie West, Kevin Heady, and Cindy Satel.

INTRODUCTION

Every day, health-conscious individuals say, "Goodbye, gluten!" For people with celiac disease, it's a no-brainer: That's when gluten, a protein found in wheat, barley, and rye, triggers an immune reaction in the gut. But celiac disease is only half of the gluten-free story. There's a whole other group of people who have discovered that they feel better or get a noticeable uptick in their health when they avoid gluten. They're kicking the gluten habit, too. It's no surprise both groups are fueling a huge interest in gluten-free products and cooking.

That's where we come in. Once married and now divorced, we got together to write this cookbook because we wanted to share what we have learned about living gluten-free and loving it. Bill was diagnosed with celiac disease 35 years ago, when it was hard to find foods that were gluten-free and the ones out there were usually dreadful. Kim went gluten-free 10 years ago at the suggestion of an alternative health practitioner after she was diagnosed with thyroid issues. She avoided surgery, and the difference in how she feels is like day and night. So we've lived the gluten-free life from both perspectives.

Few people realize how many everyday foods can contain gluten. These include breads, processed foods, condiments, salad dressings, desserts, ketchup, mustard, soy sauce, mayonnaise, sauces, gravy, cured meats, sausage, hot dogs, flavored and herbed cheeses (yes, cheeses), blue-veined (bread mold-based) blue cheeses, barbecue sauces, broth, bouillon, tamari, marinades, spice blends (ingredients used to prevent caking), spiced nuts, puddings, cocoa, vinegars, cooking wines, flavored liqueurs and spirits, some ice creams, and even vitamins.

In addition to coming up with fabulous recipes, a big part of our journey was the exhaustive search to figure out what ingredients we could safely use. Long before the Food and Drug Administration adopted the "gluten-free" labeling rule that goes into effect August 2014, we de-glutenized our worlds, and the legwork we've done—

reading labels, looking up ingredient information, writing to companies—makes it that much easier for you. And let's face it: Manufacturers aren't going to put "gluten-free" on all the labels of their gluten-free products; it's not worth it to them. We drill down beyond the "gluten free" label. As a result of our research, we name *brand names* in our recipes and include a complete Goodbye Gluten Pantry List of items you know you can trust.

But let's get down to the real reason you'll love this cookbook: It's all about good eating and not feeling deprived. Between us, we've devised more than 200 recipes for people who are gluten-intolerant but tired of missing out on their favorite foods. We've come up with a Thin and Crispy Sicilian Pizza Crust for great pizzas, Gruyère and Asiago Cheese Biscuits, and Mexican Grilled Polenta Bruschetta for bread-lovers, and Buttermilk Marinated Pan-Fried Chicken if you're missing that iconic American food. And if you're locked out of sumptuous desserts, you have only to sample our Chocolate-Chip Pecan Cookies, Buttermilk Toffee Cake, Red Velvet Cake, and Southern Belle Peach Pie to feel whole again.

Our recipes span the globe, but we're especially partial to those that connect to our Texas roots. That means lots of Southern favorites: You have to try our Havarti, Gouda and Cheddar Cheese Grits and use our New Orleans Peach Bourbon Basting Sauce on pork or chicken. We also love the bright, zesty flavors of Southwest-style Mexican, and you can taste that influence in dishes like Guadalajara Gazpacho, Lasagna with Mexican Crema—even Hoochy-Coo Hatch Green Chile Polenta. But more than anything, our recipes are just plain good eating: How about some Asian Chicken Salad with Crystallized Ginger, Beef Tenderloin Stroganoff, or Artichoke-Feta Fritters?

We started this project a few years ago. Bill called Kim to tell her he was compiling a gluten-free cookbook and asked if she'd like to co-write it. Kim was instantly on board.

We hope you enjoy cooking and eating these wonderful recipes as much as we enjoyed developing them. And we hope you're as happy as we are saying, "Goodbye, gluten!"

ABOUT BILL AND HIS JOURNEY

A fourth-generation Texan who practices law in Dallas, Bill was diagnosed with celiac disease in 1981 while attending graduate school at Georgetown University in Washington, D.C, a time when the few gluten-free foods out there were mostly terrible. Surely life would lose its meaning without pizza, cheeseburgers, fried chicken, spaghetti, and bread. His landscape of deprivation seemed endless.

Bill realized that if he wanted something really good to eat, he was probably going to have to make it himself. So he began cooking and reading recipes. Thousands of recipes. He spent hours experimenting in the kitchen. Studying recipes became a hobby, and cooking, a passion. European cuisine, Texas ranch grub, and authentic Southwest/Mexican flavors inspire him in the kitchen.

Bill's the guy whipping up Herb-Crusted Parmesan Chicken, Bacon-Wrapped Quail With Dates and Jalapeno and Gisela's Huevos Rancheros Especiale. He's also a big meat man and has included plenty of barbecued meats, rubs, and sauces. He's been perfecting gluten-free recipes for more than twenty years now, and the best of the best are in these pages.

ABOUT KIM AND HER JOURNEY

Kim is a former financial consultant who grew up in North Texas, lives in Austin and loves Southern home cooking and baking. She adores sweets, bold flavors, and zesty spices. Yes, she's the baker on the team. She would also never think of giving up pizza or desserts. Many of her recipes come from her Texas childhood, but with razzle-dazzle twists, and some of her cakes and breads are so good, she bakes them for clients.

Kim was facing surgery for a thyroid condition when she said goodbye to gluten, as well as embracing organic whenever possible. After a short time, the changes were amazing: her thyroid was healing and surgery was no longer in the picture. Her skin cleared, her allergies were 99 percent gone, her hair became thicker and shinier. In time, her energy soared and she lost unwanted pounds without conscious effort.

Kim's contributions include her very own Devil's Devil's Food Chocolate Cake, a spectacular Italian Crema Cake, breads like her Mr. Fluffy Pepper Jack and Cheddar Cheese Biscuits, main dishes that scream with flavor, sauces to make salads and vegetables come alive, and side dishes for the perfect dinner or party. But it's Kim's Famous Over-the-Top Bananas Foster Cake that will make you think you've died and gone to heaven.

THE GLUTEN-FREE LIFESTYLE

Who benefits from the gluten-free lifestyle is a moving target in medical circles.

Celiac disease is "easy" enough. Also known as "white flour disease," it is both a disease of malabsorption—meaning nutrients are not properly absorbed by the digestive system—and an autoimmune reaction to gluten, a group of related proteins found most commonly in wheat, barley, and rye.

For people with celiac disease, eating gluten-laden foods can cause real damage to the intestinal wall and the inability to absorb certain nutrients. People with celiac disease are also more susceptible to other diseases and health problems. But here's the thing: Celiac disease has certain clear-cut markers and can be diagnosed with blood tests and confirmed with a biopsy. If you have it, adopting the gluten-free lifestyle isn't optional. It's required.

A landmark 2003 epidemiological study by Dr. Alessio Fasano, founder and head of the University of Maryland Center for Celiac Research, is the source of the oft-quoted figure that one in 133 Americans have celiac disease. That number's thought to be a lot higher now.[1]

In more recent years, something called non-celiac gluten intolerance, or gluten sensitivity, has popped up on the health radar. More and more the thinking is that celiac disease is an extreme on a broad spectrum of sensitivity to gluten. But there's no tight definition of NCGI. It can have many of the same symptoms as celiac disease—diarrhea, constipation, bloating, or abdominal pain—and a lot of self-diagnosed people also mention other symptoms, like skin problems, fatigue, joint pain and headaches.

---

1 Fasano A, Berti I, Geraduzzi T, Not T, Colletti RB, Drago S, Elitsur Y, Green PH, Guandalini S, Hill ID, Pietzak M, Ventura A, Thorpe M, Kryszak D, Fornaroli F, Wassermann SS, Murray JA, Horvath K, "Prevalence of celiac disease in at-risk and not-at-risk groups in the United States: a large multicenter study," *Arch. Intern. Med.* 2003 Feb 10: 163(3): 286–92.

The key is, there's no blood marker, as with celiac disease. Dr. Daniel Leffler, M.D. told CNN in 2011, "This is something we're just beginning to get our heads around." He's an assistant professor of medicine at Harvard Medical School, a gastroenterologist at Beth Israel Deaconess Medical Center in Boston and, like Fasano, a leading voice in the gluten-free discussion. There's even debate about whether gluten sensitivity has the same cause as celiac disease, in which there's a clear erosion of the intestinal wall. Experts say that the number of people with gluten sensitivity could be many times higher than the number with celiac disease.

So what's up with this? Why this sudden uptick in gluten sensitivity? Researchers in the know generally cite two theories. First, gluten is hard to digest from the get-go—for everyone, and this may be a ramping up of that difficulty. People didn't start eating wheat—and by extension, gluten—until about 10,000 years ago with the agricultural revolution. Some guts just never fully adjusted. Add to that the fact that many modern wheat varieties contain higher levels of gluten (which artisan bakers love for the spring and elasticity it gives their bread doughs) and the greater prevalence of products containing gluten, and you have a set-up for heightened sensitivity.

The other theory is that we're too clean. You read that right. Too clean. That's the hygiene hypothesis. WebMD says, "Children aren't exposed adequately to antigens in the environment while their immune systems are developing," paraphrasing Dr. Stefano Guandalini, medical director at the University of Chicago's Celiac Disease Center and another important voice in the gluten debate. Put simply, if your gut doesn't get some practice dealing with these antigens, the immune system won't tolerate gluten. Guandalini says that celiac disease is relatively rare in less sanitary, developing countries.

All the publicity about the gluten-free lifestyle, happily encouraged by food companies making gluten-free products, has prompted a lot of people to try it when other remedies haven't helped their symptoms. But we think part of successfully adopting a gluten-free diet is also getting plenty of good, nutritious, and wholesome food. We live in a world where preserving, processing, pasteurizing, coloring, bleaching, and sterilizing often destroy or diminish the natural nutrients that otherwise would be present in foods.

Home-cooking is really the only way to guarantee tasty, gluten-free meals and the only way to assure that ingredients are gluten-free. When we cook, we use the best ingredients available, preferably fresh, either organic or from our local farmers markets, which helps us avoid pesticides, hormones, antibiotics, and other unwanted additives. We also prefer local, organic, grass-fed beef and pork, organic chicken, and other organic meats when it's possible to obtain these.

We're only too happy to point you back to the kitchen, where we've had so much fun, so let's get cooking!

TIP: We believe that limiting refined sugars and starches, corn fructose sodas (you know, the ones sweetened with high-fructose corn syrup), unhealthy saturated fats, and nutrient-bereft junk food will help heal a stressed digestive system. We also avoid artificial sweeteners and artificial sugar–based sweeteners, as our experience has been that they can cause bloating, gas, and diarrhea.

APPETIZERS

Now you can serve and enjoy gluten-free appetizers that are really appetizing. We have perfected little bites that are so good we bet they will have your guests requesting recipes. They'll forget all about gluten-free.

More than just crowd-pleasers, our appetizers are easy to make, and most can be prepared well ahead of time. Don't let the long ingredient lists fool you. Most go together quickly, whether we're talking Smoked Gouda-Cheddar Pimento Cheese spread on our Savory Tarragon Biscuits or Mexican Grilled Polenta Bruschetta. (Okay, you do have to make the bruschetta in two steps.)

Bill says, "Face it: Appetizers are party food. I don't know any families or individuals who serve appetizers before a meal on a regular basis. Kim probably does. The purpose of appetizers is to tempt your guests' palates, and prevent them from getting ravenously hungry before the meal is served, or getting too carried away with the social beverages."

Kim says that would be Bill's friends. She believes you are simply tempting and teasing your guests to stay for the incredible dinner you spent all day preparing.

We both think you just need two or three appetizers, but they'd better be top-notch. Ours will make a very good impression—even better if you pair them with good-quality beverages. We also like appetizers that can be served cold or at room temperature. After all, we want to spend as much time as we can with our guests.

SAN FRANCISCO ARTICHOKE SPINACH DIP

Not your traditional recipe for boring spinach dip, it's the perfect blend of Romano, Asiago and Parmesan cheeses that make this happen. Don't skimp on the quality of the cheese. It will really make all the difference.   YIELD: 12 TO 14 SERVINGS

¼ cup finely diced onion

1 tablespoon olive oil

2 (8-ounce) packages cream cheese, softened

½ cup mayonnaise: Hellmann's, Kraft, or Spectrum

¼ teaspoon Dijon mustard: Maille Dijon Originale Mustard or Grey Poupon

1 (10-ounce) package frozen chopped spinach, thawed and squeezed dry

1 (14-ounce) can artichoke hearts, drained, squeezed dry in paper towels: California Girl, Maria, or Reese

3 cloves garlic, minced

3 tablespoons fresh lemon juice

1½ cup grated Parmesan cheese

¾ cup grated Romano cheese

½ cup grated Asiago cheese

½ teaspoon sea salt

Preheat oven to 375 F. Lightly grease a 9 x 11-inch baking dish. In a small skillet, sauté onion in olive oil until translucent.

In a bowl, mix together cream cheese, mayonnaise, and mustard until smooth. Fold in sautéed onion, spinach, artichoke hearts, garlic, lemon juice, cheeses, and salt. Mix well and pour into baking dish.

Cover and bake 20 minutes. Remove cover. Bake for 5 to 7 minutes longer, or until top is golden. Serve with small slices of gluten-free toast, crackers, or tortilla chips.

SMOKED GOUDA-CHEDDAR PIMENTO CHEESE SPREAD

Smoky Gouda and sharp cheddar amp up this Southern staple so you just can't stop eating it. It makes an awesome sandwich on our Savory Tarragon Biscuits (see Page 203), or you can serve it as a dip with crackers or fresh vegetables.   YIELD: 2 CUPS

3 tablespoons chopped roasted red bell pepper: Mezzetta

1 jalapeño pepper or serrano chile, seeded, deveined, and finely chopped (see note)

1½ cups freshly grated smoked Gouda (see note)

1½ cups freshly grated sharp cheddar cheese: Kraft Natural or Boar's Head (see note)

1 cup freshly grated Havarti cheese (see note)

½ cup mayonnaise: Hellmann's, Kraft, or Spectrum

3 tablespoons pimentos, drained well and chopped

⅛ teaspoon cayenne pepper: McCormick or Spice Islands

½ teaspoon freshly ground black pepper

½ teaspoon fresh lemon juice

¼ teaspoon white pepper: Spice Islands

Purée red pepper and jalapeño or serrano chile. Set aside.

In a mixing bowl, blend together cheeses, mayonnaise, pimentos, cayenne pepper, black pepper, lemon juice, and white pepper. Mix well. Gently mash in puréed peppers with fork (do not use blender), and mix well. Chill. Serve with your favorite gluten-free cracker.

NOTE: Do not use pre-grated cheese. The ingredient used to prevent the cheese from sticking, often potato flour, will make it impossible to achieve the right final texture. Also, wear plastic gloves when handling hot peppers.

PEAR-BRANDIED PECAN BAKED BRIE

Awesome . . . Brie with a punch. The pear brandy and pecans make this one stand out in a crowd.   YIELD: 10 TO 12 SERVINGS.

1 tablespoon butter

1 clove garlic, finely minced

4 tablespoons chopped pecans

8 to 10 sliced, fresh mushrooms

1 tablespoon pear brandy: Clear Creek Pear Brandy

1 teaspoon chopped fresh tarragon

1 (8-ounce) wedge good quality Brie, rind removed

Preheat oven to 350 F.

Melt butter in medium, nonstick skillet over medium heat. Add garlic and pecans. Cook until lightly browned. Do not burn. Add mushrooms and cook for about 5 minutes.

Remove skillet from stove and add brandy. Sprinkle with tarragon.

Place Brie in small baking dish. Pour pecan-mushroom mixture over Brie. Bake for 20 minutes or until bubbly. Serve with small gluten-free crackers or toast.

JALAPEÑO HAVARTI DIP

Heavenly Havarti . . . with saucy jalapeño to boot. This is the most sensational dip, especially on fresh veggies, which are chock-full of vitamins, minerals, phytonutrients, and fiber.   YIELD: 1 ¼ CUP

8 ounces Havarti cheese: Boar's Head, shredded

2 ounces white cheddar cheese: Boar's Head, shredded

4 tablespoons mayonnaise: Hellmann's, Kraft, or Spectrum

1 tablespoon finely chopped fresh chives

1 jalapeño pepper, seeded, deveined, and finely chopped (see note)

⅛ teaspoon cayenne pepper: McCormick or Spice Islands

¼ cup chopped walnuts

⅛ teaspoon paprika: McCormick or Spice Islands

Pinch of sea salt

Combine all ingredients and mix well. Taste to adjust seasoning. Cover and refrigerate for at least 4 hours. Serve at room temperature with your favorite gluten-free crackers.

NOTE: Wear plastic gloves when handling hot peppers.

BLUE CHEESE ROULADE

This party pleaser is a snap to make. The flavors of roasted red peppers with the blue cheese just make this pop.

YIELD: 20 SERVINGS

1 pound blue cheese: Alouette, Boar's Head, Kraft Blue Cheese Crumbles, or Sargento Natural Blue Cheese, room temperature

2 (8-ounce) packages cream cheese, room temperature

¼ pound butter, room temperature

1 jigger whiskey: Crown Royal Blended Canadian Whiskey

2 tablespoons finely chopped chives

2 tablespoons chopped roasted red pepper

1 teaspoon Worcestershire sauce: Lea & Perrins or French's

⅛ teaspoon cayenne pepper: McCormick or Spice Islands

1 cup chopped pecans

Gluten-free crackers

In a medium mixing bowl, mash together blue cheese, cream cheese and butter. Mix well.

Add Crown Royal, chives, roasted red pepper, Worcestershire sauce, and cayenne pepper. Stir. Chill in the refrigerator 30 minutes.

Remove and roll into a cylinder 1½ to 2 inches thick. Roll in pecans, pressing them to adhere, and chill until ready to serve. Slice and serve on your favorite gluten-free crackers.

SERVING SUGGESTION   We like to pair this with some sliced Granny Smith apples and champagne or a nice red wine.

FRENCH FARMERS PÂTÉ

Rich, robust, elegant. A pâté lover's dream, yet so simple. This is Kim's most requested and favorite party recipe, especially with chilled white wine on a hot summer day. The bold flavor of dark cherries coupled with the distinction of Cognac makes this pâté absolutely magnificent. YIELD: ABOUT 3 CUPS

1 cup butter, room temperature (divided use)

¼ small onion, diced

1 pound chicken livers

1 clove garlic, minced

1 ½ teaspoon dry mustard: Colman's

¼ teaspoon cayenne pepper: McCormick or Spice Islands

Sea salt and pepper

⅛ teaspoon dried basil

¼ teaspoon dried thyme: McCormick or Spice Islands

¼ teaspoon white pepper: McCormick or Spice Islands

1 teaspoon sea salt

¼ teaspoon allspice: McCormick or Spice Islands

4 tablespoons Worcestershire sauce: McCormick or Spice Islands

3 tablespoons Cognac

⅓ cup dried dark cherries

Melt 2 tablespoons of butter in a large skillet over medium heat. Sauté the onions. Add ½ cup butter and the livers and sauté livers until brown but still a little pink in the middle. Remove from heat. Cool until butter begins to set. Partly cover pan and turn livers a few times.

Put livers with butter into blender with remaining butter. Add all remaining ingredients except cherries. Blend until smooth. Add salt and pepper to taste.

Place mixture into a well-buttered, 1-quart mold. Cover and chill overnight.

Allow the pâté to come to room temperature for 30 minutes before serving. Garnish with dried cherries.

Serve with gluten-free crackers or toasted and quartered gluten-free bread slices. This is great with icy cold champagne, too.

NEW NEW ORLEANS TAPENADE

New Orleans tapenade . . . all jazzed up. Great for an appetizer or a turkey muffaletta made with our Savory Tarragon Biscuits (see Page 203).   YIELD: ABOUT 3 CUPS

¾ cup stuffed green olives

¾ cup pitted kalamata olives

¼ cup pitted black olives

2 cloves garlic

¼ cup olive oil

2 tablespoons red wine vinegar: Heinz or Regina

½ cup gluten-free salami: Boar's Head Genoa salami or Applegate salami, finely chopped

½ cup provolone cheese, shredded

2 tablespoons finely chopped fresh parsley

1 large tomato, very finely chopped

¼ cup drained and very finely chopped sun-dried tomatoes in oil

¼ teaspoon freshly ground black pepper

Combine olives and garlic in a food processor. Cover and pulse until finely chopped, not puréed. Mix in olive oil and vinegar until well mixed.

Transfer mixture to a bowl and stir in meats, cheese, parsley, tomatoes, and pepper.

Chill up to 24 hours.

SERVING SUGGESTION   This is great with crusty gluten-free bread or crackers and, oh yeah, a glass of red wine.

SPICED EGG SALAD CANAPÉS

The perfect canapés . . . and more than just an appetizer. Serve them for a light lunch, brunch or a picnic at the park. Kim prefers them without the sweet pickles, and, of course, Bill likes them with. They are great either way. YIELD: 24 TO 30 canapés

10 hard-cooked eggs, finely chopped

1 tablespoon capers: Mezzetta, Reese, or Star (see note)

2 teaspoons Dijon mustard: Maille Dijon Originale Mustard or Grey Poupon

¾ cup mayonnaise: Hellmann's or Spectrum

⅛ teaspoon cayenne pepper: McCormick or Spice Islands

2 tablespoons fresh lemon juice

⅛ teaspoon Louisiana Hot Sauce or to taste

¼ teaspoon celery salt: Spice Island, Spice Hunter, or McCormick

1 jalapeño pepper, seeded, deveined and finely chopped

Freshly ground black pepper and sea salt to taste

6 to 8 slices Kinnikinnick's Soft White Bread or Udi's White Sandwich Bread, toasted and cut into quarters for canapés (see note)

Combine all the ingredients except the bread in a medium-size bowl and mix well. Place 1 tablespoon of egg salad on each toasted bread quarter or, our favorite, between our Savory Tarragon Biscuits (see Page 203).

NOTE: You may add an additional 1 tablespoon of capers for garnish. Kim loves them this way. Or, as Bill prefers, mix in 4 tablespoons chopped Mt. Olive sweet pickles.

SAVORY GOAT CHEESE AND CRÈME FRAÎCHE CROSTINI

Pronounced "krem fresh," crème fraîche is a rich and velvety, yet thinner form of sour cream developed by the French. It has a slightly tangy and nutty flavor that your guests will just love.   YIELD: 24 TO 32 CROSTINI

2 ounces crème fraîche or La Vaquita Crema Mexicana

1 tablespoon chopped fresh basil

1 tablespoon chopped fresh oregano

1 tablespoon chopped fresh thyme

½ teaspoon freshly ground black pepper

1 (8-ounce) package goat cheese

1 clove garlic, minced

½ teaspoon sea salt

1 teaspoon Newman's Lite Italian Salad Dressing

Pinch of red pepper flakes: McCormick or Spice Islands

1 whole garlic clove

6 to 8 slices Kinnikinnick Italian White Tapioca Rice Bread or Udi's White Sandwich Bread

1 tablespoon capers, drained: Mezzetta, Reese, or Star

Olive oil

Mix all ingredients except the bread and whole garlic clove and refrigerate.

For the crostini, place the bread slices on a baking tray. Cut garlic clove in half and rub each bread slice with a cut side. Brush bread with olive oil and broil until crispy golden brown.

Slice the bread into quarters. Spread 1 to 2 teaspoons savory goat cheese topping on each quarter. Garnish with capers.

SERVING SUGGESTION   These crostini are great with sun-dried tomatoes, shrimp or salmon on top of the savory cheese spread. They are also welcome sitting next to a salad.

MEXICAN GRILLED POLENTA BRUSCHETTA

This Mexican twist on Italian bruschetta calls for grilled white-cheddar polenta in place of French bread and makes an outstanding gluten-free dish. Queso fresco is a common Mexican cheese with a crumbly texture similar to feta cheese, but it's slightly tangier—and of course you can substitute feta if you can't find queso fresco.   YIELD: 12 TO 14 SERVINGS

½ small onion, finely grated

2 tablespoons olive oil plus more for brushing

1 clove garlic, minced

2 ¾ cups water

1 cup raw polenta

⅔ cup grated white cheddar or Manchego cheese

½ cup raw, fresh, or frozen corn kernels, thawed if frozen

1 jalapeño pepper, seeded, deveined, and finely chopped

1 teaspoon ground cumin: McCormick or Spice Islands

⅛ teaspoon cayenne pepper: McCormick or Spice Islands

1 ½ teaspoon sea salt or to taste

Tomato Topping (recipe follows)

1 cup queso fresco

Sauté onion in olive oil approximately 4 to 5 minutes. Add garlic and sauté 2 minutes.

Remove from heat and set aside.

Bring water to a boil in a medium saucepan and add polenta and onions and garlic. Return to a boil, then reduce heat and simmer 6 to 8 minutes, stirring constantly. Add cheese and continue stirring for 4 to 5 minutes. Add corn, jalapeño, cumin, cayenne pepper, and salt and stir well.

Let cool slightly.

Preheat oven to 350 F. Spread cooled polenta into a 13 x 8 x 2-inch greased baking dish. Brush top lightly with oil. Bake 38 to 40 minutes, or until edges are crispy brown. Let cool.

Cover and chill. (This can be done a day ahead.)

Cut polenta into 3 x 4-inch squares. Fire up the grill, bringing the temperature to medium. Lightly brush the grate with oil, and place squares on grill. Grill until golden brown, about 2 to 3 minutes per side. Remove to a platter.

Place 1 to 2 tablespoons of tomatoes on each square, then top with queso fresco.

TOMATO TOPPING

1 ½ cups chopped very ripe Roma tomatoes

1 teaspoon balsamic vinegar

½ teaspoon ground cumin: McCormick or Spice Islands

½ teaspoon chili powder: McCormick or Spice Islands

1 teaspoon sea salt or to taste

In a medium bowl, mix together all ingredients. Let sit at room temperature a half hour for flavors to blend.

VARIATION   If you don't want to grill, you can also place the tomatoes on top of the polenta, add the cheese on top, and run them under the broiler until crispy brown. Oh, my.

CRABMEAT AVOCADOS WITH LIME-CILANTRO-CHIVE MAYO

This very colorful and delicate combination of crabmeat, red bell pepper, and capers is a Veracruz delight. For the best flavor, always choose ripe avocados, which give just a bit when lightly squeezed. Avocados are packed with vitamins (including antioxidants C and E), nutrients, phytonutrients, and healthy fats. Glutathione, also present in avocados, has antioxidant properties.   YIELD: 10 appetizer or 5 entrée servings

2 teaspoons finely chopped cilantro plus sprigs for garnish

2 teaspoons finely chopped chives

2 tablespoons fresh lime juice (divided use)

½ teaspoon sea salt

⅛ teaspoon white pepper: Spice Islands

1 pound fresh jumbo lump crabmeat, picked completely free of shell bits

2 tablespoons chopped celery

¼ cup chopped red bell pepper

¼ cup chopped scallions, green part only

¼ teaspoon garlic powder

1 tablespoon capers: Mezzetta, Reese, or Star, drained

½ cup mayonnaise: Hellmann's, Kraft, or Spectrum

5 large ripe avocados

1 tablespoon fresh lemon juice

Lime wedges, for garnish

In a small bowl, combine cilantro and chives. Mix in 1 tablespoon lime juice, salt, and pepper. Set aside.

In a medium bowl, combine crabmeat, celery, red bell pepper, scallions, garlic powder, capers, and remaining 1 tablespoon lime juice. Mix well. Gently stir in mayonnaise.

Halve and pit avocados. Sprinkle with fresh lemon juice. Fill avocado halves with crab salad. Cover with plastic wrap. Refrigerate 1 hour. Drizzle the cilantro-chive mixture over and garnish with lime wedges and cilantro sprigs just before serving.

SERVING SUGGESTION   Great with our Romano and Oregano Crisps (see Page 196), fresh strawberries, honeydew melon, cantaloupe, and champagne.

BILL'S BLUE CLAW CRAB CAKES

If you are like us, you love a good crab cake, but don't dare order them in a restaurant because they are sure to contain bread, bread crumbs, or crackers. Now you have a recipe for crab cakes that will rival any restaurant's, thanks to Bill. Guests will never guess they are gluten-free. Buy the freshest crab meat you can find, as it will make all the difference in the world. Frozen is fine, too. YIELD: 8 CRAB CAKES

7 tablespoons butter (divided use)

¼ cup finely diced onion

¼ cup finely chopped celery

¼ cup finely chopped red bell pepper

2 tablespoons chopped fresh parsley

2 eggs

1 pound premium blue claw crab meat, thoroughly picked free of shell bits

2 tablespoons mayonnaise: Hellmann's or Kraft

2 teaspoons Dijon mustard: Maille Dijon Originale Mustard or Grey Poupon

¼ teaspoon paprika: McCormick or Spice Islands

¼ teaspoon onion powder

¼ teaspoon garlic powder

½ teaspoon celery salt: Spice Islands

¼ teaspoon cayenne pepper: McCormick or Spice Islands

2 slices gluten-free bread: Kinnikinnick's Italian White Tapioca Rice Bread or Udi's White Sandwich, processed or chopped into bread crumbs

½ teaspoon sea salt

2 teaspoons fresh lemon juice

1 teaspoon Worcestershire sauce: Lea & Perrins or French's

¼ teaspoon white pepper: Spice Islands

1 tablespoon baking powder: Clabber Girl, Hain, or Rumford

1 teaspoon Louisiana Hot Sauce

¼ cup finely chopped scallions

½ teaspoon grated fresh horseradish (a must)

1 teaspoon Old Bay Seasoning

4 tablespoons vegetable oil

Remoulade (recipe follows)

Heat 3 tablespoons of butter in small, nonstick skillet. Sauté onion, celery, red pepper, and parsley about 3 minutes over medium-high heat. Remove from burner. Let partially cool.

In large bowl, whisk eggs. Add onion-celery sauté and remaining ingredients except oil and Remoulade. Mix. Cover with plastic wrap. Refrigerate 2 hours.

Form into 3-inch patties. Melt 4 remaining tablespoons of butter and 4 tablespoons of oil in a large skillet over medium-high heat. Fry patties in small batches. If butter and oil start to burn, we like to pour it out and start with fresh. Don't overcook.

Serve with Remoulade.

TIP: The crab cakes will be ruined if not fried in hot enough oil. Be sure oil is at fry temperature before adding first cake.

SERVING SUGGESTION   Serve each crab cake on a
Bibb lettuce leaf with a tomato slice. Put 2 teaspoons of
Remoulade on top of each. They are also great with boiled
red potatoes, fresh corn on the cob, and a cold Redbridge
beer (Bill's favorite). Or, make it a meal with our Wilted
Spinach Salad (see Page 37) and Kim's Famous Over-the-
Top Bananas Foster Cake (see Page 250) for dessert, with
champagne. Kim's favorite, of course!

REMOULADE

Try this with our crab cakes, although it's
also great with fried shrimp or pan-seared sea
scallops.   YIELD: ABOUT 1¾ CUP

¼ teaspoon paprika: McCormick or Spice Islands

½ cup mayonnaise: Hellmann's, Spectrum, or Kraft

1 tablespoon chopped parsley

2 tablespoons chili sauce: Heinz Chili Sauce

1 large scallion, finely chopped (white and green parts)

2 tablespoons fresh lemon juice

1 tablespoon garlic dill pickles or cornichons, finely chopped

½ teaspoon Worcestershire sauce: Lea & Perrins or French's

¼ teaspoon celery salt: Spice Islands

¼ teaspoon finely ground black pepper

1 tablespoon tarragon white wine vinegar: Regina

1 tablespoon Dijon mustard: Maille Dijon Originale Mustard
   or Grey Poupon

1 tablespoon drained capers: Mezzetta, Reese, or Star

1 teaspoon Louisiana Hot Sauce

2 tablespoons finely chopped celery

2 tablespoons finely chopped Spanish green olives

1 clove garlic, minced

1 teaspoon sea salt

½ teaspoon thyme: McCormick or Spice Islands

1 hard-cooked egg, chopped

Mix together all ingredients in a glass bowl. Refrigerate for
1 hour before serving.

THAI SALMON CAKES WITH CILANTRO-MINT DIPPING SAUCE

A fusion of delectable Asian flavors. These are great for appetizers or an entrée.   YIELD: 6 TO 8 CAKES

3 (8-ounce) skinless salmon fillets

1 tablespoon olive oil

1 cup diced onion

2 cloves garlic, minced

1 tablespoon chopped red bell pepper

1 jalapeño pepper, seeded, deveined, and finely chopped

Juice and zest from 1 large lime

4 teaspoons soy sauce: Eden Foods Tamari Organic, La Choy, or San-J Organic Wheat Free Tamari Soy Sauce (Gold Label)

2 teaspoons brown sugar

¼ cup chopped scallion (green part only)

¼ cup chopped celery

⅛ cup chopped fresh cilantro

1 teaspoon chopped fresh basil

½ teaspoon finely chopped mint

2 eggs

3 tablespoons cornstarch

⅛ teaspoon cayenne pepper: McCormick or Spice Islands

Sea salt and Spice Islands white pepper to taste

Cilantro-Mint Dipping Sauce (recipe follows)

Lightly oil skillet, and heat over medium heat. Add fillets and a small amount of water. Heat, then reduce to a low simmer and cover. Gently poach for 3 minutes. Carefully turn fillets and cook for 5 minutes, or until brown. Remove from pan and set aside to cool. Flake with a fork.

Heat oil in small, nonstick skillet. Add onion and sauté for 2 minutes. Add garlic, red pepper, and jalapeño pepper, and cook for 1 to 2 minutes. Set aside and cool.

In a small bowl, combine lime juice, lime zest, soy sauce, brown sugar, scallions, celery, cilantro, basil, and mint. Mix well and combine with the flaked salmon.

In a larger bowl, whisk eggs. Add cornstarch, cayenne pepper, salt, and pepper. Mix well. Add the cooled onion mixture. Mix. Carefully fold in the flaked salmon. Form into 6 to 8 cakes and chill in refrigerator for 1 hour.

Pan-fry cakes over medium heat, 2 to 3 minutes per side. Serve with Cilantro-Mint Dipping Sauce.

CILANTRO-MINT DIPPING SAUCE

2 tablespoons sugar

4 teaspoons brown rice vinegar: Eden Foods Organic Brown Rice Vinegar

2 tablespoons chili sauce: Lee Kum Kee Sriracha Chili Sauce

1 teaspoon chopped fresh cilantro

½ teaspoon chopped fresh mint

In a small bowl, dissolve sugar in brown rice vinegar. Mix in chili sauce, cilantro, and mint.

SESAME CHICKEN WITH JALAPEÑO-BUTTERMILK-ROMANO DRESSING

This is Kim's version of Sesame Chicken, with a little added spice. The flavors just explode. Kids love this even more than deep-fried chicken tenders. Plus, do we even have to say that it's healthier than those processed chicken nuggets with unpronounceable additives? P.S. Adults love it, too.   YIELD: 8 TO 10 SERVINGS

1 jalapeño pepper, seeded, deveined and finely chopped (see note)

Buttermilk Romano Herb Dressing (see Page 31)

6 boneless and skinless chicken breast halves, cut into 5-to-6-inch chicken strips

1 ½ cups buttermilk

⅛ teaspoon cayenne pepper: McCormick or Spice Islands

1 teaspoon sea salt plus more for strips

1 teaspoon freshly ground black pepper plus more for strips

¾ cup Orgran Gluten-Free Bread Crumbs, other gluten-free bread crumbs or Pamela's Baking & Pancake Mix

¾ cup raw sesame seeds

1 teaspoon paprika: McCormick or Spice Islands

⅛ teaspoon white pepper: Spice Islands

1 teaspoon garlic powder

1 teaspoon onion powder

2 eggs, beaten

2 tablespoons olive oil

3 tablespoons butter, melted

Mix dipping sauce by mixing chopped jalapeno into Buttermilk Romano Herb Dressing. Refrigerate. In a zip-top plastic bag, marinate chicken in buttermilk for at least 3 hours.

Preheat oven to 350 F. Lightly oil a shallow baking pan. Remove chicken from bag. Discard buttermilk. Sprinkle chicken strips with cayenne pepper and salt and pepper to taste.

Mix bread crumbs, sesame seeds, paprika, white pepper, garlic powder, onion powder, and remaining 1 teaspoon salt and 1 teaspoon black pepper.

One at a time, dip chicken strips in eggs. Then roll in sesame-seed-bread-crumb mixture, coating each piece well. Arrange strips in a shallow baking pan, close but not touching.

Mix olive oil and butter together and drizzle evenly over coated strips. Bake 25 to 30 minutes, or until chicken is golden brown and no longer pink in the center. Serve warm with dipping sauce on the side.

NOTE: Wear plastic gloves when handling hot peppers.

GRAPE LEAVES STUFFED WITH LAMB, DILL AND MINT

Here you go: another cold appetizer that can be prepared well ahead of party time. You won't believe how good these stuffed grape leaves, or dolmas, are, and so easy to make. YIELD: 20 TO 24

1 (8-ounce) jar grape leaves

1 cup white or brown rice

1 ¼ cups water

1 pound ground lamb

2 tablespoons olive oil

½ cup diced onion

2 cloves garlic, minced

1 teaspoon dried dill

1 tablespoon chopped fresh mint

2 tablespoon chopped fresh parsley

1 teaspoon sea salt

½ teaspoon freshly ground black pepper

⅛ teaspoon cinnamon: McCormick or Spice Islands

¼ cup fresh lemon juice (divided use)

Cook rice half the amount of time given in package directions. Drain excess water and return to the pan.

In another skillet, brown lamb in olive oil; add onions and sauté until transparent. Add garlic and cook 1 to 2 minutes. Add dill, mint, parsley, salt, pepper, cinnamon, ⅛ cup lemon juice, and rice. Mix well and set aside.

Carefully remove grape leaves and cook in boiling water for 2 to 3 minutes. Drain grape leaves on paper towels.

Layer the bottom of a large Dutch oven, LeCreuset preferred, with 2 to 3 layers of grape leaves. Use those that have big veins or are damaged here. This is just the foundation.

Lay about 2 dozen young leaves without stems vein-side-up on a cutting board. If the center veins are thick, gently trim them out, cutting as close as possible. Add 1 tablespoon lamb-rice mixture to center of each leaf. Don't overfill.

To roll: Fold up the bottom. Fold sides over to tuck the filling in. Roll leaf up. Place rolls, seam side down, in the pot. Put rolls as close together as possible. Repeat in layers.

Pour remaining lemon juice into pot and cover with water.

Cover the pot and simmer over low heat for 40 to 45 minutes. Add more water, as needed, to keep rolls covered. Serve room temperature.

SOUTHWESTERN PEPPER-JACK-AND-ZUCCHINI CORN CAKES

Sweeeeeeet. The best corn cakes south of the Red River. These delectable, savory cakes make a wonderful appetizer or side dish.   YIELD: 10 TO 12 (4-INCH) CAKES

1 cup gluten-free flour: Pamela's Baking & Pancake Mix or Arrowhead Mills All Purpose Gluten Free Baking Flour

1 cup cornmeal: Lamb's Stone Ground Yellow Cornmeal, Albers Yellow Cornmeal, or Arrowhead Mills Organic Yellow Cornmeal

1 tablespoon baking powder: Clabber Girl, Hain, or Rumford

1 teaspoon paprika: McCormick or Spice Islands

⅛ teaspoon cayenne pepper: McCormick or Spice Islands

1 teaspoon cumin: McCormick or Spice Islands

1 teaspoon sea salt

2 cups coarsely grated zucchini

1 clove garlic, minced

1 egg, beaten

1 cup fresh or frozen corn kernels, thawed if frozen

1 tablespoon Worcestershire sauce: Lea & Perrins or French's

1 tablespoon Dijon mustard: Maille Dijon Originale or Grey Poupon

½ small onion, finely grated

1 cup grated pepper jack cheese

Olive oil for frying

In a large mixing bowl, combine all dry ingredients. Set aside.

Spread the grated zucchini over paper towels, fold over and squeeze out as much water as possible (the less water the better).

Add zucchini, garlic, egg, corn, Worcestershire, mustard, onion, and cheese to dry ingredients. Form into a ball, then into small patties approximately 4 inches in diameter.

Pour oil on a griddle or frying pan over medium heat. When oil slightly sizzles, place patties on griddle in batches and cook 2 to 4 minutes on each side, or until crispy brown.

ARTICHOKE-FETA FRITTERS

Greek flavors and a Texas fritter . . . now, that is what we call Texas two-steppin'. The tangy lemon zest, artichoke hearts, and feta cheese just electrify the palate and complement each other superbly in this delicious twist on traditional fritters. YIELD: 10 TO 12 FRITTERS

¾ cup gluten-free baking mix: Pamela's Baking & Pancake Mix or Arrowhead Mills All Purpose Gluten Free Baking Flour

½ cup cornmeal: Albers Yellow Stone Ground Cornmeal, fine grind

¼ teaspoon cayenne pepper: McCormick or Spice Islands

¼ teaspoon paprika: McCormick or Spice Islands

1 teaspoon chopped fresh basil

1 teaspoon baking powder: Clabber Girl, Hain, or Rumford

1 egg, beaten

1 clove garlic, minced

1 tablespoon lemon juice

½ teaspoon lemon pepper

1 teaspoon lemon zest (yellow part of peel only)

1 tablespoon Dijon mustard: Maille Dijon Originale Mustard or Grey Poupon

1 teaspoon Worcestershire sauce: Lea & Perrins or French's

½ small onion, finely grated

¼ cup half-and-half

1 (14-ounce) can chopped artichoke hearts: California Girl, Maria, or Reese, liquid squeezed out

¾ cup feta cheese

¼ cup grated Parmagiano-Reggiano cheese

½ teaspoon sea salt (optional)

Oil for frying

Mix all dry ingredients in a medium bowl. Add egg, garlic, lemon juice, lemon pepper, lemon zest, mustard, Worcestershire sauce, onion, and half-and-half. Mix well. Add remaining ingredients except oil and mix thoroughly. Refrigerate 1 to 2 hours.

Remove and form into a ball, then small patties, approximately 3 inches in diameter.

Pour oil just to cover the bottom of large frying pan and heat over medium heat. Place patties in batches of 3 or 4 in pan and cook 2 to 4 minutes on each side or until crispy brown.

TIP: Kim likes to make a ball and then form a nice round patty on wax paper She then slides a thin spatula under them and gently places them into the frying pan.

SALADS AND
SALAD DRESSINGS

We've got savory, wholesome, and delicious salads in all shapes, sizes, flavors, and colors. Some are sides, and some are meals in themselves. Some are exotic, some not. They're all fresh and unique, and our dressings just make them come alive. Even with familiar favorites, we always add our own touch just to make them interesting. Best of all, you don't have to skip the dressing. We pay special attention to dressings because, unfortunately, you just don't know what's in restaurant dressings and most of the ones from the grocery store contain gluten.

You simply have to try our Warm Brown Sugar and Applewood-Smoked Bacon Dressing; you won't believe what it does to an everyday salad. You'll never go back to ranch once you've tried our Buttermilk Romano Herb Dressing. And you'll love the Grilled Peach, Feta, and Spinach Salad with our Sherry Balsamic Vinaigrette, and our Asian Chicken Salad made with Crystallized Ginger. These creative salads add a touch of elegance to your table. Give these salads your own flair, but most of all, enjoy them. Own them.

BUTTERMILK ROMANO HERB DRESSING

Ranch, step aside. This dressing is delicious on cold spinach leaves with grated carrots, chopped mushrooms, sunflower seeds, and tomatoes. It's also great with steamed fresh artichokes, fresh vegetables, and little steamed red potatoes, or as a complement to our Southwestern Pepper Jack and Zucchini Corn Cakes (see Page 25), Red Chile Fried Green Tomatoes (see Page 170), or the Roasted Tomato and Goat Cheese Risotto Cakes (see Page 161). YIELD: 1½ CUP

½ cup mayonnaise: Hellmann's, Kraft, or Spectrum

½ cup buttermilk

1 clove garlic, minced

½ teaspoon chopped fresh oregano

½ teaspoon paprika: McCormick or Spice Islands

½ teaspoon freshly ground black pepper

½ teaspoon Dijon mustard: Maille Dijon Originale or Grey Poupon

½ teaspoon Worcestershire: Lea & Perrins or French's

Dash Louisiana Hot Sauce or Tabasco

1 teaspoon sugar

1 teaspoon fresh lemon juice

Sea salt and freshly ground black pepper to taste

1 tablespoon chopped chives

¼ cup grated Romano cheese

Mix all ingredients except chives and Romano cheese together in a blender. Blend for approximately 1 minute. Add Romano cheese and chives and mix thoroughly.

WARM BROWN SUGAR AND APPLEWOOD-SMOKED BACON DRESSING

A sensational blend of the boldest ingredients, this is one of our most unique and scrumptious dressings. You're gonna love it!   YIELD: 4 SERVINGS

4 slices thick applewood-smoked bacon

2 tablespoons minced shallots

1 to 2 cloves garlic, minced

3 tablespoons red wine vinegar: Heinz or Regina

1 tablespoon balsamic vinegar

1 teaspoon brown sugar

1 teaspoon apple juice

½ teaspoon Dijon mustard: Maille Dijon Originale Mustard or Grey Poupon

1 teaspoon Worcestershire sauce: Lea & Perrins or French's

½ teaspoon sea salt

Freshly ground black pepper

In a skillet, slowly brown bacon until crisp. Reserve 3 tablespoons of bacon drippings in the pan. Drain bacon on paper towel. Crumble.

Sauté shallot and garlic in bacon drippings for 3 minutes. Place in a stainless steel pan over low heat.

In a small nonreactive bowl, whisk together vinegars, brown sugar, apple juice, mustard, Worcestershire sauce, salt and pepper. Add to drippings.

Stir over low heat until warm. Turn off heat. Add in crumbled bacon.

Toss thoroughly with fresh spinach or salad ingredients of your choice.

SERVING SUGGESTION   We like to serve this over fresh spinach leaves, shredded carrots, chopped tomatoes, and sliced mushrooms and avocados. A meal unto itself.

CHUNKY BLUE CHEESE DRESSING

Here is a blue cheese dressing with some freshness and zing to it—perfect on a cold iceberg lettuce wedge topped with chopped ripe tomatoes, sliced hard-cooked eggs, crumbled crispy bacon and freshly ground pepper. Come to think of it, that's a meal.   YIELD: 3 CUPS

1½ cup mayonnaise: Hellmann's, Kraft, or Spectrum

¼ cup buttermilk

¼ cup sour cream or crème fraîche

½ teaspoon Worcestershire sauce: Lea & Perrins or French's

2 tablespoons fresh lemon juice

1 teaspoon grated shallot

½ teaspoon sea salt

¼ teaspoon hot sauce: Louisiana Hot Sauce or Tabasco

1 tablespoon white wine vinegar: Regina

1 teaspoon Dijon mustard: Maille Dijon Originale Mustard or Grey Poupon

⅛ teaspoon white pepper: Spice Islands

1 cup crumbled blue cheese: Boar's Head, Kraft, or Sargento All-Natural

Blend all ingredients except blue cheese together in a blender. Whisk in blue cheese by hand.

GARLICKED PARMESAN DRIZZLE

Garlic dressing with a twist. Serve this on just about any dark leafy greens, on cucumber salad, or as a flavorful dip for fresh vegetables. Bill has been known to dab this on freshly grilled steaks and veggies.   YIELD: 1 ½ CUPS

2 cloves garlic, peeled and chopped

1 teaspoon coarse sea salt

½ cup red wine vinegar: Heinz or Regina

¾ cup extra virgin olive oil

¼ cup grated Parmesan cheese

A couple twists of freshly ground black pepper

With the back of a fork, mash and work together garlic with salt into a paste. Put garlic/salt mixture into a mixing bowl. Add vinegar. Slowly add the olive oil. Whisk. Add Parmesan cheese; whisk well. Serve at room temperature.

SERVING SUGGESTION   After we've dressed some greens, we like to serve them with our Sicilian-style Veal Scaloppini (see Page 100), Mr. Fluffy Pepper Jack and Aged Cheddar Biscuits (see Page 199), fresh blackberries, and a nice dry white wine.

BETTER-THAN-A-FRENCH-KISS FRENCH DRESSING

This is our flirty American version of classic French dressing—like the original, only better. So much better, in fact, it just makes you want to pucker your lips! YIELD: ABOUT 3 CUPS

¾ cup sugar

1 cup vegetable or other oil

1 cup ketchup: Heinz

4 tablespoons apple cider vinegar: Heinz

½ teaspoon paprika: McCormick or Spice Islands

2 cloves garlic, minced

½ cup fresh lemon juice

¼ teaspoon cayenne pepper: McCormick or Spice Islands

1 teaspoon Dijon mustard: Grey Poupon or Maille Dijon Originale

¼ teaspoon chopped fresh parsley

Place all ingredients except parsley into a blender and mix for 90 seconds. Add parsley and mix again. And you're done.

POPPYSEED DRESSING

Bill likes this dressing drizzled over grapefruit wedges and sliced avocados on baby spinach or mixed greens with our Savory Tarragon Biscuits (see Page 203) on the side. He also likes it on a turkey sandwich with lettuce, tomato, onion, and avocado. You name it—he puts it on everything. It's that good! YIELD: 3 ½ CUPS

1 ½ cup sugar

2 teaspoons dry mustard: Colman's

2 teaspoons sea salt

⅔ cup apple cider vinegar: Heinz

2 tablespoons onion juice: Howard's

1 cup vegetable oil

3 tablespoons poppyseeds: Spice Islands

Mix sugar, mustard, salt, and vinegar in blender. Add onion juice. Blend well. With blender running, add oil very slowly in constant drizzle (takes a couple of minutes). Add poppyseeds and blend well. Use immediately or refrigerate.

TIP: Before serving, remove from refrigerator and allow to come to room temperature. Shake or mix well before serving.

SAUCE VINAIGRETTE (FRENCH VINAIGRETTE)

The classic French salad dressing, the real thing. When you eat it, imagine yourself at a small bistro on the bank of the Seine in Paris. We add a south-of-France touch with the addition of garlic. Real French dressing does not contain Worcestershire sauce, cheese, tomato, or sugar—ingredients you commonly see in store-bought French dressing. The key is using the finest ingredients and freshest, seasonal herbs. This is what you will find in French restaurants.   YIELD: 1 CUP

2 tablespoons red wine vinegar: Heinz or Regina

1 tablespoon fresh lemon juice

½ teaspoon sea salt

½ teaspoon dry mustard: Colman's

¼ teaspoon freshly ground black pepper

⅔ cup olive oil

2 tablespoons chopped fresh herbs (parsley, chives, tarragon, or basil)

Place everything in blender except oil. Blend. Slowly, very slowly, add oil with the blender running at low until all the oil is incorporated.

VARIATION   You can also add 1 teaspoon chopped capers and 1 teaspoon finely chopped shallots.

KIM'S FRESH GINGER VINAIGRETTE

This vinaigrette is just full of flavor, and great on spinach salads or as a marinade. It's slightly tangy, with a hint of sweetness and lots of fresh ginger goodness. It's even delicious on salmon.   YIELD: 1½ CUPS

1 tablespoon fresh lemon juice

2 tablespoons Dijon mustard: Maille Dijon Originale Mustard or Grey Poupon

3 tablespoons grated fresh ginger

3 tablespoons red wine vinegar: Heinz or Regina

2 tablespoons soy sauce: Eden Foods Tamari Organic Soy Sauce, La Choy, or San-J Organic Wheat-free tamari: Gold Label

2½ teaspoons brown sugar or to taste

1 cup extra virgin olive oil

½ teaspoon sea salt

Freshly ground black pepper

Combine all ingredients in a bowl, except the olive oil, salt, and pepper. Whisk until well blended. Slowly add olive oil 1 drop at a time until it starts emulsifying, then mix vigorously while adding in a thin stream. Add salt and pepper to taste.

SERVING SUGGESTION   Drizzle over a salad of fresh baby spinach leaves, grated carrots, chopped tomatoes, sliced cucumbers, feta cheese, and black olives. Or, marinate salmon in the dressing for 3 to 4 hours, and baste after salmon is almost cooked.

NOTE: Kim likes to substitute honey for sugar.

CRANBERRY WALDORF SALAD

Fine tartness and crunchy texture with crisp green apples, pecans, and cranberries pump up this twist on the classic Waldorf salad. We just know you will agree that it's as delicious as it is healthy.   YIELD: 4 SERVINGS

Juice of 1 lemon

2 cups unpeeled, cored, and diced Granny Smith apples

1 cup chopped celery, strings removed

¼ cup broken pecan pieces

¼ cup dried sweetened cranberries

½ cup mayonnaise: Hellmann's, Kraft, or Spectrum

4 cups Bibb lettuce, rinsed, spun dry, and torn into pieces

Lemon wedges for garnish

Squeeze lemon juice over apples in a medium mixing bowl to prevent browning. Mix apples with celery, pecans, and cranberries. Mix in mayonnaise. Serve on bed of Bibb lettuce with lemon wedges.

WILTED SPINACH SALAD

This is one of our most popular salads—the perfect combination of colorful and flavorful spinach, feta cheese, cranberries, and crunchy pecans. And even though its ingredients say fall, you can enjoy this light and delicious salad any time of year. We also like to sprinkle crispy bacon on top. YIELD: 6 TO 8 SERVINGS

3 to 4 cups fresh spinach, rinsed, spun dry and torn into pieces

6 ounces feta cheese

¼ cup sweetened dried cranberries

1 cup chopped pecans

¾ cup Kim's Fresh Ginger Vinaigrette (see Page 36), heated to very warm

Toss spinach with cheese, cranberries, and pecans. Drizzle with hot vinaigrette.

Toss again and serve. Note: The spinach should retain some crunch.

SERVING SUGGESTION   This is excellent with our Beef Tenderloin with Brandied Peppercorn Sauce (see Page 84) and for dessert our Buttermilk Toffee Cake with Chocolate Buttercream Frosting (see Page 256).

HEARTS OF PALM AND SPINACH SALAD

We really like this refreshing salad. The hearts of palm, walnuts, grated carrots, blue cheese and sliced mushrooms tossed with Kim's Fresh Ginger Vinaigrette are over the top. YIELD: 6 SERVINGS

3 cups fresh spinach, rinsed, dried, and torn into bite-size pieces

½ cup chopped walnuts

¾ cup sliced hearts of palm

½ cup grated carrots

½ cup sliced fresh mushrooms

1 medium chopped Roma tomato

½ cup blue cheese: Boar's Head, Kraft, Primo Taglio Crumbled, or Sargento All Natural Blue Cheese or feta cheese

¾ cup Kim's Fresh Ginger Vinaigrette (see Page 36)

Sliced cucumbers (optional)

Toss and serve.

SERVING SUGGESTION   We like this with grilled lobster tails and Kim's glorious and oh, so decadent Over-the-Top Bananas Foster Cake (see Page 250).

ASIAN CHICKEN SALAD WITH CRYSTALLIZED GINGER

With crunchy puffed rice noodles, this salad is easy to prepare and makes for a great, refreshing, and nutritious spring or summer lunch.   YIELD: 6 TO 8 SERVINGS

¼ cup sugar

4 tablespoons brown rice vinegar: Eden Foods Organic Brown Rice Vinegar

3 tablespoons vegetable or olive oil plus olive oil for frying (divided use)

1 teaspoon soy sauce: Eden Foods Tamari Organic Soy Sauce, La Choy, or San-J Organic Wheat-free Tamari Soy Sauce (Gold Label)

¾ cup shredded, cooked free-range chicken

1 cup shredded romaine lettuce

2 tablespoons minced crystallized ginger

2 tablespoons toasted sesame seeds

2 minced green onions (green parts only)

1½ cup rice vermicelli noodles

Blend sugar, vinegar, oil, and soy sauce in a small saucepan and heat to dissolve sugar.

Allow to cool.

Combine chicken, lettuce, ginger, sesame seeds, and green onions in a medium bowl. Set aside.

In a skillet, fry noodles in oil for about 2 minutes or until "puffed" and remove from skillet. Combine chicken mixture with noodles and toss with dressing.

WALNUT-DILL CHICKEN SALAD

Great with a glass of fresh lemonade on a warm summer day. Truth is, it's good all year. It's best if you let the chicken marinate for 24 hours before baking it and chill the salad another 12. But you don't have to.   YIELD: 4 TO 6 SERVINGS

2 pounds boneless, skinless free-range organic chicken breasts

1 cup salad dressing: Newman's Own Lite Italian Dressing or Newman's Own Parmesan and Roasted Garlic Dressing

½ cup diced onion

1 cup chopped celery

1 teaspoon garlic powder

1½ teaspoon seasoned salt: Lawry's

3 teaspoons chopped fresh dill

5 teaspoons red wine vinegar: Heinz or Regina

1 cup mayonnaise: Hellmann's, Kraft, or Spectrum

¼ cup chopped walnuts

Marinate chicken in dressing for at least 12 hours and up to 24. Drain and discard marinade.

Preheat oven to 350 F. Place chicken in a baking dish and bake 45 minutes to 1 hour, or until done. Remove from oven and let cool.

When chicken is cool enough to handle, dice and put in a large mixing bowl. Add remaining ingredients. Mix well.

Chill another 12 hours before serving.

SERVING SUGGESTION   We like to serve this salad on a bed of Bibb lettuce surrounded by grapes and cherry tomato halves. Try as a snack or light lunch on Kim's Mr. Fluffy Pepper Jack and Cheddar Cheese Biscuits (see page 199).

SEARED AHI TUNA NIÇOISE SALAD WITH DIJON HERB VINAIGRETTE

An absolutely monumental gourmet salad. This is one of Kim's favorites, made with seasoned roasted potatoes, oven-roasted balsamic tomatoes, haricot verts drizzled with the most magnificent Dijon Vinaigrette, all topped by succulent, seared ahi tuna. This is indeed the mother of all salads. We know, the recipe looks long and tedious, but it is really quite easy to make. Start with the dressing, then make your hard-cooked eggs so they have time to cool. Prepare the tomatoes and potatoes, then the haricots verts. All those elements will be served room temperature. Prepare the ahi tuna last. Plate the salad as it cooks. Then you have only to top your masterpiece. Voilà! **YIELD: 3 SERVINGS (BILL, KIM, AND KIM'S MOTHER)**

---

4 cups baby spinach, rinsed and dried

Dijon Herb Vinaigrette (recipe follows, divided use)

2 hard-cooked eggs, peeled and quartered

Roasted Potatoes (recipe follows)

Balsamic Roasted Tomatoes (recipe follows)

Haricots Verts (recipe follows)

½ cup pitted Niçoise olives

3 tablespoons capers: Mezzetta, Reese, or Star

Seared Ahi Tuna (recipe follows)

¼ teaspoon paprika: McCormick or Spice Islands

In medium mixing bowl, toss spinach with ¼ cup Dijon Herb Vinaigrette. Divide the dressed spinach among 3 plates.

Arrange ⅓ of the egg quarters, potatoes, tomatoes, and haricots verts around rim of each plate. Top each salad with ⅓ each of the Niçoise olives and capers.

Arrange a tuna fillet in center on top of each salad. Drizzle with Dijon Herb Vinaigrette to taste and add a dash of vinegar. Sprinkle with paprika and serve.

HARICOTS VERTS

Rinse and trim ends of a handful of fresh haricots verts (very small) or green beans. Blanch in boiling water for 4 to 5 minutes, then plunge into a bowl of ice water to stop the cooking. When cool, remove and pat dry with a paper towel.

DIJON HERB VINAIGRETTE

¼ cup fresh lemon juice

2 tablespoons Dijon mustard: Maille Dijon Originale Mustard or Grey Poupon

2 cloves garlic, minced

½ teaspoon sea salt

¼ teaspoon freshly ground black pepper

1 anchovy fillet, mashed

1 tablespoon red wine vinegar: Heinz or Regina

⅛ teaspoon thyme

⅛ teaspoon oregano

½ cup extra-virgin olive oil

Mix all ingredients except olive oil in a glass bowl. Very slowly whisk in olive oil, literally one drop at a time at first until it emulsifies. Store in the refrigerator until needed.

BALSAMIC ROASTED TOMATOES

6 Roma tomatoes, sliced in quarters

¼ cup high-quality olive oil

1 tablespoon chopped fresh basil

1 tablespoon chopped fresh oregano

2 cloves garlic, minced

½ teaspoon sea salt

½ teaspoon freshly ground black pepper

2 tablespoons balsamic vinegar

Preheat oven to 400 F. Combine ingredients and toss. Arrange tomatoes, cut side up, on a baking sheet in a single layer. Roast for 25 to 30 minutes on rack second from top. Remove from oven and cool to room temperature.

ROASTED POTATOES

4 small red potatoes

1 tablespoon extra-virgin olive oil

1 teaspoon sea salt

2 to 3 cloves garlic, minced

1 tablespoon minced shallot

Preheat oven to 400 F. Rinse and quarter potatoes. Toss with olive oil, salt, garlic and shallot. Place potatoes in a baking dish and roast on rack second from top, uncovered, for 25 to 30 minutes, or until done. Remove from oven and cool to room temperature.

SEARED AHI TUNA

3 (6-ounce) center-cut ahi tuna fillets

1½ teaspoons Spice Islands Beau Monde Seasoning or our Authentic Atchafalaya Blackened Cajun Spice (see Page 212) to taste

Freshly ground black pepper

2 tablespoons olive oil

Season each tuna fillet with ½ teaspoon Beau Monde or Cajun seasoning and freshly ground black pepper.

Heat olive oil in skillet over medium-high heat. Sear tuna, 2 minutes on each side, until all sides are brown, keeping the centers rare. Remove from heat.

SERVING SUGGESTION   We like to serve this entrée salad with our Savory Goat Cheese and Crème Fraîche Spread Crostini (see page 17) and Devil's Devil's Food Cake with Chocolate Fluff Frosting (see Page 244).

GRILLED PEACH, FETA, AND SPINACH SALAD WITH SHERRY BALSAMIC VINAIGRETTE

Now here's a peachy-keen salad… and if peaches are not in season, we substitute grilled apples. Both are amazingly good. Get the sweetest, juiciest, and freshest peaches you can find, preferably from your farmers market. Store this in your fridge because you'll want to use it to jazz up a salad everyday!   YIELD: 6 SERVINGS

3 large, almost ripe Freestone peaches, cut into halves and pitted

Olive oil

3 to 4 cups baby spinach

1 cup feta cheese

1 cup coarsely chopped pecans

Sherry Balsamic Vinaigrette (recipe follows)

Fire up the grill, bringing the temperature to medium. Lightly brush the grate with oil. Brush both sides of peaches with oil. Place peaches on grill, cut side down, and grill until golden brown.

Meanwhile, toss the spinach, feta, and pecans with just enough dressing to moisten the ingredients. Plate the salads and top each with a grilled peach half. Drizzle a little more dressing over the peach. Save any leftover dressing for another use.

SHERRY BALSAMIC VINAIGRETTE

2 tablespoons fresh lemon juice

1 teaspoon sherry

2 tablespoons balsamic vinegar

2 tablespoons red wine vinegar: Heinz or Regina

1½ tablespoons Dijon mustard: Maille Dijon Originale or Grey Poupon

1 tablespoon brown sugar

1 clove garlic, smashed

½ teaspoon sea salt

½ teaspoon freshly ground black pepper

¼ teaspoon dried thyme: McCormick or Spice Islands

½ teaspoon dried oregano: McCormick or Spice Islands

½ teaspoon dried basil: McCormick or Spice Islands

¼ cup extra virgin olive oil

Combine all ingredients in a food processor except the oil. While the processor is running, slowly add the oil—drop by drop at first until the mixture emulsifies. Then add the rest very, very slowly. If it tastes too pungent, add a little more brown sugar. Note: Be sure to taste it on a spinach or lettuce leaf, to better approximate its flavor on a salad.

ROASTED BEET SALAD WITH GOAT CHEESE AND PECANS

In this nutritious (and delicious) beet salad, the goat cheese and pecans add unique yet subtle flavor. Don't be put off by the beet prep—it's easy! It just takes a little time. But oh, is the end salad worth it. YIELD: 6 SERVINGS

4 beets

½ cup chopped pecans

2 teaspoons olive oil

½ teaspoon sea salt

½ teaspoon freshly ground black pepper

1 cup water

½ cup apple cider vinegar: Heinz

½ cup sugar

4 whole cloves

½ cup thinly sliced red onion

6 cups mixed greens, rinsed and spun dry

10 ounces goat cheese, or as desired

Garlic Vinaigrette (recipe follows)

Preheat oven to 350 F.

Wash and trim top and stem off beets. Wrap each beet in foil. Put on a baking sheet and bake for 1½ to 2 hours. Remove beets from oven. Open foil. Let beets cool 20 to 30 minutes. Rub skins off under running water (so everything doesn't turn pink) and slice beets into ½-inch rounds. Set aside.

Keep oven on. Combine pecans, olive oil, salt, and pepper in a bowl. Mix well. Spread pecans evenly on baking sheet. Bake 10 minutes. Remove from oven. Let cool.

In medium saucepan, combine water, vinegar, sugar, cloves, sliced beets, and onions. Bring to a boil, then reduce heat to medium-low. Simmer for 30 minutes. Remove from heat. Let cool 1 hour. Remove beets from liquid. Cut into ½-inch cubes.

To finish salads, divide mixed greens among 6 salad plates. Top with cubed beets and then desired amount of goat cheese. Drizzle 1 tablespoon of Garlic Vinaigrette over each plate. Top with roasted pecans. Serve immediately.

GARLIC VINAIGRETTE:

¼ cup fresh lemon juice

2 cloves garlic (minced)

2 tablespoons finely chopped parsley

¼ teaspoon sea salt

2 anchovy fillets (optional), mashed with a fork

¼ cup extra virgin olive oil

Whisk together in a glass bowl lemon juice, garlic, parsley, sea salt, and anchovy fillets if using. Slowly drizzle in olive oil, first by droplets, whisking constantly to set up the emulsion.

SERVING SUGGESTION   We like to pair this with our Pecan-Crusted Salmon (see Page 147). Add a side of steamed asparagus and you have a gourmet meal. Great with a dry, cold, and very crisp chardonnay.

LEMON CAPER VINAIGRETTE GREENS WITH BAKED GOAT CHEESE ROUNDS

Distinctively different and loaded with flavor. We also like to marinate tilapia or redfish fillets in this dressing for 15 minutes and bake for 20 minutes.   YIELD: 6 SERVINGS

½ cup red wine vinegar: Heinz or Regina

2 tablespoons fresh lemon juice

2 teaspoons Dijon mustard: Maille Dijon Originale Mustard or Grey Poupon

¼ teaspoon sea salt

2 tablespoons brown sugar

¼ teaspoon freshly ground black pepper

½ cup olive oil

4 teaspoons capers: Mezzetta, Reese, or Star, drained

12 cups salad greens, rinsed and spun dry

3 fresh summer tomatoes, sliced or chopped

1 (14-ounce) can hearts of palm

Black olives for garnish

Baked Goat Cheese Rounds (recipe follows)

Place vinegar, lemon juice, mustard, salt, brown sugar, and pepper in a food processor and mix. With the food processor running, slowly add the oil drop by drop to emulsify. Then slowly add the rest of the oil. Pour into a bowl. Add the capers and mix. Refrigerate. When ready to use, whisk again.

Mound the greens on 6 salad plates. Arrange tomatoes and hearts of palm on top. Add a few black olives. Drizzle with dressing to taste. Garnish with Baked Goat Cheese Rounds.

BAKED GOAT CHEESE ROUNDS

½ cup finely ground pecans or walnuts (see note)

1 teaspoon chopped fresh chives

1 teaspoon chopped fresh tarragon

1 teaspoon chopped fresh thyme

1 teaspoon sea salt

Dash of cayenne pepper

1 teaspoon paprika: McCormick or Spice Islands

8 to 10 ounces goat cheese

2 large eggs, beaten

Preheat oven to 375 F.

Mix finely ground nuts with the fresh herbs and spices. Set aside.

Roll cheese into small 1¼-inch balls and flatten into patty. Dip patty into beaten egg, then into nut-spice mixture.

Place on a cookie sheet lined with parchment paper and bake for 8 to 12 minutes. Let cool and place on top of salad.

NOTE: Place pecans in food processor only until fairly finely ground. Don't process into pecan dust.

MEDITERRANEAN QUINOA SALAD

So what the heck is quinoa? Pronounced "keen-wa" and neither cereal, grain, nor grass, it's a seed that's been grown in the Andes for six thousand years. The Incas considered it sacred. It is a complete, easy-to-digest protein, something the celiac person desperately needs, and it has a neutral, slightly nutty flavor. Like rice or pasta, it absorbs the flavors of whatever you add to it, and it's a natural with Mediterranean ingredients. YIELD: 6 TO 8 SERVINGS

1 cup quinoa

2 cups water

½ cup sun-dried or roasted tomatoes, chopped in small pieces

⅔ cup crumbled feta cheese

¼ cup pitted kalamata olives, roughly cut (add more if desired)

¼ cup toasted pine nuts

1 tablespoon finely chopped fresh oregano

1 tablespoon finely chopped fresh basil

3 tablespoons extra-virgin olive oil

2 cloves garlic, minced

1 teaspoon freshly ground black pepper

Sea salt to taste

12 to 16 Bibb lettuce leaves, rinsed and spun dry

Bring quinoa and water to a boil, cover, and simmer on low heat for 18 to 20 minutes. Fluff with a fork. Let cool to room temperature.

Mix remaining ingredients except Bibb lettuce leaves in a large mixing bowl. Add quinoa and refrigerate for 4 to 6 hours so flavors can blend. Place lettuce leaves on each salad plate. Add quinoa salad.

ROASTED ASPARAGUS, TOMATO, AND MUSHROOM SALAD

This is the best asparagus salad ever and a delicious accompaniment to any entrée.

When selecting asparagus, choose firm green spears with tightly closed tips. Before cooking, take each spear and bend it gently. It will snap at the point where the tenderness begins. Just discard the hard ends. When not roasting asparagus, we like to place it in a pot of salted boiling water for about 1 to 4 minutes, then plunge it into ice water. This will stop the cooking process and enhance the luscious green color, which makes for an attractive salad and makes you look like an attractive host.   YIELD: 6 TO 8 SERVINGS

2 tablespoons olive oil

2 tablespoons balsamic vinegar

2 cloves garlic, minced

1 tablespoon Italian herb seasoning: Spice Islands

1 cup fresh mushrooms, gently rinsed and halved

1 cup cherry tomatoes, halved

1 bunch asparagus, rinsed, with tough ends broken off

Sea salt to taste

Grated aged Parmesan cheese

Preheat oven to 400 F.

Whisk together olive oil, balsamic vinegar, garlic, and seasoning. Toss with mushrooms, tomatoes, and asparagus. Place on a parchment-lined baking sheet and roast for 12 to 18 minutes. Season with salt, if desired. Cool and serve. Garnish with grated aged Parmesan cheese.

SERVING SUGGESTION   This is great with grilled chicken and our Mr. Fluffy Pepper Jack and Aged Cheddar Biscuits (see Page 199). Oh, just have one of our Pecan Chocolate-Chip Cookies (see Page 240) afterward. We won't tell.

TOASTED PECAN, PEAR, AND BLUE CHEESE SALAD

This simple yet elegant salad is perfect for that "important" dinner. We top it with blue cheese and crunchy toasted pecans for a wonderful look and taste. YIELD: 4 SERVINGS

½ cup pecans

3 tablespoons white wine vinegar: Regina

1 teaspoon Dijon mustard: Maille Dijon Originale Mustard or Grey Poupon

½ teaspoon fine sea salt

4 teaspoons fresh lemon juice

⅛ teaspoon white pepper: Spice Islands

¼ cup extra-virgin olive oil

4 cups Bibb or other young lettuce, rinsed, spun dry, and torn into pieces

2 fresh ripe pears, cored and sliced

1 cup blue cheese: Boar's Head, Kraft, or Sargento All-Natural

Preheat oven to 350 F. Spread pecans on a baking sheet and roast for 10 to 15 minutes. Set aside.

In bowl, whisk together vinegar, mustard, salt, lemon juice, and pepper. Slowly whisk in olive oil until dressing is emulsified.

Divide lettuce among 4 plates. Place sliced pear on top of the lettuce. Divide the blue cheese and pecans among the salads. Drizzle with vinaigrette to taste.

SERVING SUGGESTION   We like this with our Beef Filets with Champagne Cream Sauce (see Page 85) and a hearty bottle of red wine.

ALMOND-AND-RED-PEPPER CABBAGE SLAW

This healthy, crunchy, slightly sweet salad stores well for a few days, as the flavors marry nicely. Also, we use much less oil than a traditional Southern cabbage slaw. In fact, you can omit the oil altogether and it's just as good. YIELD: 2 TO 3 QUARTS

1 cup sugar

1 cup apple cider vinegar: Heinz

1½ teaspoons mustard seed

1 tablespoon celery seed: Spice Islands

2 teaspoons sea salt

¼ cup olive oil

1 large head cabbage, thinly sliced

1 large carrot, coarsely grated

½ medium green bell pepper, sliced in matchstick pieces

½ medium red bell pepper, sliced in matchstick pieces

1 medium white onion, diced

½ cup slivered almonds: Blue Diamond Smoked Almonds

Prepare dressing by bringing the sugar, cider vinegar, mustard seed, celery seed, salt, and olive oil to a boil.

Mix prepared vegetables in a large bowl. Pour boiling-hot dressing over all and mix well. Store in glass container in refrigerator, where it will keep for a week. Serve topped with almonds.

SERVING SUGGESTION Try it with our Texas Oven-style Barbecue Brisket (see Page 80) and corn tortillas. It's also good with an icy cold Redbridge beer and sliced avocados with fresh lime juice.

MEXICAN CAESAR SALAD WITH CHILE POLENTA CROUTONS

Kim says you will want to bring out the Tijuana Brass for this zesty twist on a Caesar salad. The star of the show: Chile Polenta Croutons, which you make ahead. Finally, here is your crouton. Gluten-intolerant people no longer have to push them to the side. You can pile 'em high and enjoy.   YIELD: 8 TO 10 SERVINGS

2 chopped anchovy fillets, mashed well (see note)

1 cup mayonnaise: Hellmann's, Kraft, or Spectrum

1 tablespoon red wine vinegar: Heinz or Regina (add more depending on taste)

1 teaspoon Dijon mustard: Maille Dijon Originale Mustard or Grey Poupon

¼ teaspoon sea salt

⅛ teaspoon white pepper: Spice Islands

1 tablespoon Worcestershire sauce: Lea & Perrins or French's

3 cloves garlic, finely minced

2 to 3 teaspoons fresh lemon juice

½ teaspoon taco seasoning: McCormick Mexican Seasoning, Paul Prudhomme Ground Dried Magic Chile/New Mexico (mild) or our Mexican Seasoning (see Page 214)

½ teaspoon Tabasco sauce, or to taste

1 teaspoon chopped fresh oregano

1 teaspoon chopped fresh thyme

1 tablespoon chopped fresh parsley

1 tablespoon chopped capers

½ cup extra-virgin olive oil

16 to 20 cups fresh Romaine lettuce, rinsed, spun dry, and torn into pieces

½ cup grated Parmigiano-Reggiano cheese

½ cup crumbled cotija cheese (Mexican white cheese)

½ cup frozen corn kernels, room temperature

Chile Polenta Croutons (recipe follows)

Purée together anchovy, mayonnaise, vinegar, mustard, salt, pepper, Worcestershire, garlic, lemon juice, taco seasoning, Tabasco, fresh herbs, and capers. Slowly add the olive oil with processor on low.

Mix lettuce and Parmigiano-Reggiano in a large bowl; toss with enough dressing to coat. You may have some dressing left over for another use.

Plate the salads individually. Top with crumbled cotija, corn, and Chile Polenta Croutons.

NOTE: If the anchovies are too fishy-tasting, soak them in milk or buttermilk for 1 hour. Drain and mash.

ADDITIONS: You may add any of the following to make your salad even more festive: Pine nuts, red, green, or yellow peppers, avocado, black olives, chopped tomatoes, chopped egg or poached egg, roasted red pepper, or sun-dried or roasted tomatoes.

CHILE POLENTA CROUTONS

Olive oil

1¼ cup water

1 teaspon sea salt

½ cup polenta or yellow corn grits

1 tablespoon butter

1 teaspoon ground cumin: McCormick or Spice Islands

1 teaspoon chili powder: McCormick or Spice Islands

½ cup grated Parmesan or extra-sharp cheddar cheese

1 clove garlic, minced

½ ear of corn, kernels sliced off the cob, or frozen corn kernels

2 eggs, beaten

½ teaspoon freshly gound black pepper

Preheat oven to 360 F. Use olive oil to generously grease an 8x11-inch pan. Set aside.

In a small saucepan over high heat, bring water with salt to a boil. Quickly whisk in the polenta until fully incorporated.

Lower the heat to a low simmer. Add the butter, cumin, and chili powder and allow the polenta to cook, stirring often, for 5 minutes, or until very thick. (It has to be thick.) Finish by stirring in the cheese, garlic, corn kernels, and salt and pepper to taste.

Pat the thickened polenta into the prepared pan and bake for 30 to 38 minutes, or until the top is a bit crispy and the edges are golden brown. Remove from oven, let cool, then place in refrigerator until cold.

Preheat oven to 425 F. Gently remove from pan in large pieces. Lightly brush top and bottom of polenta with olive oil. Cut into 1-inch croutons. Bake for 10 to 12 minutes, or until crispy brown.

NOTE: Kim likes to keep polenta croutons on hand because who knows when a dinner party just happens to pop up! The croutons freeze quite well so just thaw'em to soften them up, broil 'em to crisp them up, and toss'em to perk up that salad! Try it!

SOUPS

Soups are good for the soul and so beneficial for a healthy gluten-free lifestyle. Our mouthwatering soups are filled with fresh vegetables, savory meats, and an array of bold herbs and spices to make them interesting and scrumptious. For a light, refreshing lunch on a warm summer day, chilled Guadalajara Gazpacho, with just a little spicy heat, is perfect.

For recipes that would ordinarily call for wheat flour, like our decadent Potato Leek Soup with Watercress, we've substituted gluten-free flours in just the right proportion. You would be shocked to find out how many of the canned soups on the market contain gluten.

Our delicious soups, which liberate you forever from canned mediocrity, are substantial, rich, and tasty. In fact, if we're going to serve soup, it's going to be the meal, not an appetizer. After you try these, we think you'll agree it's the only way to go.

POTATO LEEK SOUP WITH WATERCRESS

Hot and satisfying . . . perfect for that chilly winter day. We love the flavor that leeks bring to soup—similar to their cousin, the onion, but with a milder, sweet taste that adds depth to any dish. They are great in brunch dishes sautéed or braised, or they can fly solo on their own when soup's not on the menu. But when you're ready for a rich, warming meal-in-a-bowl, try this.   YIELD: 10 SERVINGS

2 cloves garlic, minced

½ cup carrot, thinly sliced into rounds

1 cup chopped leeks (white part only, see note)

1 cup finely chopped celery

1 tablespoon olive oil

5 cups chicken broth: Health Valley Fat-free, Pacific Natural Foods Organic, or Swanson Natural Goodness

6 cups peeled, diced russet potatoes

2 bay leaves

⅔ cup butter

⅔ cup Bob's Red Mill White Rice flour

5 cups whole milk

1 cup half-and-half

1 cup sour cream

1 teaspoon sea salt

1 teaspoon pepper

1 cup shredded Boar's Head Vermont cheddar cheese

4 slices bacon, cooked and crumbled

½ cup chopped chives

¼ cup finely chopped watercress

In a large pot, sauté garlic, carrot, leek, and celery in olive oil until translucent, 7 to 10 minutes. Add chicken broth, potatoes, and bay leaves. Add water to cover. Bring to a boil, then reduce heat and simmer 15 to 20 minutes, or until potatoes are done.

In double boiler, melt butter, then whisk in rice flour until smooth. Add milk, stirring until mixture is smooth. Add half-and-half and sour cream. Whisk until smooth. Set aside.

Measure and set aside 1 or 2 cups of liquid from vegetable pot.

Purée about two-thirds of vegetables and liquid in blender or with a handheld blender until smooth. Don't overblend; you want to retain some texture.

Return puréed liquid to vegetable pot. Stir well. Add milk-flour mixture to vegetable pot. Stir until soup thickens. Add salt and pepper. Cook over medium heat until well blended and heated thoroughly.

Serve in individual bowls garnished with cheddar cheese, crumbled bacon, chives, and watercress.

NOTE: To clean leeks well, cut off the root and part of the green top. Slice the white part lengthwise into halves, separate the layers, and wash under cold running water. Pat dry.

SERVING SUGGESTION   We like big bowls of this soup with our Southwestern Pepper-Jack-and-Zucchini Corn Cakes (see Page 25), a baby spinach salad dashed with our Poppyseed Dressing (see Page 34) and a dry white wine.

CREAMY TOMATO BASIL SOUP

This is a delicious recipe that is rich and velvety. But the real secret to its great taste is using Pastene brand San Marzano plum tomatoes with a basil leaf. These are some of the finest-tasting tomatoes in the world, grown in nutrient-dense volcanic soil in the San Marzano region of Italy, and Pastene is the oldest Italian specialty importing company in America. Although *Cook's Illustrated* magazine punched some holes in the San Marzano mystique in a 2012 taste test, we still love our Pastenes. They also carry the elite European Union Denominazione d'Origine Protella (D.O.P.) seal, which guarantees that they are real San Marzanos grown in the Sarnese-Nocerino area.   YIELD: 6 SERVINGS

1 (28-ounce) can Pastene San Marzano Italian plum tomatoes, crushed by hand in a bowl

1 tablespoon finely chopped shallot

4 cups tomato juice

10 fresh basil leaves, minced

1 tablespoon sugar

1 cup heavy whipping cream

3 tablespoons butter

Basil for garnish

In a large nonstick pot, bring crushed tomatoes, shallots, and tomato juice to a very light boil.

Reduce heat to low/medium-low. Cover pot and simmer very slowly for 45 minutes to 1 hour.

Add minced basil and sugar. Stir. Pour in blender and purée, or use a handheld blender. (Be very careful blending hot liquids. Put a towel or thick cloth on top of blender when you are blending.)

Return mixture to pot. Increase heat to medium. Stir in cream and butter. When butter has melted, give it another quick stir and serve. Garnish with fresh basil leaves.

SERVING SUGGESTION   This is awesome with our Artichoke-Feta Fritters (see Page 27) or our Romano and Oregano Crisps (see Page 196) with a light salad.

DADDY'S POBLANO-AND-MONTEREY-JACK CORN CHOWDER

Daddy-o, Daddy-o. Daddy's corn chowder tops them all. Bill dedicates this recipe to his daughter, Jeni.

YIELD: 6 TO 8 SERVINGS

4 strips applewood-smoked bacon, diced

½ cup diced onion

½ cup finely chopped carrot

½ cup finely chopped celery

3 teaspoons finely chopped jalapeño pepper

4 tablespoons finely chopped poblano pepper

2 cloves garlic, minced

2 cups peeled and diced russet potatoes, cut in ½-inch cubes

2½ cups chicken broth: Health Valley 100 Percent Natural, Pacific Natural Foods, or Swanson Natural Goodness

1 teaspoon sea salt (divided use)

¼ teaspoon ground paprika: McCormick or Spice Islands

1 bay leaf

4 tablespoons Bob's Red Mill White Rice Flour

½ cup cold whole milk

1½ cup hot (not boiling) half-and-half

2 cups fresh or frozen premium white corn, thawed if frozen

1 (15-ounce) can Del Monte yellow corn

¼ teaspoon freshly ground black pepper

1 cup grated Monterey Jack cheese

Sauté bacon until semi-crisp. Add onion, carrot, celery, peppers, and garlic and sauté 5 minutes. Add potatoes, broth, ½ teaspoon salt, paprika, and bay leaf and simmer 45 minutes.

Remove and discard bay leaf. Stir in the rice flour and cold whole milk and heat 5 minutes.

Add hot half-and-half. Add corn and black pepper. Reheat. Do not boil.

Divide among 4 large soup bowls. Sprinkle with remaining ½ teaspoon salt.

Top with cheese.

SERVING SUGGESTION   This is great in the fall served with our Artichoke-Feta Fritters (see Page 27) and a spinach salad topped with our Better-Than-a-French-Kiss French Dressing (see Page 34) and a sprinkling of sunflower seeds.

WEAVER FAMILY CHICKEN-AND-RICE SOUP

Every family has a recipe that they will defend to their death. This is it for Bill. This recipe is a hand-me-down from his grandmother Mimi and his mother, Adrienne. It's a household staple. You can't buy chicken soup this good.   YIELD: 10 TO 12 SERVINGS

---

4 whole bone-in, skin-on chicken breasts

1 cup diced onion

2 garlic cloves, minced

9 cups water

4 to 6 carrots, peeled and chopped

1 cup chopped celery (use green leafy parts, too)

3¼ cups chicken broth: Health Valley Fat-free, Pacific Natural Foods Organic, or Swanson Natural Goodness

½ teaspoon sea salt or to taste (see note)

½ teaspoon poultry seasoning: Spice Island or Paul Prudhomme Poultry Magic

⅛ teaspoon celery powder: Spice Island

1 tablespoon chopped fresh parsley

1 cup cooked rice

In a large pot over medium heat, boil chicken, onion, and garlic in water 45 minutes to 1 hour. Remove chicken and let cool. Remove skin and bones. Chop chicken into bite-size pieces.

Add chicken and all remaining ingredients except the rice to the pot. Bring to a boil, reduce heat, then cook on low for 2 to 3 hours. Add rice 10 minutes before serving.

NOTE: Go easy on the salt. You can always adjust to taste just before serving.

GUADALAJARA GAZPACHO

This chilled tomato soup, a gazpacho of sorts, makes a refreshing addition to a summer lunch. We like to serve it with guacamole, Authentic Fresh Pico de Gallo, grilled shrimp, and our Mr. Fluffy Pepper Jack and Aged Cheddar Biscuits (see Page 199). You also might just want to serve it with an icy cold Redbridge Beer (Bill's favorite) and large grilled shrimp with quartered limes.   YIELD: 8 servings

2 to 3 pounds plum tomatoes, washed, cored, and chopped

⅔ cup diced yellow onion

1 red bell pepper, diced

½ green bell pepper, diced

½ teaspoon ground cumin: McCormick or Spice Islands

1 teaspoon chopped fresh oregano

Dash of cayenne pepper: McCormick or Spice Islands

4 cloves garlic, minced

1 mild pepper (poblano or serrano), seeded and halved

1 jalapeño pepper, seeded and halved

¼ cup chopped fresh cilantro

4 cups chicken broth: Health Valley Fat-free, Pacific Natural Foods Organic, or Swanson Natural Goodness

Sea salt and pepper to taste

½ cup finely diced cucumber

Avocado Purée using 2 avocados (recipe follows)

1 cup fresh roasted corn kernels (see note)

Purée all ingredients except Avocado Purée and corn in blender. Strain through fine sieve.

Adjust seasoning with salt and pepper. Pour into a glass container. Chill in refrigerator for 5 hours before serving. Serve with small dollops of avocado purée and sprinkle with roasted corn.

NOTE: To roast corn, preheat oven to 375 F. Slice kernels off cob and lightly toss with olive oil, salt, and pepper. Spread in a single layer in a pan and roast for 7 to 10 minutes.

AVOCADO PURÉE

Peel, pit, and quarter 2 ripe avocados. Place in a blender with 3 tablespoons fresh lime juice.

EGGS, CHEESE, AND PASTA

Our egg, cheese, and pasta dishes are distinctly creative, healthy, and guaranteed to keep you going all day . . . or night. Many cultures around the world serve egg dishes for breakfast, lunch, and dinner. The French are especially appreciative of beautiful eggs. And why not? Eggs are a rich, gluten-free source of protein and adaptable in so many recipes. We prefer fresh, local, organic, cage-free eggs. For breakfast, Gisela's Huevos Rancheros Especiales is always a favorite. Our Feta, Spinach, Artichoke, and Sun-Dried Tomato Frittata has just enough kick for that morning jump-start. Or, to keep it simple, add our Gruyère and Asiago Cheese Biscuits to straight-up bacon and eggs.

We also love cheese, as you can see. Eggs-and-cheese and pasta-and-cheese are naturals together. But many cheeses and especially packaged shredded cheeses include gluten as an anti-caking agent. So when you shop, look for aged block cheeses; try a good cheddar, Parmesan or Romano. Just check the labels for additives and flavorings. If you are a blue cheese addict, you may also want to check the source of mold.

As for pasta, remember that semolina, spelt, and whole-wheat pasta, including couscous, are not gluten-free. Thank goodness there are some really great gluten-free pastas on the market these days. We have every reason to believe that the number of delicious gluten-free pasta products will increase in the future, which means your options are only going to improve. Our Boursin Fettucine Alfredo with Pancetta is great as an entrée and, of course, we couldn't leave out the good old American Mac and Cheese that kiddos love— and adults crave. Just remember: Do not overcook your pasta. You want it to be al dente, as it will continue to cook in its sauce.

GISELA'S HUEVOS RANCHEROS ESPECIALES

We are Texans. Hear us loud and clear: We love our huevos rancheros, or "ranch-style" eggs. Our version of the classic Mexican favorite starts with sunny-side-up eggs that are topped with spicy Ranchero Sauce and a sprinkling of cotija cheese. We like to round out the platter with fresh fruit, avocado slices, salsa, and skillet potatoes, hash browns, or refried beans. Oh, and don't forget some warm corn tortillas.   YIELD: 4 SERVINGS

4 slices bacon

5 teaspoons oil (divided use)

½ onion, diced

½ teaspoon sea salt

¼ teaspoon cumin: McCormick or Spice Islands

1½ clove garlic, minced

⅛ teaspoon oregano: McCormick or Spice Islands

⅛ teaspoon white pepper: Spice Islands

1 tablespoon finely chopped, mild pickled jalapeños

½ cup mild Rotel brand tomatoes and diced green chiles

½ cup tomato sauce: Contadina, Del Monte Organic, or Hunt's

1 cup chicken broth: Health Valley Fat-free, Pacific Natural Foods Organic, or Swanson Natural Goodness

¼ teaspoon cayenne pepper: McCormick or Spice Islands

4 corn tortillas: Mission, El Lago, or Sonoma Organic

2 to 4 tablespoons unsalted butter for frying

8 large eggs (see note)

½ cup warm refried beans: El Paso fat-free

1 cup cotija cheese (Mexican cheese)

Cook bacon in large cast-iron skillet over medium-high heat. Remove with a slotted spoon. Drain on paper towels and chop fine. Set aside.

Drain bacon grease and add 3 teaspoons oil to skillet. Cook onion in oil 3 to 5 minutes, stirring. Add salt, cumin, garlic, oregano, white pepper, and jalapeño pepper. Cook for 30 seconds.

Add Rotel tomatoes with diced chiles and tomato sauce. Cook for 2 minutes. Add the chopped bacon. Add chicken broth and cayenne pepper. Bring to a boil and reduce heat, simmering for 10 to 15 minutes, or until flavors are well blended. Cover sauce and keep warm.

Preheat oven to 200 F.

In nonstick skillet, heat ½ teaspoon of oil over medium-high heat for each tortilla. When hot, cook the tortillas, 1 at a time, 8 to 10 seconds on each side until just warmed through and starting to bubble. Add ½ teaspoon of oil and heat for each tortilla. Tortillas should be pliable and not crispy. Wrap tortillas in foil, placing paper towels between them. Keep warm in oven.

Heat butter in large nonstick skillet. Gently fry eggs until the whites are almost set, about 1 minute. Keep the eggs separate. Pour 1 cup of the Ranchero Sauce over the eggs and cook over low heat for 2 to 3 minutes.

Place 1 tortilla on each of 4 warmed plates. Spread 2 tablespoons of warm refried beans on each tortilla. Put 2 eggs on each tortilla. Top with remaining Ranchero Sauce and cotija cheese. Serve immediately.

NOTE: We like eggs kind of runny, so the yolks enhance the texture of the sauce. They can be poached, too.

NEW YEAR'S DAY BRUNCH CASSEROLE

Celebrate New Year's every day. This very delicious brunch dish is always a crowd-pleaser. Actually, this can be eaten at all hours of the day or night. We like it spicy, so we add 2 teaspoons of chopped jalapeño pepper. Of course we do. YIELD: 6 SERVINGS

¼ cup unsalted butter

10 slices gluten-free bread: Kinnikinnick's Soft White Bread, Udi's White Sandwich Bread (crusts cut off)

1½ pounds pork sausage: J. C. Potter's

½ pound sharp cheddar cheese, grated: Kraft Natural or Boar's Head

½ pound Monterey Jack cheese, grated: Kraft Natural or Boar's Head

1 (4-ounce) can green chiles, drained

3 tablespoons finely sliced green onion

12 eggs

¼ teaspoon dry mustard: Colman's

2 dashes Louisiana or Cholula hot pepper sauce

2 tablespoons grated onion

½ teaspoon garlic powder

3 cups milk (or ½ milk and ½ half-and-half)

½ teaspoon paprika: McCormick or Spice Islands

1 teaspoon Worcestershire sauce: Lea & Perrins or French's

Sea salt and pepper to taste

Butter de-crusted bread. Cube each slice of bread into 9 pieces. Set aside.

Brown sausage well (do not fully cook). Drain on paper towel.

Preheat oven to 350 F. Butter a 9 x 13 x 3-inch baking dish.

In the dish, layer ½ of the bread, ½ of the sausage, ½ of the cheeses, ½ of the chiles and ½ of the green onions.

In a large mixing bowl, mix eggs, mustard, hot sauce, grated onion, garlic powder, milk, paprika, Worcestershire sauce, salt, and pepper. Pour over casserole and lightly dust with paprika. Add the other layer of ingredients, starting with the bread.

Wrap with plastic wrap and refrigerate overnight.

When ready to bake, preheat oven to 375 F. Bake 1½ hours, or until a fork comes out clean.

TORTILLA, GREEN CHILE, AND MANCHEGO CHEESE STRATA

Spain meets Mexico in Santa Fe. The delicious and slightly piquant nutty taste of the Spanish Manchego cheese combined with traditional Mexican ingredients and New Mexico green chiles make this uniquely, wonderfully flavorful—and perfect for brunch. Assemble it the night before, and all you have to do is pop it in the oven. Then you can spend your time concentrating on the rest of the brunch. Or not.   YIELD: 8 TO 10 SERVINGS

1 cup diced onion

2 tablespoons butter

1 (4-ounce) can green chile peppers, drained, or 1 fresh medium to large mild green chile pepper, chopped

1 (10-ounce) can Rotel brand tomatoes and diced green chiles, drained

8 ounces sharp cheddar cheese, grated: Kraft Natural or Boar's Head

8 ounces La Vaquita (Mexican style cream) or sour cream

4 ounces Manchego cheese, grated

2 tablespoons salsa: Valentina Mexican Salsa Picante or Ortega Medium Picante Sauce

8 eggs, beaten

1 teaspoon dry mustard: Colman's

½ teaspoon sea salt

½ teaspoon pepper

1 teaspoon garlic powder

8 to 10 drops of Louisiana Hot Sauce

1 cup half-and-half

1 cup fresh or frozen corn

9 corn tortillas, cut in half: Mission, El Lago, or Sonoma Organic

Nonstick cooking spray

Sauté onion in 2 tablespoons butter.

In a medium bowl, mix together all ingredients except tortillas and cooking spray. Reserve a little of grated Manchego cheese for the top.

Spray a 9 x 13-inch baking dish with nonstick cooking spray. Line bottom in a single layer with 9 tortilla halves, then ½ of mixture and repeat. Cover with plastic wrap and refrigerate overnight.

Preheat oven to 350 F. Remove the dish from refrigerator and remove plastic wrap. Cover top with foil and bake 30 minutes. Remove foil and bake another 15.

SERVING SUGGESTION   We like this with our Cranberry Waldorf Salad (see Page 36).

POBLANO PEPPER FRITTATA WITH RED ONION, POTATO, AND PARMESAN

This is worth getting outta bed for. We guarantee this is the best frittata this side of the border. If you enjoy the spice of life early in the day, add our Authentic Fresh Pico de Gallo (see Page 209)   YIELD: 4 SERVINGS

4 tablespoons olive oil (divided use)

2 russet potatoes, peeled and thinly sliced (¼ inch)

4 poblano peppers, cored, seeded, and chopped

½ cup diced red onion

1½ cup hot water

8 eggs

1 tablespoon finely minced fresh oregano

¼ teaspoon sea salt

¼ teaspoon cayenne pepper: McCormick or Spice Islands

¼ teaspoon white pepper: Spice Islands

1 tablespoons grated Parmesan cheese

Preheat broiler.

Heat 2 tablespoons olive oil in cast-iron skillet over medium-high heat. Add potatoes, peppers, and onion. Fry for 5 minutes. Add water and stir. Cover skillet and reduce heat. Cook 10 to 15 minutes, or until vegetables are cooked and liquid evaporates. Add more water, if necessary. Remove to a bowl and set aside.

Wipe the skillet clean with paper towel. Add remaining 2 tablespoons oil over medium heat.

In a medium mixing bowl, beat together eggs, oregano, salt, cayenne pepper, and white pepper. Add egg mixture to skillet. Tilt to coat pan.

Add fried vegetables, distributing them evenly. Reduce heat to medium-low. Cook frittata, without stirring, for about 10 minutes. Run the frittata under the broiler, about 5 inches from the heat source until top is lightly browned, 1 to 2 minutes.

Remove frittata to a platter. Top with Parmesan cheese and serve immediately.

SERVING SUGGESTION   We like this with a spinach salad drizzled with our Warm Brown Sugar and Applewood-Smoked Bacon Dressing (see Page 32), and fresh berries and melon.

FETA, SPINACH, ARTICHOKE, AND SUN-DRIED TOMATO FRITTATA

This easy and elegant Mediterranean-flair frittata is light and flavorful, yet refined. It is always satisfying. Although it's a brunch natural, it makes a tasty lunch or light dinner.   YIELD: 6 TO 8 SERVINGS

2 tablespoons salted butter

1 cup fresh spinach, rinsed and dried

¼ cup chopped sun-dried tomatoes (in olive oil)

2 finely chopped scallions

½ cup chopped fresh mushrooms

¼ teaspoon sea salt or to taste

¼ teaspoon freshly ground black pepper

1 teaspoon chopped fresh basil

1 teaspoon chopped fresh thyme

1 teaspoon chopped fresh oregano

8 eggs

2 tablespoons half-and-half

½ cup feta cheese, crumbled

¼ cup black olives, pitted and sliced

½ cup chopped canned artichokes: California Girl, Maria, or Reese

Preheat oven to 350 F.

Heat butter in nonstick, ovenproof skillet (we mean it, as this will go in the oven) over medium heat. Add spinach, tomatoes, scallions, mushrooms, salt, pepper, and herbs. Stir.

In a medium mixing bowl, whisk eggs with half-and-half. Add egg mixture to skillet. Add feta, black olives, and artichokes. Reduce heat to low. Tilt skillet to coat and cook for 3 minutes.

Place skillet in oven and bake for 6 to 8 minutes. Remove skillet from oven. Allow frittata to rest for 5 minutes before serving.

SERVING SUGGESTION   We like this for Saturday brunch with a mixed-green salad topped with our Buttermilk Romano Herb Dressing (see Page 31), some fresh raspberries, our Blueberry Crumb Muffins (see Page 200), and, yeah . . . some pink champagne.

CHEDDAR AND JALAPEÑO GRATIN

Let this gratin light your fire. It's great for brunch, lunch, or dinner. It's easy to make the night before: You can just pop it into the oven. It's also an ideal party food, because it can be served at room temperature on a buffet. Think Christmas morning. Or any Sunday morning. YIELD: 6 SERVINGS

Nonstick cooking spray

10 to 12 eggs

4 cups milk

½ teaspoon sea salt

½ teaspoon white pepper: Spice Islands

10 to 12 slices gluten-free bread: Kinnikinnick's Italian White Rice Tapioca, or Udi's white sandwich bread, crusts cut off

1 pound bacon, cooked crisp and crumbled

1 bunch green onions, white and green parts, sliced into ½-inch pieces

3 cups shredded sharp cheddar cheese: Kraft Natural or Boar's Head

1 jalapeño pepper, seeded, deveined, and finely chopped

½ cup grated Parmesan cheese

Preheat oven to 350 F (unless you are making the dish ahead).

Generously spray a 9 x 13 x 3-inch baking dish with cooking spray. In bowl, mix eggs, milk, salt, and pepper until blended. Set aside.

Line the bottom of the prepared dish with 6 pieces of bread. Crumble ½ of the bacon over layer. Sprinkle ½ of the onion, ½ of the cheddar cheese, and ½ of the jalapeño pepper over bacon. Pour ½ egg mixture over layer.

Repeat bread, onion, bacon, and cheese layers and pour remaining milk-egg mixture over top.

Sprinkle with Parmesan cheese. Bake uncovered for 45 minutes to 1 hour or until a knife inserted in the center comes out clean.

If you refrigerate the gratin overnight, give it 30 minutes at room temperature before popping in the 350 F oven. It will probably take the longer baking time.

ASPARAGUS GRATIN

Asparagus isn't just for dinner anymore. This luscious dish works as a side or a light entrée, depending on your mood. Great with fresh, sliced tomatoes. Simple and gourmet and packed with fresh flavor. YIELD: 4 SERVINGS

1 bunch fresh asparagus, tough ends snapped off

Nonstick cooking spray

4 eggs

1 egg white

1 cup whole milk

¼ cup grated Parmigiano-Reggiano cheese

Pinch sea salt

⅛ teaspoon white pepper: Spice Islands

In a large saucepan, boil asparagus in salted water about 5 minutes. Let it go a little beyond al dente but don't overcook. Remove and set aside.

Adjust oven rack to middle and preheat oven to 400 F. Spray a 9 x 13-inch baking pan with nonstick cooking spray. Set aside.

In a medium mixing bowl, whisk together eggs, egg white, milk, cheese, salt, and pepper.

Lay asparagus across the bottom of prepared pan. Pour egg mixture over asparagus. Bake 20 to 25 minutes, or until done and light brown on top.

SERVING SUGGESTION   We like this with our Beef Filets with Champagne Cream Sauce (see Page 85), a salad of mixed greens with our *Sauce Vinaigrette* (French Vinaigrette) (see Page 35), red wine and our Lemon-Sour-Cream Pound Cake (see Page 236).

LORRAINE . . . THE QUICHE

Lorraine has outdone herself. Here's our version of a tried-and-true. Served warm or at room temperature, it's a crowd-pleaser.   YIELD: 1 (9-INCH) QUICHE

8 strips of bacon, cooked crisp

Piecrust for Quiche (recipe follows)

¼ cup diced smoked Virginia ham: Boar's Head

½ cup diced Swiss cheese: Boar's Head

4 to 5 eggs

½ teaspoon sea salt

¼ teaspoon white pepper: Spice Islands

¼ teaspoon cayenne pepper: McCormick or Spice Islands

¾ cup whipping cream

¾ cup half-and-half

Preheat oven to 350 F.

Crush bacon and scatter over bottom of pie shell. Scatter ham and Swiss cheese evenly.

Place eggs, spices, cream and half-and-half in blender. Blend thoroughly. Pour into pie shell.

Bake for 35 to 40 minutes, or until top is golden and eggs are set. Ovens may vary.

Serve warm or at room temperature.

PIECRUST FOR QUICHE

Finally, a gluten-free piecrust worth eating. This freezes beautifully, so we like to leave one or two in our freezer. That way, when we need it, all we have to do is thaw one out.   YIELD: 1 (9-INCH) PIE SHELL

Nonstick cooking spray

1½ cups gluten-free flour: Bob's Red Mill Biscuit

7 tablespoons butter

4 tablespoons cold water

Preheat oven to 400 F. Grease a 9-inch pie plate with nonstick cooking spray or butter. Set aside.

Blend together flour and butter with a pastry cutter or food processor until well cut. Add water and knead with oiled hands until it forms a ball, approximately 1 minute.

Continuing with oiled hands, shape and press evenly into the bottom and up the sides of prepared pie plate. Protect crust with pie shield or strips of aluminum foil. Bake 10 to 12 minutes. Cool completely.

BISQUICK VARIATION   Follow directions above, except use 1 cup gluten-free Bisquick, ¼ cup plus 1 tablespoon shortening and 3 to 4 tablespoons cold water.

GRUYÈRE AND APPLEWOOD-SMOKED BACON QUICHE

Now, here's to the top of the morning. The flavor of gruyère is just so mouthwatering. Unbelievable. And now you don't have to leave the crust on your plate anymore. YIELD: 1 (9-INCH) QUICHE

|||||||||||||||||||||||||||||||||||||||||||||||||||||||||||||||||||||||||||||||||||||||||||||||||||||||||||||||||||||||||

4 to 5 eggs

2 tablespoons minced chives

¼ teaspoon paprika: McCormick or Spice Islands

⅛ teaspoon cayenne pepper: McCormick or Spice Islands

¼ teaspoon dry mustard: Colman's

½ teaspoon sea salt

¼ teaspoon white pepper: Spice Islands

¾ cup whipping cream

¾ cup half-and-half

¼ teaspoon Tabasco sauce

5 strips of applewood-smoked bacon, cooked crisp and crumbled

1 cup grated gruyère cheese

1 Piecrust for Quiche (see Page 69)

½ very thinly sliced tomato

Preheat oven to 350 F.

Place eggs, chives, spices, cream, half-and-half, and Tabasco sauce in a mixing bowl and blend very thoroughly. Add bacon and cheese. Pour into piecrust. Place tomato slices on top.

Bake for 35 to 40 minutes, or until top is golden and mixture is set. Protect crust with pie shield or strips of aluminum foil, if needed. Serve warm or at room temperature.

SERVING SUGGESTION   We like this with a mix of blueberries and sliced strawberries and a simple salad of mixed greens tossed with our Lemon Caper Vinaigrette with Baked Goat Cheese Rounds (see Page 45).

ALL-AMERICAN MACARONI AND CHEESE

We all grew up eating that concoction out of a box laden with preservatives and powdery faux cheese sauce. And it seemed good. But it's not good for you. Drum roll, please: This is the grown-up, all-American mac-and-cheese you have been waiting for. It's simple and tasty, and it's real. And because gluten-free pastas have come such a long way, you don't have to miss out. You'll love it, and the kids will love it, too. Kim likes to add chopped green chiles. Because she's a Texan, that's why. YIELD: 4 SERVINGS

2 tablespoons butter, plus a little extra for dish

Nonstick cooking spray

2 tablespoons white rice flour: Bob's Red Mill

1¼ cups milk

2 eggs

1 cup grated cheddar or American cheese: Boar's Head

¼ teaspoon sea salt

⅛ teaspoon paprika: McCormick or Spice Islands

½ teaspoon Worcestershire sauce: Lea & Perrins or French's

2 drops Tabasco sauce or Cholula hot sauce

2 tablespoons chopped green chiles (optional)

1¼ cup cooked gluten-free noodles tossed with 1 tablespoon oil (we like Mrs. Leeper's organic corn noodles)

Preheat oven to 350 F. Butter a baking dish or spray with nonstick cooking spray.

Melt butter in the top of double boiler. Add flour; whisk until well blended. Add milk, stirring constantly. Cook until smooth.

In a mixing bowl, beat eggs slightly. Stir 2 tablespoons cooked milk mixture into eggs. Gradually stir egg mixture into double boiler. Stir in cheese, salt, and paprika until dissolved. Add Worcestershire, Tabasco, or Cholula and chopped green chiles, if using.

Pour cooked macaroni in baking dish. Spread evenly. Pour cheese mixture over macaroni and bake for 25 to 30 minutes until top begins to turn lightly brown.

MEXICAN QUICHE WITH POBLANO-CHEDDAR POLENTA CRUST

With loads of flavor, this recipe is just divine, and it makes a beautiful quiche that's perfect for a brunch. It's very versatile, as you can use our chorizo recipe, pork or turkey sausage, or, if you are a vegetarian, skip the meat. Not only is it a meal in itself, but it is outrageous with a gluten-free crust that's better than any traditional crust —hands down. YIELD: 1 (11-INCH) QUICHE

CRUST:

1¼ cup plus 2 tablespoons water

½ cup polenta

2 tablespoons chopped poblano pepper, cored and seeded

1 tablespoon oil

½ tablespoon baking powder: Clabber Girl, Hain, or Rumford

½ cup gluten-free flour: Arrowhead Mills All Purpose Gluten Free Baking Flour

or Pamela's Baking & Pancake Mix

½ teaspoon xanthan gum

1 teaspoon sea salt

3 tablespoons butter, room temperature

1 egg

½ cup aged white cheddar cheese

1 tablespoon red chile peppers, cored, seeded, and finely chopped, optional

FILLING:

¼ cup diced white onion

¼ pound sausage: J. C. Potter's Regular Country Sausage, Johnsonville Chorizo, or our chorizo (see Page 103), or ground sirloin

5 large eggs, beaten

½ teaspoon ground cumin: McCormick or Spice Islands

½ teaspoon chili powder: McCormick or Spice Islands

½ teaspoon sea salt

⅛ teaspoon cayenne pepper: McCormick or Spice Islands

1 tablespoon Valentina Mexican Salsa Picante or dash of Tabasco or Cholula hot sauce

¼ cup diced green chilies (canned is okay)

¼ cup black olives

½ cup chopped firm and very ripe Roma tomatoes

½ cup fresh or high-quality frozen corn kernels, thawed if frozen

½ cup sharp cheddar cheese or Monterey Jack cheese

½ cup Havarti cheese (we use Havarti with jalapeño peppers)

Bring water to a boil in a small saucepan. Add the polenta very, very slowly, stirring constantly until smooth. Reduce heat to low and cook 3 to 5 minutes, constantly stirring until it becomes thick. (It will become very thick.) Let cool to room temperature.

Sauté the poblano pepper in oil. Set aside.

In a medium mixing bowl, mix the baking powder, gluten-free flour, xanthan gum, and 1 teaspoon salt. Add butter and egg. Mix well. Add white cheddar cheese and poblano and mix into dough "flour mixture." Set aside.

Blend together the flour mixture with the polenta and red chile peppers, if using, until it almost forms a ball.

Dust the pan with gluten-free flour or use oiled hands and press dough into bottom and up sides of pan. Set aside while you make the filling.

Preheat oven to 350 F.

Sauté onions with beef or chorizo. Drain.

In a bowl, mix together the eggs, cumin, chili powder, remaining ½ teaspoon salt, cayenne and picante or Mexican hot sauce. Add the green chilies, olives, tomatoes, corn, cheeses, and meat mixture with onions.

Fill the crust with the quiche filling. Bake for 22 to 27 minutes, or until a knife inserted in center comes out clean and the eggs are set and the crust is golden brown. If the crust is getting too brown, cover with foil after 15 minutes.

PASTA WITH LEMON-CAPER SAUCE

This is a delicious lemony, buttery, garlicky treat. It makes a scrumptious summer or spring dinner, especially when paired with our Jalapeño Pecan Cornbread-Crusted Fillets (see Page 151) or grilled salmon.   YIELD: 4 SERVINGS

2 tablespoons extra-virgin olive oil

4 tablespoons butter (divided use)

3 cloves garlic, minced

1 tablespoon chopped shallots

¼ cup capers, drained: Mezzetta, Reese, or Star

1 teaspoon chopped fresh basil

1 teaspoon chopped fresh thyme

½ teaspoon chopped fresh oregano

1 teaspoon lemon zest (yellow part only)

¼ teaspoon white pepper: Spice Islands

¼ teaspoon sea salt

Pinch of freshly ground black pepper

1 cup chicken broth: Health Valley Fat-free, Pacific Natural Foods Organic, or Swanson Natural Goodness

Juice of 1 lemon

½ cup dry white wine

8 ounces Orgran Tomato and Basil Corn Pasta or Mrs. Leeper's Organic Corn Pasta, cooked al dente in salted water with 1 tablespoon olive oil

2 tablespoons grated Romano cheese

3 tablespoons grated Parmesan cheese

Place olive oil in a large skillet over medium-high heat. Add 2 tablespoons of the butter, and garlic and shallots. Cook until golden brown. Don't overcook.

Add capers, basil, thyme, oregano, lemon zest, white pepper, salt, and black pepper. When capers sizzle, immediately add the chicken broth and lemon juice and bring to a boil.

Add wine and cook until sauce is reduced by one-half, or until thick. Finish sauce with remaining 2 tablespoons butter and stir until melted. Pour over drained pasta and mix. Add more lemon juice to taste. Top with cheese and serve.

SERVING SUGGESTION   This is great with grilled chicken, Sicilian-Style Veal Scaloppini (see Page 100), or grilled shrimp.

BOURSIN FETTUCCINE ALFREDO WITH PANCETTA

This is the best twist on Boursin cheese and pancetta ever. As the Boursin melts in your mouth, the delicious blend of grated cheeses and Italian herbs and spices with crispy pancetta will take your breath away. It's creamy, rich, and so decadent.   YIELD: 6 TO 8 SERVINGS

1½ cups heavy cream (divided use)

2 tablespoons unsalted butter

1 tablespoon plus ¼ teaspoon sea salt (divided use)

¼ teaspoon white pepper: Spice Islands

9 ounces gluten-free fettuccine

½ cup grated Parmigiano-Reggiano cheese

½ cup grated Romano cheese

½ cup Boursin cheese

¼ cup pancetta, diced and pan-fried crisp

1 teaspoon chopped fresh oregano

Bring 1 cup of the heavy cream and butter to a simmer in a large saucepan over medium heat.

Reduce heat to low and simmer gently for 12 to 15 minutes, or until the mixture reduces to ⅔ cup.

Off the heat, stir in the remaining ½ cup cream, salt, and pepper.

While the cream reduces, bring 1½ quarts of water to a rolling boil, covered, in a large stockpot.

Add 1 tablespoon salt and pasta to the pot of boiling water. Cook the pasta until just shy of al dente. Drain.

Meanwhile, return the cream mixture to a simmer over medium-high heat. Reduce the heat to low and add the pasta, Parmigiano-Reggiano, Romano cheese, Boursin, pancetta, and oregano to the cream mixture.

Cook over low heat, tossing pasta with tongs in sauce to combine until the cheese is melted, 1 to 2 minutes. Serve immediately.

SERVING SUGGESTION   It's great with a fresh spinach salad with sliced mushrooms, grated carrots, chopped tomatoes, our Sherry Balsamic Vinaigrette (see Page 43), and a bottle of champagne.

BEEF, PORK, AND LAMB

Thank goodness meat doesn't punish the gluten-free diet. Plain meat—preferably local, organic, and pasture-raised beef, pork, lamb, and venison—is naturally gluten-free. It's the added sauces, broths, seasonings, rubs, and marinades that you have to watch out for.

We're Texans, and we are not giving up meat. Period. We also don't cotton to wimpy flavors, so you'll find an abundance of Tex-Mex and Southwestern influences in our beef, pork, and lamb recipes. That means red chiles, green chiles, ancho chiles, jalapeños, and bold, flavorful spices. We Texans also love our barbecue, and we've included some great recipes for those backyard feasts, plus a few for oven-barbecue lovers. Our Lasagna with Crema Mexicana sauce is a new Tex-Mex classic, while Stuffed Orange Bell Peppers with Homemade Chorizo and Authentic Fresh Pico de Gallo is more free-form.

Yes, we know there's a world beyond Texas, and we haven't forgotten that. Our Sicilian-style Veal Scaloppini is superb. Beef Tenderloin with French Gourmet Brown Sauce and Oktoberfest Best Wiener Schnitzel are classic European delights. And our Caramelized Onion and Applewood-Smoked Bacon Meatloaf with Homemade Ketchup is the best you will ever put in your mouth. We hope you have some fun with these delicious, easy-to-prepare entrées.

TEXAS OVEN-STYLE BARBECUE BRISKET

Yee-haw. Let's have some real brisket, Texas style . . . well, sorta. This is an easy-to-make, authentic-tasting brisket for those who can't hang out tending the smoker for 24 hours. Bill loves to grill, and while he is not giving up his Texas ways, this an indoor version of a Texas barbecue brisket. (Master grillers will insist that doing a brisket in the oven is heresy.) There are a number of plain to fancy cuts of brisket. Odds are, if you buy a fancy cut, you'll probably get a tough brisket. **YIELD: 10 SERVINGS**

2 tablespoons plus 1 teaspoon liquid smoke (divided use): Wright's or Colgin's

1 (10-pound) brisket, commercial cut

1 tablespoon onion salt

1 tablespoon garlic salt

2 tablespoons brown sugar

1 cup ketchup: Heinz

3 tablespoons butter

¼ cup water

½ teaspoon celery powder

2 tablespoons Worcestershire sauce: Lea & Perrins or French's

1½ teaspoon dry mustard: Colman's

Sea salt and pepper to taste

Sprinkle 2 tablespoons liquid smoke evenly over brisket. Rub meat with onion salt and garlic salt. Wrap brisket in plastic wrap and refrigerate overnight.

Preheat oven to 300 F.

Unwrap and place brisket in a large roasting pan. Cover and bake for 5 to 6 hours. Remove from oven, cool, and then slice. Leave oven on.

Meanwhile, empty pan drippings and put slices back into pan.

In a medium saucepan, combine brown sugar, ketchup, butter, water, celery powder, remaining 1 teaspoon liquid smoke, Worcestershire sauce, mustard, salt, and pepper. Stir and cook until boiling. Pour sauce over meat slices in pan. Cover with foil and bake for 1 more hour.

SERVING SUGGESTION   Great with our Hoochy-Coo Hatch Green Chile Polenta (see Page 156) and our Brown Sugar, Bacon, and Jalapeño Beans (see Page 179) and a cooler full of Bill's favorite iced Redbridge beer. With some sliced dill pickles and onions on the side, that is some of Texas's finest eating.

MEMPHIS-STYLE BARBECUE BRISKET

Memphis? Okay, it's not Texas... but it is still incredibly good. Our homemade "rub" is what puts this one over the top. The secret to its supreme tenderness is the long, slow roasting. Allow seven hours, and don't skimp.   YIELD: 14 SERVINGS

½ cup North Texas Barbecue Beef Brisket Rub (see Page 213)

1 (7-pound) beef brisket

3 cups of your favorite barbecue sauce or Bill's Better Bourbon Barbecue Sauce (see Page 220)

2 medium onions, sliced ½-inch thick

The night before serving, rub barbecue rub onto brisket. Wrap in plastic. Refrigerate and let marinate overnight.

Preheat oven to 225 F.

Line large shallow baking dish with foil. Make sure foil seam does not leak. Unwrap brisket and place in dish. Pour barbecue sauce over it. Place onion slices (in rings) all over the top.

Seal dish well with foil.

Cook for 2 hours. Never open foil until through. Increase oven temperature to 300 F. Cook for 2 more hours.

Reduce heat to 200 F and cook 3 more hours. Remove brisket from foil. Pour juices into a gravy boat. Slice brisket across the grain and serve with juices.

BEEF TENDERLOIN STROGANOFF

Many countries have stroganoff recipes, and we have tried a lot of them. We think our recipe is the best. You will think you are in a Hungarian restaurant. YIELD: 6 TO 8 SERVINGS

¾ cup butter (divided use)

2½ pounds beef tenderloin, cut into 1-inch cubes

1 tablespoon olive oil

1 large onion, diced

2 cups fresh mushrooms, rinsed clean and quartered

4 cloves garlic, minced

1 (10-ounce) can mushroom stems and pieces

2 tablespoons paprika: McCormick or Spice Islands

1 teaspoon dry mustard: Colman's

¼ cup Worcestershire sauce: Lea & Perrins or French's

1 cup sour cream

1 tablespoon chopped fresh parsley

Sea salt and pepper to taste

Melt 2 tablespoons of the butter in a skillet over medium-high heat. Gently cook beef tenderloin for about 2 minutes, just until seared on all sides. Remove from pan and set aside in a dish to collect juices.

Melt remaining butter in the skillet and add olive oil. Sauté onion. Add fresh mushrooms and garlic, stirring constantly for 2 minutes. Add mushroom stems and pieces, including liquid, paprika, mustard, and Worcestershire sauce. Stir well.

Boil for 4 to 6 minutes; reduce heat and simmer on low for 30 minutes. Add sour cream and parsley, stir to blend. Add beef and juices, stir over medium heat just until warmed through. Serve.

SERVING SUGGESTION We like this with rice or Mrs. Leeper's organic corn pasta. Add our Roasted Asparagus, Tomato, and Mushroom Salad (see Page 47) along with some fresh, organic pears poached in white wine.

BEEF TENDERLOIN WITH BRANDIED PEPPERCORN SAUCE

Perfect. Elegant. Rich. Luxurious. For beef lovers, nothing sounds better than beef tenderloin with a deep, rich sauce made by reducing the pan drippings and flavoring with brandy. This recipe will impress both your friends and your enemies.   YIELD: 6 TO 8 SERVINGS

¼ cup Worcestershire sauce: Lea & Perrins or French's

¼ cup olive oil

¼ cup balsamic vinegar

¼ cup soy sauce: Eden Foods Tamari Organic, La Choy, or San-J Organic Wheat-free Tamari (Gold Label)

1½ tablespoon kosher salt

3 tablespoons freshly ground tricolored pepper (black, green, and red peppercorns)

4 cloves garlic, minced

2 tablespoons Dijon mustard: Maille Dijon Originale Mustard or Grey Poupon

1 tablespoon chopped fresh rosemary

1 tablespoon chopped fresh tarragon

1 (5-pound) beef tenderloin

100 percent cotton kitchen string

Brandied Peppercorn Sauce (recipe follows)

Mix Worcestershire sauce, olive oil, balsamic vinegar, and soy sauce to make a marinade. Set aside.

Make a paste of salt, pepper, garlic, mustard, rosemary, and tarragon. Rub paste on tenderloin.

Place tenderloin in a glass dish. Pour marinade over all and refrigerate for 2 hours.

Preheat oven to 500 F.

Remove tenderloin from refrigerator, discarding marinade. Fold over the thin end of tenderloin and secure with cotton kitchen string.

Gently rub tenderloin with oil and pan-sear so that it's really brown on all sides.

Place meat on roasting pan. Do not cover or baste. Immediately reduce oven heat to 400 F. Bake tenderloin 18 to 23 minutes per pound for rare to medium-rare. Keep in mind ovens will vary and the meat will continue cooking after you take it out.

Remove from oven. Let stand 15 minutes before serving with Brandied Peppercorn Sauce.

BRANDIED PEPPERCORN SAUCE:

Pan drippings

1 cup beef broth: Health Valley Fat-Free Beef-flavored Broth, Pacific Natural Foods, or Wolfgang Puck Organic

½ cup butter

1 cup heavy cream

1 tablespoon finely crushed black peppercorns

½ cup brandy

In a saucepan, combine pan drippings, beef broth, and butter. Bring to a boil. Reduce heat, and reduce until thick (an eternity, or about 20 minutes). Add cream, black peppercorns, and brandy. Continue reducing until thick, about 5 minutes.

SERVING SUGGESTION   Serve this with our Rosemary Roasted Red Potatoes (see Page 174), steamed asparagus, a green salad topped with our Chunky Blue Cheese Dressing (see Page 33), red wine, and our Devil's Devil's Food Cake with Chocolate Fluff Frosting (Page 244) for dessert.

BEEF FILETS WITH CHAMPAGNE CREAM SAUCE

Stand up . . . take a bow. These filets are not just fancy; they are extraordinarily pleasing.   **YIELD: 4 SERVINGS**

3 tablespoons butter (divided use)

1 (8-inch) beef tenderloin, cut into 4 (1½-inch) slices

½ cup champagne or sparkling wine

½ cup French Gourmet Brown Sauce (see Page 228)

1 cup sliced mushrooms

½ cup heavy cream

4 slices gluten-free bread, toasted: Kinnikinnick Italian White Tapioca Rice Bread or Udi's White Sandwich

Parsley for garnish (optional)

In a skillet large enough to hold tenderloin slices in a single layer, melt 1 tablespoon butter over medium-high heat. Gently sauté tenderloin for about 2 minutes on each side for rare tenderloin, until just seared on all sides. Sauté longer if you like yours more done.

Remove from pan, cover, and set aside to collect juices for 10 minutes.

In the skillet, bring champagne, remaining 2 tablespoons butter, French Gourmet Brown Sauce, mushrooms, and cream to a light boil. Don't scorch.

Place a piece of toast on each of 4 plates. Top with steak and juices. Drizzle with sauce. Garnish with parsley, if desired.

SERVING SUGGESTION   We like to garnish with parsley and serve with our Golden Brown Belgian Potato Patties with Chives (see Page 177), steamed asparagus, and a nice cabernet sauvignon.

BEEF TENDERLOIN WITH FRENCH GOURMET BROWN SAUCE

This is our Texas take on classic French beef tenderloin—so decadent that you should probably go to confession before and after eating it. The brown sauce makes the dish. Novice cooks and even a lot of chefs fear preparing the sauce. Don't worry. Making brown sauce is fun and very, very rewarding. It also freezes well.   YIELD: 4 SERVINGS

½ cup French Gourmet Brown Sauce (recipe on Page 228)

4 pieces prime beef tenderloin, sliced 1½ inch thick

Pinch of sea salt

Pinch of white pepper: Spice Islands

2 tablespoons unsalted butter

2 tablespoons olive oil

¼ cup champagne

1 cup sliced baby bella mushrooms

¼ cup heavy cream

4 slices gluten-free bread, toasted: Kinnikinnick's Italian White Tapioca Rice Bread or Udi's White Sandwich Bread

Parsley for garnish

Make French Gourmet Brown Sauce. Preheat oven to 400 F.

Sprinkle the tenderloin steaks with salt and white pepper. Preheat a cast-iron skillet in the oven to medium-hot.

Brown steaks in 2 tablespoons butter and oil until done, turning once (usually 2 to 3 minutes per side, depending upon taste). Be careful not to burn the butter. (And remember: The steaks will continue cooking after you remove them from the oven.)

Remove steaks to warm platter and cover.

Slice toasts the same size as the steaks so that the steak will sit on them nicely. Set aside.

In the same cast-iron skillet over medium-high heat (be careful not to burn your hands), bring the champagne, ½ cup brown sauce, mushrooms, and cream just to the medium boiling point. Do not overcook.

On 4 plates, arrange steaks on toast. Pour sauce over each steak. Garnish with fresh parsley. Serve immediately.

SERVING SUGGESTION   This pairs beautifully with our Wilted Spinach Salad (see Page 37), Asparagus and Blue Cheese Risotto (see Page 155), and a nice glass of merlot.

TAMARI-GRILLED RIB EYE

Bill really got it right—really. This is one fine steak. When summer tomatoes are at their best, just slice any leftover steak into ¼-inch-thick strips and toss in a bowl with lots of fresh lettuce and chopped tomatoes drizzled with our Chunky Blue Cheese Dressing (see Page 33). Finish with a sprinkling of crumbled blue cheese and candied walnuts. Oh, yeah. YIELD: 4 SERVINGS

4 (1¼-inch thick) rib-eye steaks

Freshly ground black pepper

Garlic powder

Soy sauce: Eden Foods Tamari Organic, La Choy, or San-J
  Organic Wheat-free Tamari (Gold Label)

2 onions, halved

2 green bell peppers, halved, seeded, and membrane removed

Olive oil

8 teaspoons butter

Sprinkle steak with pepper and garlic powder to taste. Coat generously with soy sauce, rubbing into the meat. Cover and leave at room temperature for 30 minutes before grilling.

Fire up the grill, bringing the temperature to medium-high, or white-hot embers . (Bill refuses to grill over charcoal. He prefers mesquite or pecan wood. He hopes you know to never, ever poke a fork into meat. Use tongs.)

Brush onion and bell pepper lightly with olive oil. Place on grill, cut side down, and grill until fork tender.

Grill meat to medium-rare, about 7 minutes per side. Remove to hot platter. (Never remove to a cold plate.) Rub 1 teaspoon butter on each side of each steak. Serve immediately with grilled onion and bell pepper.

SERVING SUGGESTION   So good with our Havarti, Gouda, and Cheddar Cheese Grits (see Page 158) and Southern Belle Peach Pie (see Page 247). You can also cut up the steak and eat it on some steamed corn tortillas with our Authentic Fresh Pico de Gallo (see Page 209) or Feta, Roasted Tomato, and Pine Nut Mediterranean Salsa (see Page 206).

TEXAS CHICKEN-FRIED STEAK WITH POBLANO GRAVY

A Texas classic . . . with poblano gravy to boot. The love affair between Texans and their chicken-fried steaks is legendary, as it should be. Chicken-fried steak, when done right, is quite the entrée. There are many ways to make it. Some people don't dip the steak in egg and milk. Some just lightly flour the meat. Cuts of meat vary. It is the spice blend that sets our recipe apart. A nap is probably in order afterward. And note: Kim prefers Pamela's Gluten-free Baking & Pancake Mix while Bill prefers Bob's Red Mill White Rice Flour. You'll just have to decide which one suits you. Try extra light olive oil for high-heat frying.   YIELD: 4 SERVINGS

2 teaspoons sea salt

2 teaspoons freshly ground black pepper

2 teaspoons garlic powder

¼ teaspoon ground cumin: McCormick or Spice Islands

2 teaspoons onion powder

4 large pieces of cube steak (flap meat is good, too)

1 cup half-and-half

3 eggs, slightly beaten

2 cups gluten-free baking mix: Bob's Red Mill White Rice Flour or Pamela's Gluten-free Baking & Pancake Mix

Vegetable oil for frying

Poblano Gravy (recipe follows)

Sprinkle salt, pepper, garlic powder, cumin, and onion powder on both sides of each piece of meat. Combine milk and eggs.

Dip each piece of meat in milk and egg. Then dip in flour or baking mix, coating well. Shake off excess. Set aside on wax paper.

In large cast-iron skillet, heat 1 inch of oil to the point where a drop of water flicked into it pops. Slowly add meat. Don't crowd the pan. Fry on both sides until meat is done and has a nice brown crust. Remove to paper towel to drain and keep warm. Pour off all but 4 tablespoons of drippings so you can make the gravy in the same pan. Make gravy, and serve.

POBLANO GRAVY

1 fresh poblano pepper

1½ tablespoons cornstarch

¼ cup cold water

1 cup cold milk

Preheat oven to 425 F. Roast poblano 8 to 10 minutes. Let cool enough to handle. Peel, seed, and finely chop. In the same pan you used for frying, reduce heat to medium and scrape bits of meat off bottom and sides of pan. Dissolve cornstarch in cold water. Use a wire whisk to blend into the drippings. Slowly add milk, stirring constantly. Add poblano pepper and continue stirring until thick and hot.

Add more milk to thin to desired consistency. Add salt and pepper to taste. Serve in a separate sauceboat or bowl.

SERVING SUGGESTION   We like this with homemade mashed potatoes, an iceberg lettuce wedge with our Better -Than-a-French-Kiss French Dressing (see Page 34) and our Lemon-Sour-Cream Pound Cake (see Page 236).

PICKAPEPPA-STUFFED BELL PEPPERS

These are truly Texas-style stuffed peppas—"peppa." An easy Sunday-night dinner. Pick your pepper, then Pickapeppa.   YIELD: 4 SERVINGS

4 large flat-bottomed green bell peppers, seeded, stems removed, caps cut off and reserved for top

4 tablespoons Pickapeppa Sauce plus additional (divided use)

1 crushed garlic clove

½ pound ground beef

½ pound ground sirloin (or ground turkey, buffalo, or chorizo)

1 teaspoon sea salt

1 teaspoon freshly ground black pepper

1 clove garlic, minced

1 cup diced sweet onion

1 teaspoon dry mustard: Colman's

2 tablespoons Worcestershire sauce: Lea & Perrins or French's

½ cup water

Preheat oven to 350 F.

Place 1 tablespoon of Pickapeppa Sauce inside bottom of pepper and sprinkle with crushed garlic.

In a bowl, combine meat, salt, pepper, minced garlic, onion, mustard, and Worcestershire sauce. Mix well by hand, but don't overmix. Overmixing makes the meat texture tough.

Loosely stuff each pepper with the mixture. Pour additional Pickapeppa Sauce on top of meat. Put the cap back on each pepper (try to match them exactly).

Place peppers in baking dish and add ½ cup water in bottom of pan; bake uncovered for 1½ hours until done.

SERVING SUGGESTION   We like this with our Havarti, Gouda, and Cheddar Cheese Grits (see Page 158).

RIO GRANDE VALLEY SWISS STEAK

Here's a deep South Texas family recipe for tender and juicy Swiss steak. And you just thought you had to live without it! For some of us, the notion conjures up scary (or cozy) memories of the school cafeteria: that big serving pan filled with little cardboard patties drenched in faux mushroom soup. Our recipe is completely different. Trust us: Even if you have a good family recipe for Swiss steak, you've got to try this one. YIELD: 4 SERVINGS

¼ cup oil

2 tablespoons butter

1 cups gluten-free flour: Bob's Red Mill White Rice Flour

1 teaspoon sea salt

½ teaspoon freshly ground black pepper

4 cube steaks

Tomato Sauce (recipe follows)

Heat oil and butter in a large skillet over medium-high heat.

Mix flour, salt, and pepper in a gallon zip-top plastic bag. Add pieces of meat 1 at a time and shake. Shake off excess flour.

Brown each piece of meat on both sides. Remove from skillet. Drain on paper towels. Pour excess grease out of skillet, and return meat to skillet. Pour Tomato Sauce over meat and simmer on low heat for 1 hour.

TOMATO SAUCE

1 cup ketchup: Heinz

1 (6-ounce) can tomato paste: Del Monte Organic, Hunt's, or Muir Glen (rinse can);

1 tablespoon apple cider vinegar: Heinz

1 tablespoon yellow mustard: French's Classic Prepared Mustard

1 stalk celery, chopped

Dash Louisiana Hot Sauce

1 white onion, diced

1 green bell pepper, diced

1 tablespoon Worcestershire sauce: Lea & Perrins or French's

1 tablespoon sugar

In a large saucepan, combine all the ingredients. Cook sauce until it comes to a boil.

SERVING SUGGESTION   This is great with our Southwestern Pepper-Jack-and-Zucchini Corn Cakes (see Page 25) and Kim's Warm Chocolate Pudding Cake with Kahlua Whipped Cream (see Page 243).

ITALIAN MEATBALLS

Passed down for generations, this kid-tested and mother-approved recipe works—a traditional Italian recipe that won't disappoint.   YIELD: 6 LARGE MEATBALLS

Nonstick cooking spray

1½ pounds ground beef (¾ pound sirloin, ¾ pound ground chuck)

1 slice gluten-free bread, soaked in milk: Kinnikinnick's Italian White Tapioca Rice Bread or Udi's White Sandwich

2 eggs, beaten

3 tablespoons butter (divided use)

¼ cup finely diced yellow onions

1 clove garlic, minced

¼ teaspoon paprika: McCormick or Spice Islands

1 teaspoon fresh lemon juice

3 tablespoons grated Parmesan or Parmigiano-Reggiano cheese

3 tablespoons chopped fresh parsley

1 (28-ounce) can tomato sauce: Contadina, Del Monte Organic, or Hunt's (see note)

1 tablespoon chopped fresh oregano

Preheat oven to 350 F. Spray a small baking dish with nonstick cooking spray.

Place meat in large mixing bowl. Squeeze the milk out of bread over the bowl, and grind bread with fingers into meat. Add the eggs to the meat mixture. Set aside.

In a small nonstick skillet, melt 1 tablespoon butter and sauté the onions and garlic until golden. Add to the meat.

Add paprika, lemon juice, cheese, and parsley and mix just enough to blend, not overworking the meat. Form into 2-inch meatballs.

Heat remaining 2 tablespoons of butter in a skillet. Lightly brown meatballs on at least 2 sides.

Arrange meatballs in the prepared baking dish, not too far apart. Pour tomato sauce over meatballs. Add oregano. Cover with foil. Bake for 30 to 35 minutes. Remove from oven.

We prefer to lift the meatballs out of the pan and sauce and place them on a platter after removing them from the oven. (The tomato sauce is only for baking.)

Meatballs may be frozen in good-quality zip-top freezer bags. (Squeeze all the air out.) They will freeze for up to 4 weeks and are great thawed for a quick meal or meatball sandwich.

SERVING SUGGESTION   We serve these with our Basil-Black-Pepper Italian Tomato Sauce (see Page 227). Try it with a spinach garden salad topped with Kim's Buttermilk Romano Herb Dressing. Kids love 'em both!

CARAMELIZED ONION AND APPLEWOOD-SMOKED BACON MEATLOAF WITH HOMEMADE KETCHUP

We call this meat loaf "old glory" as it's a glorified version of everyone's age-old favorite. President Ronald Reagan loved meatloaf, and why not? Doesn't everyone love a good meatloaf? And okay, you got it—it goes great with some pink champagne. That's right. We like our meat loaf with pink champagne. You will definitely want to use the leftovers for meatloaf sandwiches with our Savory Tarragon Biscuits (see Page 203), sliced tomatoes, Bibb lettuce, sliced onion, and a thinly sliced cornichon pickle, mayo, and a tad of Grey Poupon Dijon mustard. Unbelievable! YIELD: 6 SERVINGS

---

1 tablespoon butter

1 tablespoon olive oil

1 teaspoon brown sugar

1 cup thinly sliced sweet onion

6 crimini mushrooms, rinsed clean and coarsely chopped

1 pound ground sirloin

1½ pounds ground chuck

1 teaspoon sea salt

1 teaspoon freshly ground black pepper

3 cloves garlic, minced

1 tablespoon Worcestershire sauce: Lea & Perrins or French's

1 teaspoon dry mustard: Colman's

½ cup Homemade Ketchup (recipe follows)

3 slices applewood-smoked bacon

Preheat oven to 350 F.

Heat butter and oil in thick-bottomed sauté pan over medium-high heat. Add brown sugar, onion, and salt to taste, if desired.

Reduce heat to medium-low and brown onion until caramelized, about 30 minutes. Add mushrooms and turn heat off. Let cool.

In a large mixing bowl, add onion-mushroom mixture to meat. Add salt, pepper, garlic, Worcestershire sauce, and mustard. Mix well.

Mold mixture into a rectangular loaf and place in a baking dish. Brush loaf with Homemade Ketchup.

Top with bacon. Bake, uncovered, for 1½ hours.

Remove from oven. Let rest 10 minutes. Slice and serve with more Homemade Ketchup.

SERVING SUGGESTION We like to serve meatloaf with our Gruyère-Jalapeño Scalloped Potatoes with Caramelized Onions (see page 173) and haricots verts drizzled with a little melted butter and fresh lemon juice. And then for dessert, our Pineapple Upside-down Cake (see page 248).

HOMEMADE KETCHUP

(see page 248).

YIELD: ABOUT 1 CUP

1 (20-ounce) Pastene San Marzano Italian plum tomatoes with basil leaf, puréed in blender

½ cup apple cider vinegar: Heinz

½ cup brown sugar

1 teaspoon celery seed: McCormick or Spice Islands

1 teaspoon freshly ground black pepper

1 tablespoon garlic powder

1 tablespoon onion powder

½ teaspoon ground cinnamon: Spice Islands

⅛ teaspoon ground cloves: Spice Islands

⅛ teaspoon ground mace: McCormick or Spice Islands

⅛ teaspoon ground allspice: Spice Island

½ teaspoon sea salt

⅛ teaspoon red pepper flakes: Spice Island

½ teaspoon dry mustard: Colman's

1½ bay leaves

Combine all ingredients in a large saucepan and simmer over low heat for about 30 minutes. Remove and discard bay leaves before using.

MAPLE-GLAZED BARBECUE RIBS

Slow-cook heaven. Maple-Glazed Barbecue Ribs are for those occasions when you don't have the time or inclination to smoke ribs all day on the smoker, but you just gotta have ribs. Get your slow cooker out, because this is a great recipe for it. It's so easy . . . and the meat just falls right off the bone.   YIELD: 4 TO 6 SERVINGS

1½ pounds boneless pork country-style ribs

1 tablespoon garlic powder

1 teaspoon seasoning salt: Lawry

1 medium white onion, sliced thick

1 can (10.5 ounces) beef broth: Health Valley Fat-free Beef-flavored Broth, Pacific Natural Foods, or Wolfgang Puck Organic

3 tablespoons honey mustard: French's Honey Mustard

¼ cup honey

½ cup water

¼ cup Kraft Honey Mustard barbecue sauce

¼ cup soy sauce: Eden Foods Tamari Organic, La Choy, or San-J Organic Wheat-free Tamari (Gold Label)

¼ cup real maple syrup

Rub meat with garlic powder and a little seasoning salt. Layer onions in bottom of slow cooker. Place meat on top of onions.

Mix liquids, and pour over meat to cover. (Bill likes to add a Redbridge beer.)

Cook 6 hours on Low. Remove meat. Cover loosely with foil. Let rest 20 minutes, then slice.

SERVING SUGGESTION   We like this with our Creamed Sweet Corn with Bacon and Jalapeño (see Page 154). You can also make a barbecue sandwich: Simply chop the meat and place between pieces of toasted, gluten-free bread with a slice of Texas 1015 sweet onion.

HUNGARIAN PAPRIKA-STUFFED CABBAGE

If you think stuffed cabbage is boring, try this one. Hearty and delicious, it's what stuffed cabbage is supposed to taste like. But here's the key: Love your big cabbage leaves, which means treat them gently—and carefully trim out the tough veins. You have to roll these babies.   YIELD: 6 TO 8 SERVINGS

1 large head cabbage

1 large yellow onion, diced

3 tablespoons olive oil

1 tablespoon paprika: McCormick or Spice Islands

1½ pound ground beef (¾ pound of ground sirloin and ¾ pound of ground chuck)

½ cup of uncooked white or brown rice

1½ teaspoons sea salt

½ teaspoon freshly ground black pepper

2 eggs

Cotton kitchen string

1 (15-ounce) can Pastene San Marzano Italian plum tomatoes with basil leaf, chopped

Water

Cut bottom inch off cabbage and place head in a pot of boiling water. Remove outer leaves as they wilt.

Lay the leaves on a flat surface, rib up, and trim off just the top of the thick rib on the leaves. You don't want to cut through the leaves; you want them to stay intact. You'll want to prepare at least 2 dozen leaves plus several extra, since some cabbage rolls might require 2 leaves. Set aside.

Heat oil in a small skillet and sauté onion and paprika.

In a large bowl, combine beef, rice, salt, pepper, eggs, and paprika onions.

To make the rolls, place 2 to 4 tablespoons meat mixture (depending on the size of your leaves) crosswise at the thick end. Fold the 2 sides over toward the middle and roll from the bottom. Tie with cotton kitchen string.

Chop remaining cabbage and place half in the bottom of large pan. Lay the cabbage rolls on top (it's OK to have more than 1 layer) and pour tomatoes and remaining chopped cabbage on top.

Add enough water to cover and bring to a boil. Reduce heat and simmer until done, 1½ to 2 hours.

SERVING SUGGESTION   Try these with a mixed green salad topped with our Lemon Caper Vinaigrette with Baked Goat Cheese Rounds (see Page 45) and our Chocolate-Chip Pecan Cookies (see Page 240).

LASAGNA WITH CREMA MEXICANA

Bella meets olé. This recipe is feisty and has a rich and creamy sauce. The blend of tasty Mexican cheeses and spicy fresh herbs makes it absolutely mouthwatering. This recipe also works well with shredded chicken or pork, jalapeño sausage or our Chorizo (see Page 103). Or, if you are a vegetarian, use vegetable broth and skip the meat. Thick, rich Crema Mexicana (Mexican sour cream) is "crema de la crema" and very popular in Mexican kitchens. Kim likes to also use another Mexican cheese, queso panela, in this recipe. Bill prefers fontina. We agree to disagree. Although we know Kim is always right. **YIELD: 8 TO 10 SERVINGS**

1¼ pound ground sirloin or a blend of ¾ pound ground sirloin and ¾ pound Johnsonville chorizo

1 medium onion, diced

1 (6-ounce) can tomato paste: Del Monte Organic, Hunt's, or Muir Glen

2 (8-ounce) cans tomato sauce: Contadina, Del Monte Organic, or Hunt's

1 teaspoon cumin: McCormick or Spice Islands

1 to 2 cloves garlic, minced

1 teaspoon oregano: McCormick or Spice Islands

2 tablespoons chili powder: McCormick or Spice Islands

1 cup beef stock: Kitchen Basics or Maxwell's Kitchen

Dash of cayenne pepper: McCormick or Spice Islands

1 teaspoon sea salt

1 teaspoon freshly ground black pepper

¼ cup sliced black olives

10 to 12 corn tortillas, cut in half: Mission, El Lago, or Sonoma Organic

1 cup La Vaquita Crema Mexicana, sour cream, or crème fraîche

4 ounces shredded cotija cheese (divided use)

4 ounces shredded queso panela cheese (divided use)

2 ounces of shredded Havarti cheese with jalapeño: Boar's Head Creamy

Sea salt to taste

Roasted tomato slices (optional)

Homemade Sangria (recipe follows)

In a large skillet, brown the ground beef and onion. Drain thoroughly.

Add tomato paste, tomato sauce, cumin, garlic, oregano, chili powder, beef stock, cayenne pepper, salt, and black pepper. Bring to a low boil and simmer for 15 to 20 minutes, or until thickened. Add olives.

For the sauce, mix together in a bowl the Crema Mexicana with the cotija cheese, panela cheese, and Havarti cheese, reserving 2 tablespoons each of the cotija and panela for topping.

Preheat oven to 350 F.

Spread a thin layer of meat sauce in a 9 x 13-inch baking dish.

Place a layer of 3 to 4 tortillas in the bottom of the pan.

Fill in remaining spaces with quartered tortillas, if desired. Don't overlap, as it is okay to have gaps between tortilla edges. Spread a layer of the cheese mixture over it.

Repeat with 2 more layers, starting with meat sauce, until you have used all the ingredients, ending with meat sauce on top.

Bake for 18 to 24 minutes. Remove from oven and top with remaining cheeses. Bake for 10 additional minutes, or until cheese is melted. We like to place a few roasted tomatoes on top.

SERVING SUGGESTION   This is great served with our Homemade Sangria and fresh, sliced fruit in season.

HOMEMADE SANGRIA

Every Texas ranch has its own recipe for sangria, and we present to you ours (even if we're not ranchers). Sangria is a Spanish punch traditionally made with red wine from the Rioja region of Spain. Always use a good-quality red wine, and use fruit that you enjoy. Serve cold. Sangria can also be made with white wine, so we give you a white-wine option. Kim likes to add ¼ cup of Damiana, a Mexican liqueur that a groom's parents traditionally give their daughter-in-law in hopes of a baby.   **YIELD: 8 TO 10 SERVINGS**

1 (750-ml) bottle good-quality pinot noir or dry white wine

1 orange, quartered and squeezed into pitcher

1 lemon, quartered and squeezed into pitcher

1 lime, quartered and squeezed into pitcher

1 cup fresh strawberries, halved

1 peach, peeled, pitted, and thinly sliced

2 tablespoons sugar

¼ cup fresh orange juice

¼ cup Southern Comfort or apricot brandy

¼ cup triple sec

1 (8-ounce) can Dole's sliced pineapple with juice or ½ sliced fresh pineapple

1 quart Canada Dry Diet Ginger Ale

Add everything but ginger ale in a large glass pitcher. Mix well. Cover with plastic wrap. Refrigerate 24 hours. Immediately before serving, add ginger ale.

STUFFED ORANGE BELL PEPPERS WITH HOMEMADE CHORIZO

We would go to the far corners of Mexico for this one. Simple, spicy, and *muy sabroso*. You gotta love it.

YIELD: 4 TO 6 SERVINGS

4 to 6 orange bell peppers

1 pound Homemade Chorizo (see Page 103)

¾ cup homemade Authentic Fresh Pico de Gallo (see Page 209)

Preheat oven to 350 F.

Cut the tops off the peppers horizontally and set aside. Remove seeds and membrane.

Gently mix chorizo and pico de gallo. Stuff bell peppers. Put pepper tops back on. Arrange in baking pan.

Bake for 1½ hours. Remove and let rest for 5 minutes.

SERVING SUGGESTION   This is great with our Monterey Fried Rice (see Page 164) and mixed green salad drizzled with our homemade Buttermilk Romano Herb Dressing (see Page 31).

SICILIAN-STYLE VEAL SCALOPPINI

At last . . . veal scaloppini, just as you remember it: lemon, capers, and Parmesan cheese all fused together. Ask the butcher to cut the veal scaloppini, or buy veal already cut up scaloppini style. The trick? Don't overcook.　YIELD: 6 TO 8 SERVINGS

½ cup gluten-free baking mix: Bob's Red Mill White Rice Flour or Pamela's Gluten-Free Baking and Pancake Mix

½ cup grated Parmesan cheese

1 teaspoon sea salt

⅛ teaspoon pepper

1½ pounds veal, cut into 2-inch strips ¼-inch thick

2 tablespoons olive oil

1 clove garlic, minced

½ cup sauvignon blanc

½ cup chicken broth: Health Valley Fat-free, Pacific Natural Foods Organic, or Swanson Natural Goodness

1 tablespoon fresh lemon juice

1 tablespoon capers: Mezzetta, Reese, or Star

Chopped parsley for garnish

Combine rice flour or baking mix, cheese, salt, and pepper together in a bowl. Sprinkle meat with flour mixture and pound in.

In a large skillet, heat oil with garlic; brown meat, 1 to 2 minutes on each side. It needs to be just beyond rare. Don't overcook.

Add wine, stock, and lemon juice. Reduce heat and cover. Simmer on medium-low heat for 12 minutes. Sprinkle with capers and parsley and serve.

SERVING SUGGESTION　We like this with any of Mrs. Leeper's organic corn pastas and a spinach salad with our Chunky Blue Cheese Dressing (see Page 33), chopped tomatoes, and chopped boiled egg. Pair with champagne or a dry sparkling wine.

TARRAGON VEAL CHOPS

This one has the "wow" factor. Veal chops with that smooth, silky taste and texture that just seems to melt.

YIELD: 4 SERVINGS

3 tablespoons butter

½ teaspoon sea salt

½ teaspoon white pepper: Spice Islands

4 (1½-inch-thick) veal chops

1 tablespoon chopped fresh tarragon (dried tarragon cannot be substituted)

1 cup gluten-free flour or baking mix: Bob's Red Mill Biscuit and Baking Mix or Pamela's Baking & Pancake Mix

½ cup champagne

¾ cup French Gourmet Brown Sauce (recipe on Page 228)

Melt butter in nonstick skillet over medium-high heat. Salt and pepper the chops. Mix tarragon with flour on a plate.

Dredge chops in flour mixture. Brown chops 4 to 5 minutes on each side, turning once. Transfer chops to hot platter.

Add champagne and French Gourmet Brown Sauce to skillet. Cook 3 to 4 minutes.

Place chops on serving plates and pour sauce over it.

SERVING SUGGESTION   We like this with one of Mrs. Leeper's pastas that has been buttered and sprinkled with chopped fresh parsley, our Grilled Peach, Feta, and Spinach Salad with Sherry Balsamic Vinaigrette (see Page 43), and a fine pink champagne.

OKTOBERFEST BEST WIENER SCHNITZEL

Texas has a large German population, and we love attending Oktoberfest deep in the heart of Texas' Hill Country. That's where you find the best Wiener schnitzel the Lone Star State has to offer because that's where the Germans settled. This one might even make you want to polka.   YIELD: 4 SERVINGS

4 eggs

2 tablespoons whole milk

4 veal cutlets or veal steaks nicely pounded to ½-inch thickness

1½ cups gluten-free flour or baking mix: Arrowhead Mills All Purpose Gluten Free Baking Flour or Pamela's Baking & Pancake Mix

2 teaspoons sea salt

½ teaspoon pepper

½ teaspoon paprika: McCormick or Spice Islands

½ teaspoon garlic powder

½ teaspoon onion powder

1½ cup gluten-free bread crumbs made from finely chopped gluten-free bread, or Orgran Gluten-free bread crumbs

¼ cup olive oil

4 tablespoons butter

Lemon wedges, chopped parsley for garnish

Sour cream (optional)

In shallow baking dish, beat eggs and milk. Set aside.

Salt and pepper both sides of veal.

In 1-gallon zip-top plastic bag, place flour, salt and pepper, paprika, garlic powder, and onion powder. Shake well. Add veal to flour mixture and shake until well coated. Remove cutlets.

Place bread crumbs on a plate. Dip cutlets in egg mixture. Dip both sides of cutlet into bread crumbs. Place on a platter and chill uncovered for 1 hour.

Heat oil and butter in heavy skillet over medium-high heat. When oil is hot but not smoking and foam from butter has subsided, add cutlets to skillet. Fry on first side until golden, about 3 to 4 minutes. Turn over and fry for an additional 3 to 4 minutes.

Remove to paper towels and drain. Salt to taste while still warm. Serve on warm platter with plenty of lemon wedges. Garnish with parsley. You can also add a small dollop of sour cream on top of each cutlet.

SERVING SUGGESTION   This is traditionally served with our Potato Pancakes with Shallot. We also like it with homemade mashed potatoes and red cabbage.

EAST AUSTIN TRAILER PARK SPICY HOMEMADE CHORIZO

Chorizo is a chile-spiced Mexican sausage that we love. But we hate the greasy commercial brands that almost always contain gluten, preservatives, glands, and who knows what. So we came up with this easy recipe. You can also substitute ground turkey, and you can add more chile powder if you like. We do.   YIELD: 3 POUNDS

2 pounds ground pork

1 pound sausage package: J. C. Potter's Regular or Hot

1 teaspoon sea salt

3 tablespoons chili powder: McCormick or Spice Islands

1 teaspoon garlic powder: McCormick or Spice Islands

1 teaspoon onion powder: McCormick or Spice Islands

1 teaspoon oregano: McCormick or Spice Islands

1 teaspoon ground cumin: McCormick or Spice Islands

1 teaspoon freshly ground black pepper

1 teaspoon brown sugar

4 tablespoons water

2 teaspoons paprika: McCormick or Spice Islands

⅛ teaspoon cinnamon: McCormick or Spice Islands

1 teaspoon Paul Prudhomme Ground Dried Magic Chile, mild

2 tablespoons Red Pepper Vinegar (recipe follows)

Combine all ingredients except vinegar and mix well with a wooden spoon. Then mix in the Red Pepper Vinegar well. Refrigerate overnight. We also like to refrigerate or freeze it in 1-cup portions.

RED PEPPER VINEGAR:

2 teaspoons crushed red pepper: Spice Islands

½ cup apple cider vinegar: Heinz

Combine crushed red pepper and vinegar. Refrigerate overnight.

SERVING SUGGESTION   We like to cook up chorizo and add it to scrambled eggs served on a corn tortilla with our fresh Authentic Fresh Pico de Gallo. Also great with a side of refried beans or black beans.

FEBE'S ROCKIN' TACOS

We think tacos are the perfect food, and this is our basic recipe. These are great served with soft-fried corn tortillas or crisp Ortega taco shells. Febe's Cocina Mexicana Sauce is our secret weapon: It's a basic Mexican sauce that elevates these tacos out of the ordinary.   YIELD: 10 SERVINGS

1 tablespoon olive oil

¼ cup diced onion

3 tablespoons Febe's Cocina Mexicana Sauce (see Page 222)

1 pound ground sirloin

1 (16-ounce) can Frito-Lay Bean Dip or Old El Paso Fat-free Refried Beans

1½ cups chopped tomato

1½ cup grated sharp cheddar cheese: Boar's Head or Kraft

10 Ortega taco shells, or 10 softly fried corn tortillas

1½ cups chopped lettuce

Preheat oven to 375 F.

Heat oil in a large nonstick skillet over medium-high heat.

Add onion. Cook 2 minutes. Add Febe's Cocina Mexicana Sauce and cook 2 more minutes. Add ground sirloin and brown.

Meanwhile, put taco shells in pan and heat in the oven for 4 to 5 minutes. Remove.

Spread refried beans on bottom of each shell. Add meat and tomato. Top with cheese.

Return to oven until cheese melts. Stuff with lettuce and serve hot.

SERVING SUGGESTION   We like to serve these with our Monterey Fried Rice (see Page 164). A pitcher of our Homemade Sangria (see Page 97) is not altogether disturbing with tacos.

CAJUN-STYLE BALSAMIC ROASTED PORK LOIN

This is New Orleans fine dining . . . at home. Incredibly rich in flavor, our tender pork loin marinated in tangy balsamic vinegar is an excellent party dish. So simple and delicious, and so easy to prepare ahead of time. YIELD: 4 TO 6 SERVINGS

2 tablespoons Healthy Solutions Cajun-style Pork Seasoning or Emeril's Original Essence

½ cup high-quality balsamic vinegar

½ cup high-quality extra virgin olive oil plus extra for roasting

2 pounds pork loin

1 tablespoon garlic powder

1 small onion, minced

Mix pork seasoning, vinegar, and oil in a large, zip-top plastic bag.

Rub loin with garlic powder. Add loin to bag. Marinate 24 hours, turning occasionally.

Preheat oven to 350 F. Remove loin from plastic bag and place loin on rack, reserving marinade. Sprinkle loin generously with additional olive oil. Add minced onion on top. Place into oven.

Put marinade in a bowl and microwave on high (100 percent power) for 1 minute. Baste loin and every 30 minutes thereafter. Roast loin for a total of 1 hour and 15 minutes.

Increase oven to 425 F. Bake 15 minutes longer.

Remove from oven. Let rest for 15 minutes.

SERVING SUGGESTION   Great with our Hatch Green Chile Cheese Muffin Soufflés (see Page 166). Have Kim's Red Velvet Cupcakes for dessert (see Page 255).

ROASTED PORK LOIN WITH RED CURRANT-POMEGRANATE GLAZE AND PORTABELLA MUSHROOMS

Unique, exotic, succulent, delicious—need we say more? This recipe will bring the house down. YIELD: 8 TO 10 SERVINGS

1 cup pomegranate juice: Smart Juice Organic Pomegranate Tart Cherry or POM

1 tablespoon balsamic vinegar

1 teaspoon chopped shallot

2 tablespoons red currant jelly or jam

1 (2-pound) pork tenderloin

4 tablespoons butter, room temperature

2 tablespoons garlic, minced

1 teaspoon sea salt

½ teaspoon freshly ground black pepper

100 percent cotton kitchen string

Olive oil

4 large portabella mushrooms, halved vertically

In a small saucepan, combine pomegranate juice, balsamic vinegar, shallot, and red currant jelly. Mix well. Bring to a boil. Reduce heat to low. Reduce by almost half, stirring occasionally. Remove from heat. Let rest 10 minutes.

Preheat oven to 350 F.

Split loin lengthwise but not all the way through and flatten with a cleaver. Evenly spread butter and garlic over pork loin. Season with salt and pepper. Roll and tie with cotton kitchen string.

Put loin on baking rack over a baking pan. Brush with olive oil. Arrange mushrooms around baking pan. Generously glaze tenderloin with pomegranate mixture.

Place tenderloin in oven and roast about an hour (25 to 30 minutes per pound). Remove from oven. Let rest 10 minutes.

Serve on platter garnished with portabella mushrooms.

We like to serve this with our Hoochy-Coo Hatch Green Chile Polenta (see Page 156) and our Cranberry Waldorf Salad (see Page 36) and a nice rosé wine.

ROSEMARY RACK OF LAMB AU JUS

The perfect combination of herbs and spices—and finally, a recipe that won't smother the delicate flavor of roasted lamb. YIELD: 2 SERVINGS

1 rack of lamb

1 tablespoon sea salt

½ teaspoon freshly ground black pepper

2 cloves garlic, cut into 6 slivers

2 tablespoons olive oil

1 tablespoon chopped fresh rosemary

1 tablespoon chopped fresh parsley

2 cups hot and ½ cup cold water (divided use)

2 tablespoons cornstarch

Preheat oven to 375 F.

Season lamb with salt and pepper. With a knife, cut 6 holes in the fat of the meat and insert the slivers of the garlic. Rub the lamb with olive oil.

Place in roasting pan, and add rosemary on top. Cook 20 minutes on each side, or to your taste. Add the parsley 5 minutes before removing from oven.

Remove lamb to a hot platter and cover with foil, leaving 4 tablespoons of juice in pan and place it on a burner over medium heat.

Add the 2 cups hot water. Stir and scrape meat bits on the sides and bottom of the pan to dissolve them. Cook over medium heat; stir slowly but constantly.

Dissolve cornstarch in ½ cup cold water. Remove au jus from heat. Stir in the cornstarch mixture slowly until au jus is desired thickness. Bring to boil for 1 minute.

Adjust seasoning with salt and pepper to taste. Strain and pour into sauceboat or serving bowl. Stir and serve with the lamb.

SERVING SUGGESTION   We like this with our Roasted Beet Salad with Goat Cheese and Pecans and our Garlic Vinaigrette Dressing (see Page 44). Top it off with our recipe for the Best Little Coconut Cream Cake in Texas (see Page 239). Chill some champagne, and your palate will be so satisfied. We dare ya.

NORTH INDIAN ROGAN JOSH (LAMB CURRY)

Bring the taste of India to your dining table. But don't be put off by that long recipe. It's all about the perfect combination of spices that makes this so flavorful. And you can substitute tofu—really. We believe homemade curry is a work of art. YIELD: 6 TO 8 SERVINGS

4 tablespoons vegetable oil

1 large onion, diced

3 cloves garlic, crushed

1 tablespoon grated fresh ginger

2 tablespoons coriander: McCormick or Spice Islands

1 teaspoon paprika: McCormick or Spice Islands

¼ teaspoon cardamom: McCormick or Spice Islands

½ teaspoon cayenne pepper: McCormick or Spice Islands

¼ teaspoon freshly ground black pepper

1 pinch ground cloves: McCormick or Spice Islands

1 pinch ground nutmeg: McCormick or Spice Islands

1 pinch ground mace: McCormick or Spice Islands

1 pinch saffron: McCormick or Spice Islands

1 teaspoon ground cumin: McCormick or Spice Islands

1 teaspoon turmeric: McCormick or Spice Islands

1 tablespoon poppyseeds: Spice Islands, crushed

2 pounds leg of lamb, cubed in 1-inch squares

1 cup chicken broth: Health Valley Fat-free, Pacific Natural Foods Organic, or Swanson Natural Goodness

½ cup yogurt

1½ teaspoon sea salt

3 large tomatoes, peeled and chopped

½ cup water

Heat the oil in a large skillet over medium-high heat and brown the onion. Add garlic, ginger, coriander, paprika, cardamom, cayenne, pepper, cloves, nutmeg, mace, saffron, cumin, turmeric, and poppyseeds.

Add the lamb (or cubed tofu). Sauté for 3 minutes on medium and then cook on medium-high for 5 to 6 minutes or until no longer pink.

Add chicken broth. Stir in yogurt; then add the salt, tomatoes, and water. Reduce heat to medium-low, cover and simmer, stirring occasionally, about 1½ hours, or until meat is tender.

SERVING SUGGESTION   Try this with basmati rice and Indian raita. It's also great with an icy cold Redbridge beer.

LAMB SHISH KEBABS

Sheesh—another shish kebab. It's the marinade that makes these special, so just give it a try. Lamb Shish Kebabs are perfect when you want something different. YIELD: 8 TO 10 SERVINGS

1 cup soy sauce: Eden Foods Tamari Organic, La Choy, or San-J Organic Wheat-free Tamari (Gold Label)

1 teaspoon balsamic vinegar

2 tablespoons finely grated onion

3 tablespoons fresh lemon juice

1 teaspoon dry mustard: Colman's

4 pounds lamb, cut into 1-inch cubes

6 to 8 long skewers

Garlic powder to taste

Black pepper to taste

Fresh pineapple chunks

Green pepper chunks

Red pepper chunks

Onion chunks

Cherry tomatoes

Combine soy sauce, balsamic vinegar, onion, lemon juice, and dry mustard in a large zip-top plastic bag. Add the lamb. Refrigerate for 1 hour. Remove lamb and reserve marinade.

Fire up the grill, bringing the temperature to medium. Lightly brush the grate with oil.

Thread all the pineapple on 1 skewer, all the green pepper on 1, all the red pepper on 1 and so forth. You'll need more than 1 for all the meat.

Grill the skewers, turning until done. Baste every 15 minutes with reserved marinade. Don't overcook.

Note: Each skewer will be done at a different time. Remove each skewer when done. The tomatoes take the shortest time. The meat will take the most. The rest are in between.

Remove fruits, vegetables, and meats from skewers and serve.

SERVING SUGGESTION   How about a cold lettuce wedge topped with our Chunky Bleu Cheese Dressing accompanied by our Romano and Oregano Crisps? That will impress your crowd!

CHICKEN
AND GAME

We make some unbelievable chicken recipes, plain and simple. Chicken is so versatile, whether roasted, grilled, broiled, or fried. It makes a great salad, or makes a good salad even better. Our chicken dishes will captivate your guests or simply make you the family hero—dishes like Bourbon-Soaked Chicken with Applewood-Smoked Bacon and Vermont Cheese. We have "Real" Oven-Fried Chicken, and yes, it really works without frying. Your kids will love it. Then, of course, there's our Herb-Crusted Parmesan Chicken. That's right, gluten-free Parmesan chicken. We think it's about time.

We also recommend this very important step: Use only organic, free-range chickens that are plump, with a creamy appearance, no visible blemishes and definitely no odor. Bonus: You'll be amazed at the wholesome flavor and supple texture of fresh organic pasture-raised chicken. Before cooking, place the chicken in a nonreactive bowl and cover with apple cider vinegar for 20 minutes to remove any impurities. We use the vinegar as a cleaner, not as a flavor. Rinse, pat dry, and refrigerate until ready to use.

BUTTERMILK-MARINATED PAN-FRIED CHICKEN

Bill says there are few things that give a Southern boy on a gluten-free diet more anxiety than the thought of life without fried chicken. That is almost un-American. Since we gluten-free folks can't just pop into the Colonel's for a fix . . . lo and behold, we have a Buttermilk-Marinated Pan-Fried Chicken. This is a very traditional Southern recipe. Instead of using a whole, cut-up chicken, you may want to opt for all thighs, all breasts, etc. We like to marinate our chicken in buttermilk, as this gives it a much richer flavor. We also like to use a big, old black cast-iron skillet. If you really want to do it the classic way, drain on brown paper bags instead of paper towels. Good served hot or at room temperature.   YIELD: 4 SERVINGS

1 medium chicken, cut up, or 6 chicken thighs or half breasts, bone-in

1 quart buttermilk

Louisiana Hot Sauce or Tabasco

2 eggs

2 cups whole milk

2 cups gluten-free flour: Bob's Red Mill White Rice Flour or Pamela's Baking & Pancake Mix

1 teaspoon sea salt

½ teaspoon freshly ground black pepper

½ teaspoon garlic powder

½ teaspoon baking powder: Clabber Girl, Hain, or Rumford (only needed if you use Bob's Red Mill White Rice Flour)

Vegetable oil for frying

Gravy (recipe follows)

Soak chicken in buttermilk for 4 hours in refrigerator, then pat it dry. Discard buttermilk. Sprinkle a few drops of hot sauce on each piece of chicken.

Lightly beat eggs and whole milk in a bowl. Combine flour, salt, pepper, garlic powder, and baking powder, if using, in a doubled brown grocery bag.

Dip each piece of chicken in milk-and-egg mixture. Shake chicken in the bag of flour, one piece at time. Remove chicken to platter and refrigerate uncovered for 1 hour to set.

Pour enough oil in a deep cast-iron skillet to almost cover chicken. Heat oil over medium-high to 365 F using a fryer thermometer.

Cut a small piece of skin off a piece of chicken. Oil is ready if the skin sizzles.

Gently add chicken pieces to hot oil. Do not crowd. Cooking time will vary with the size of each piece of chicken. Do not allow to burn. Cook in batches. Try to turn only once, when golden brown on one side.

Remove and drain chicken on paper towels or flattened-out brown grocery bags. Sprinkle with salt and keep warm. Make gravy and serve.

GRAVY

4 tablespoons pan drippings

2 tablespoons Bob's Red Mill All-purpose Flour

1 cup cold whole milk

In the cast-iron skillet, bring pan drippings to medium to medium-high heat. Scrape browned bits off bottom and sides. Sprinkle with flour. Stir to mix well. Slowly whisk in milk. Cook as it thickens, stirring, to desired consistency. Add salt and pepper to taste.

SERVING SUGGESTION We like it with homemade red mashed potatoes and fresh green beans with our Southern Belle Peach Pie (see Page 247) for dessert.

"REAL" OVEN-FRIED CHICKEN

The name says it all. It's real. It's easy. It works. It tastes great. The key to this recipe is our buttermilk marinade. Bill likes to cook the chicken on a wire rack over a baking pan, because it allows the heat to circulate. This is what makes the skin crispy. You will want to give this one a try. Like, a thousand times. YIELD: 4 TO 6 SERVINGS

4 chicken breast halves (bone-in with skin) or 6 thighs (see note)

Apple cider vinegar: Heinz

1 quart buttermilk

1 egg

2 tablespoons milk

1 teaspoon garlic powder

1 teaspoon onion powder

1 teaspoon paprika: McCormick or Spice Islands

Dash of cayenne pepper: McCormick or Spice Islands

1 teaspoon seasoning salt: Lawry's

1 teaspoon freshly ground black pepper

1 cup Instant mashed potato buds: Betty Crocker

¼ cup melted butter plus more for drizzling, if desired

Soak the breasts in the vinegar for 20 minutes. Remove breasts and discard vinegar. Marinate chicken in buttermilk for 24 hours. Remove, pat dry, and discard buttermilk.

Preheat oven to 375 F.

Whisk egg and whole milk together in a bowl. In another bowl, mix spices with potato buds.

Dip chicken in egg mixture, then roll each piece in potato bud mixture, then roll in butter.

Coat well.

Place the coated chicken pieces in pan skin-side-up. Kim likes to drizzle 3 tablespoons of butter or olive oil over the chicken at this point for extra crispiness. Bake until done and crispy brown, approximately 40 to 45 minutes.

NOTE: You can also make chicken tenders this way. Tenders are great served with our Buttermilk Romano Herb Dressing. (see Page 31).

HERB-CRUSTED PARMESAN CHICKEN

It's finally here: Chicken Parmesan for the gluten-freed society. Lightly battered with a crunchy herb-seasoned Parmesan crust, this chicken makes a nice change of pace. It's also easy and mouthwatering. YIELD: 8 SERVINGS

½ cup butter

½ cup olive oil

2 cloves garlic, finely minced

½ cup gluten-free bread crumbs made from finely chopped gluten-free bread or Orgran Gluten-free Bread Crumbs

½ cup Pamela's Gluten-free Baking & Pancake Mix

1½ cup Parmesan cheese, coarsely grated

¼ teaspoon cayenne pepper: McCormick or Spice Islands

1 tablespoon sea salt

½ teaspoon paprika: McCormick or Spice Islands

¼ teaspoon freshly ground black pepper

¼ cup minced fresh parsley

1 tablespoon Italian herb seasoning: Spice Islands

¼ teaspoon dry mustard: Colman's

6 boneless, skinless chicken breast halves

Preheat oven to 350 F. Lightly grease a baking dish that will hold the breasts in a single layer, not touching if possible.

Melt butter and combine with oil and garlic. Set aside.

Combine bread crumbs, baking mix, cheese, cayenne pepper, salt, paprika, black pepper, parsley, Italian herb seasoning, and mustard in a paper sack and shake well.

Dip each piece of chicken in the melted butter and oil, shake in the bag, then arrange in the prepared baking dish. Drizzle with any remaining butter and oil.

Bake uncovered for 38 to 46 minutes, or until golden brown. Do not overcook or Parmesan cheese will turn bitter. Remove. Serve immediately.

SERVING SUGGESTION We like this with a side of our Roasted Tomato and Goat Cheese Risotto (see Page 161) and some steamed broccolini.

COQ AU VIN
(CHICKEN COOKED IN WINE)

A French classic, chicken cooked in wine. Now there's a gluten-free version. Slowly simmered to perfection, the warm, pleasant aromas of onions, thyme, bay leaf, and red wine make a delicious hearty meal in fall or winter. Slow-cooking allows the flavors to fully develop, producing tender, succulent chicken every time. This is best when cooked in a large cast-iron Dutch oven or heavy Le Creuset pot. We also think good-quality organic chicken is essential. YIELD: 8 TO 10 SERVINGS

Sea salt and pepper to taste

1 (2½-to-3-pound) chicken, cut into serving pieces

5 tablespoons plus 4 teaspoons butter (divided use)

3 tablespoons chopped shallots

2 sprigs parsley

2 bay leaves

⅛ teaspoon thyme: McCormick or Spice Islands

1 (750ml) bottle of Sebastiani Cabernet Sauvignon or your favorite full-bodied red

10 baby onions, peeled

10 mushroom caps, dirt brushed off

¼ teaspoon sugar

4 (½-inch-thick) slices salt pork, cut in cubes (No substitutes. No. No.)

1 tablespoon Bob's Red Mill Gluten-free All-purpose Baking Flour

Preheat oven to 325 F. Rub salt and pepper on chicken pieces.

Melt 4 tablespoons butter in a Dutch oven or Le Creuset. Add chicken and brown on all sides, approximately 10 minutes.

Add shallots, parsley, bay leaves, thyme, and wine. Cover and simmer.

In another pan, melt 4 teaspoons butter over medium-high heat. Brown onions, mushrooms, sugar, and salt pork. Add to pot.

In a small skillet, melt 1 tablespoon butter over medium heat. Stir in flour. Whisk continuously for several minutes to make a lightly browned roux. Add to the Dutch oven.

Cover and bake in oven for 2 hours, until tender.

SERVING SUGGESTION   We like this with our Rosemary Roasted Red Potatoes (see Page 174) and our Italian Crema Cake (see Page 252) for dessert. Red wine is a very nice accompaniment, too.

LEMON ZEST CHICKEN PICCATA

How can you not just love this savory Italian classic dish? Our Chicken Piccata, a "serve immediately" recipe, is very elegant, and always a hit. YIELD: 6 TO 8 SERVINGS

½ cup milk

3 large eggs, beaten

1½ cup gluten-free bread crumbs made from finely chopped gluten-free bread or Orgran Gluten-free Bread Crumbs

2 teaspoon grated lemon zest (yellow part only)

½ teaspoon sea salt

¼ teaspoon white pepper: Spice Islands

½ teaspoon garlic powder

½ teaspoon onion powder

1½ pounds boneless, skinless chicken breast halves, pounded ¼ to ½ inch thick

3 tablespoons unsalted butter

Juice of 1 lemon

Whisk together milk and eggs in bowl. Mix bread crumbs and lemon zest in shallow baking dish. Set these aside.

Mix together salt, white pepper, garlic powder, and onion powder. Season both sides of chicken with seasoning mixture.

In nonstick skillet, heat butter over medium heat. Dip breasts in eggs, then bread crumbs.

Pan-fry chicken in butter, about 4 minutes on each side. Remove and drain on paper towels.

Sprinkle with lemon juice and serve immediately.

SERVING SUGGESTION We like this with our Pasta with Lemon-Caper Sauce (see Page 75) and a spinach salad with some Mandarin oranges, chopped walnuts, and feta cheese drizzled with some of our Poppyseed Dressing (see Page 34). A nice dry Italian wine or pink champagne is terrific with this.

CHICKEN-STUFFED ZUCCHINI WITH TOMATO AND FETA CHEESE

So light and flavorful—perfect for a warm summer day. This will really put some zing in your zucchini.   YIELD: 6 SERVINGS

6 large zucchini squash, sliced in half

Olive oil

2 large chicken breast halves, cooked and shredded

2 chopped Roma tomatoes (very ripe)

1¼ cup feta cheese

1 tablespoon seasoned salt: Lawry's

1 cup fresh or frozen corn kernels, thawed if frozen

1 tablespoon capers, drained: Mezzetta, Reese, or Star

1 clove garlic, minced

2 tablespoons chopped chives

Preheat oven to 350 F.

Scoop out some of the zucchini to make a boat. Brush the bottoms with olive oil.

In a bowl, mix together chicken, tomatoes, feta, seasoned salt, corn, capers, garlic, and chives. Divide among zucchini boats.

Bake for 20 to 22 minutes, and serve.

SERVING SUGGESTION   Great served with our Savory Tarragon Biscuits (see Page 203) and a fresh fruit salad.

MARVELOUS MAPLE-MUSTARD CHICKEN

Our own Mr. Mustard displays his mastery with this simple yet splendid recipe made special with the addition of our Tarragon Spiced Mustard. Let us tell you, maple syrup and our Tarragon Spiced Mustard take this recipe beyond fabulous. Make the mustard first so the flavors blend overnight in the fridge. YIELD: 6 SERVINGS

6 large chicken legs or thighs

2 teaspoons garlic powder

2 teaspoons onion powder

½ teaspoon sea salt

¼ teaspoon cayenne pepper: McCormick or Spice Islands

1 cup Tarragon Spiced Mustard (recipe follows)

3 tablespoons maple syrup

¼ teaspoon fresh or dried tarragon: McCormick or Spice Islands

Nonstick cooking spray

Sprinkle chicken generously on all sides with garlic powder, onion powder, salt, and cayenne pepper. In a small bowl, combine mustard, maple syrup, and tarragon.

Spray nonstick cooking spray in a shallow pan large enough to hold the chicken without crowding. Lay the chicken in the pan and pour mustard-maple mixture over all. Marinate in refrigerator for 2 hours.

Preheat oven to 350 F. Bake chicken 90 minutes. Baste every 20 minutes with mustard mixture.

TARRAGON SPICED MUSTARD

2 tablespoons fresh tarragon

¼ cup apple cider vinegar: Heinz

1 teaspoon dry mustard: Colman's

5 teaspoons Dijon mustard: Grey Poupon

5 teaspoons coarse-grain mustard: Grey Poupon

In a small, nonreactive bowl, lightly crush tarragon with back of fork and combine with apple cider vinegar. Let steep for 4 hours. Remove and discard tarragon. Add dry mustard, Dijon mustard, and coarse-grain mustard. Cover and refrigerate overnight.

SERVING SUGGESTION This mustard is great on sandwiches, baked ham, or avocados. It will keep, refrigerated, 1 month. Put it in some unique jars for nice gifts.

CHICKEN CORDON BLEU WITH WHITE WINE AND PAPRIKA

No more Cordon Bleu blues. Here's a gluten-free dish as good as any you will find at a fancy restaurant, now available in your own kitchen. For this classic combination of chicken, ham, and cheese, take our advice and use only the highest-quality ingredients available. We prefer Boar's Head smoked Virginia ham and Swiss cheese. You won't regret it.   YIELD: 4 SERVINGS

8 boneless, skinless chicken breast halves

8 slices ham: Boar's Head smoked Virginia ham

8 good-quality Swiss cheese slices

1 teaspoon sea salt

½ teaspoon freshly ground black pepper

1½ cup gluten-free flour: Bob's Red Mill Biscuit and Baking Mix or Pamela's Baking & Pancake Mix

1 teaspoon paprika: McCormick or Spice Islands

½ teaspoon garlic powder

8 tablespoons butter

½ cup dry white wine

¼ cup chicken broth: Health Valley Fat-free, Pacific Natural Foods Organic, or Swanson Natural Goodness

1 tablespoon cornstarch

1 cup heavy cream

Chopped parsley

Pound chicken to ¼-inch thickness, but no thinner. On each breast layer as follows: 1 slice ham, 2 slices cheese, 1 slice ham. Top with a second chicken breast. Salt and pepper both sides. Secure edges of 4 serving pieces well with toothpicks.

Mix flour, paprika, and garlic powder together in a plate. Dredge chicken pieces in mixture.

Melt butter in heavy nonstick skillet over medium-high heat. Add chicken. Cook 4 to 5 minutes on each side or until browned.

Add wine and chicken broth. Reduce heat to low. Simmer, covered, for 30 minutes, or until chicken is no longer pink and juices run clear.

Remove chicken from pan with tongs to a warm platter. Remove and discard toothpicks. Keep warm.

Blend cornstarch and cream in mixing bowl. Slowly whisk into the skillet. Cook over medium heat, scraping up any solid bits from the bottom of the skillet. Stir until thickened.

Pour over chicken and serve immediately. Garnish with chopped parsley.

SERVING SUGGESTION   We like this with our Cranberry Waldorf Salad (see Page 36), Savory Tarragon Biscuits (see Page 203) and white wine.

BOURBON-SOAKED CHICKEN BREASTS WITH APPLEWOOD-SMOKED BACON AND VERMONT CHEESE

Magnificent. That is the only word to describe this superb dish that will have your guests clamoring for more. It is the "barbecue sauce" that makes this dish so spectacular. And even the pickiest of little kids will love this recipe, too. YIELD: 4 SERVINGS

4 boneless, skinless chicken breast halves

1 teaspoon sea salt

½ teaspoon freshly ground black pepper

½ pound sharp cheddar cheese, grated: Boar's Head Vermont

½ pound Monterey Jack Cheese, grated: Boar's Head

4 tablespoons butter

2 tablespoons olive oil

⅔ cup Bill's Better Bourbon Barbecue Sauce (see Page 220)

8 slices applewood-smoked bacon, cooked crisp

½ cup chopped scallions (green parts only)

Preheat oven to 375 F.

Pound chicken breasts until flattened (¼- to ½-inch thick). Season with salt and pepper. In a small bowl, mix the cheeses and set aside.

Melt butter and add olive oil in a nonstick skillet over medium-high heat. Sauté the chicken breasts 3 to 4 minutes on each side; remove and drain on paper towels.

Place the cooked breasts in a pan that will hold them in a single layer. Top each breast with 2 to 2 ½ tablespoons barbecue sauce, 2 slices of bacon, ¼ cup of cheese mixture, and scallions.

Bake in oven only until cheese melts. Serve immediately.

SERVING SUGGESTION   Great served with our Red Chile Fried Green Tomatoes (see Page 170) and our Ooey Gooey Brownies (see Page 246).

POLLO EN SALSA DE TOMATE

No Tex-Mex here. Pollo en Salsa de Tomate (chicken in tomato sauce) is a real Mexican dish, common in many regions of Mexico. YIELD: 4 TO 6 SERVINGS

1 medium-size chicken or 6 thighs

1 tablespoon bacon drippings or olive oil

½ cup minced onion

1 clove garlic, minced

1½ cup chopped tomatoes

½ cup chopped bell pepper

¼ teaspoon ground cumin: McCormick or Spice Islands

¼ teaspoon paprika

½ teaspoon Mexican oregano

½ teaspoon freshly ground black pepper

1 teaspoon sea salt

Corn tortillas

Use the Best Homemade Chicken Stock Recipe Ever (Page 134) to cook the chicken. Shred the meat, once it's cooked.

In a large skillet, melt the bacon drippings or heat the olive oil over medium-high heat. Sauté the vegetables for 2 minutes. Add chicken and add enough water to cover the chicken halfway (about 1½ cups).

Add cumin, paprika, oregano, black pepper, and salt. Bring to a boil. Reduce heat to low and simmer until the water is almost gone. Serve with corn tortillas.

SERVING SUGGESTION We like this with homemade corn tortillas, our Monterey Fried Rice (see Page 164), black beans, guacamole, and our Homemade Sangria (see Page 97).

SPICED TEQUILA CHICKEN

This is just a crazy-good recipe. It turns out best when the chicken has marinated in the mix for two hours, then grilled. You can also bake it if you prefer. YIELD: 6 SERVINGS

6 chicken breast halves (not skinless)

1 tablespoon garlic powder

1 teaspoon Oriental five-spice seasoning: McCormick or Spice Islands

1 teaspoon cayenne pepper: McCormick or Spice Islands

½ cup local honey

¼ cup tequila: Jose Cuervo Gold tequila

Juice of 4 limes

4 tablespoons chopped fresh cilantro

2 tablespoons water

1 cup canned crushed Dole pineapple with juice

½ teaspoon freshly ground black pepper

½ cup soy sauce: Eden Foods Tamari Organic, La Choy, or San-J Organic Wheat-free Tamari (Gold Label)

Rub chicken breasts with garlic powder and Oriental five-spice powder. Lightly sprinkle with cayenne pepper. Arrange chicken in a large baking or dish.

In a bowl, mix together honey, tequila, lime juice, cilantro, water, pineapple and juice, black pepper, and soy sauce. Pour mixture over chicken. Marinate for 2 hours in the refrigerator, then grill.

BAKING OPTION: To bake, preheat oven to 350 F. Lightly grease a baking pan large enough to hold the breasts in a single layer. Season, then add the marinade. Bake 1½ hours, or until tender.

SERVING SUGGESTION   We like this with our Artichoke-Feta Fritters (see Page 27) and our Mexican Brownies (see Page 246).

SHERRIED GINGER CHICKEN

For an elegant change of pace, give this Asian-inspired chicken a try.   YIELD: 4 TO 6 SERVINGS

1 teaspoon sea salt

¼ teaspoon freshly ground black pepper

⅛ teaspoon garlic powder

¾ cup gluten-free flour: Bob's Red Mill Biscuit and Baking Mix or Pamela's Baking & Pancake Mix

1 (2½-to-3-pound) chicken, cut up

1 cup butter (divided use)

1½ tablespoons soy sauce: Eden Foods Tamari Organic, La Choy, or San-J Organic Wheat-free Tamari (Gold Label)

¾ cup sherry

1 tablespoon finely chopped fresh ginger

1 tablespoon fresh lemon juice

1 tablespoon chopped fresh parsley

Preheat oven to 350 F.

Combine salt, pepper, garlic powder, and flour in a small paper sack. In batches, shake the chicken parts well in the bag.

Melt ½ cup of the butter in cast-iron skillet over medium-high heat. Add chicken pieces and brown lightly on all sides.

Remove and place in a baking dish large enough to hold the chicken pieces.

In saucepan, combine remaining ½ cup of butter, soy sauce, sherry, ginger, and lemon juice. Stir slowly, bringing to a light rolling boil. Remove from heat; pour over chicken.

Cover and bake for 1 hour, or until tender. Remove. Garnish with chopped parsley.

SERVING SUGGESTION   Serve with basmati rice sprinkled with chopped scallions and our Hearts of Palm and Spinach Salad (see Page 37). Oh, go ahead . . . have our Pineapple Upside-down Cake (see Page 248) for dessert.

MESQUITE-GRILLED ASIAN CHICKEN AND VEGETABLES

This is probably our favorite healthy, low-carb meal. We like to serve it with fresh seasonal fruit. For the best flavor, Bill insists you grill it over mesquite wood.   YIELD: 6 SERVINGS

1 teaspoon sea salt

1 teaspoon freshly ground black pepper

1 teaspoon garlic powder

1 cup soy sauce: Eden Foods Tamari Organic, La Choy, Premier Japan Organic Wheat-free Teriyaki Sauce, or San-J Organic Wheat-free Tamari (Gold Label)

6 chicken breast halves (not skinless)

3 tablespoons olive oil

3 tablespoons balsamic vinegar

1 onion, peeled and halved

1 green bell pepper, cored, seeded, and halved

1 red bell pepper, cored, seeded, and halved

3 zucchini squash, halved lengthwise

In a bowl mix salt, pepper, garlic powder, and soy sauce. Place chicken in shallow baking dish. Pour soy sauce mixture over chicken. Cover with plastic wrap. Refrigerate 1 hour.

Fire up the grill, bringing the temperature to medium-high.

Mix olive oil and balsamic vinegar together with salt and pepper to taste. Brush vegetables with this basting mixture.

Remove chicken from marinade. Brushing occasionally with marinade, grill chicken on each side, approximately 8 to 10 minutes, or until cooked thoroughly.

Grill vegetables 2 to 4 minutes, basting occasionally.

CHICKEN TANDOORI

Even though we don't have a tandoor oven, the flavor of our chicken tandoori is as tantalizing as any Indian restaurant's, and you won't find any red dye here.   YIELD: 4 SERVINGS

1 whole chicken, cut up, skin removed

2 to 3 cloves garlic, crushed

1-inch piece fresh peeled ginger

¾ cup plain yogurt

1 teaspoon chile powder: McCormick or Spice Islands

1 teaspoon ground cumin: McCormick or Spice Islands

¾ teaspoon turmeric: McCormick or Spice Islands

2 teaspoons fresh lemon juice

4 whole cloves

1 cinnamon stick

½ teaspoon sea salt

Thinly sliced onions and lemon wedges for garnish

Rinse the chicken pieces and pat dry. Place in single layer in a shallow dish.

Place remaining ingredients in a small blender, and mix to prepare a paste. Apply paste to chicken and cover with plastic wrap. Marinate refrigerated overnight.

Fire up the grill, bringing the temperature to medium or slower.

Remove the chicken from the marinade, shaking off any excess, and grill over a slow fire until the meat is cooked all the way through.

Serve hot with thinly sliced onions and fresh lemon wedges.

SERVING SUGGESTION   We like this with basmati rice and our Hearts of Palm and Spinach Salad (see Page 37). Good served with a cold Redbridge beer.

PEPPERCORN AND HERB-ROASTED TURKEY

Being the one gluten-free eater at the Thanksgiving table is like being the 800-pound gorilla in the room, unless you have someone who loves you enough to make you separate gravy, separate dressing, separate dessert, etc. Here is a recipe for roast turkey that makes its own gravy, thickened with cornstarch. And we have a Thanksgiving dressing that is better than your mother's. Serve this to friends and family. They will never know that they've been secretly "gluten-freed." YIELD: 10 TO 12 SERVINGS

1 (14-pound) turkey, defrosted (see note)

2 cups sea salt

2 tablespoons black peppercorns

3 large oranges (2 cut in half and juiced, divided use)

1 (750ml) bottle dry white wine

Salt and pepper

2 tablespoons seasoned salt: Lawry's

1 stick butter, softened, plus additional (divided use)

1 onion

3 tablespoons chicken bouillon: Herb-Ox or Le Kum Kee Chicken Bouillon Powder

2 tablespoons dried parsley: McCormick or Spice Islands

2 tablespoons onion flakes

4 cups warm water

4 small carrots

Sea salt

¼ cup cornstarch

¼ cup cold water

Remove turkey from refrigerator. Rinse. Remove bag of parts—the neck and loose organs—in cavity. Pat dry well inside and out.

Place the turkey in large plastic container with kosher salt, peppercorns, 2 oranges and their juice, white wine, and enough ice water to cover. Mix well. Refrigerate and brine for 6 to 8 hours.

Remove turkey, and discard brining solution. Pat dry very well, including cavity.

Preheat oven to 450 F. Adjust rack in oven to bottom ¼ position.

Truss drumsticks and wings. Season cavity with salt and pepper. Sprinkle seasoned salt all over turkey. Rub butter thoroughly all over turkey.

Cut remaining orange and onion in 8 pieces. Stuff inside cavity.

Add bouillon, parsley, and onion flakes to 4 cups warm water. Mix well.

Place turkey, breast side down, on V-rack set inside a large baking pan. (Note: If you use a disposable foil roasting pan, be sure to set on a nonflexible baking sheet.) Arrange carrots around turkey in pan.

Spoon parsley and water mixture over turkey. Put turkey in oven.

Immediately reduce heat to 350 F.

After 1 hour, turn turkey breast side up. Baste. Rub more butter on breast side. Bake for 2½ hours more, basting every 30 minutes with water-and-parsley mixture.

Remove turkey from oven. Let rest 20 to 30 minutes. Remove carrots from roasting pan to a serving dish. Keep warm.

While the turkey is resting, put the roasting pan over one or two burners and spoon off excess fat. Mix cornstarch in cold water to dissolve. Add to pan drippings. Stir over medium heat, scraping up any browned bits in the pan, until thickened. Pour into a gravy boat; add any remaining juices from the turkey platter.

Carve the turkey and serve with the carrots and gravy.

NOTE: For best results, defrost turkey for 3 days in refrigerator.

SERVING SUGGESTION   Try this with our Apple Sausage Thanksgiving Dressing (see Page 191), steamed broccoli, our Cranberry Waldorf Salad (see Page 36) and our Italian Crema Cake (see Page 252).

SPICY CHOLULA APRICOT CHICKEN

Some like it hot, and we've got it right. We don't know who invented apricot chicken, but it seems like everyone has a version. Here's one for the gluten-freed society. It's sweet, salty, and fruity.   YIELD: 8 SERVINGS

1 tablespoon onion flakes

1 teaspoon onion salt

1 teaspoon garlic powder

½ bottle Russian dressing: Wishbone

1 jar (16 ounces) apricot preserves or jam: Polaner

1 teaspoon Cholula hot sauce

8 chicken breast halves

Preheat oven to 325 F. Mix all ingredients except chicken. Pour over chicken in a shallow baking dish. Bake 1½ hours, or until done.

SERVING SUGGESTION   We like this with our Almond-and-Red-Pepper Cabbage Slaw (Page 49).

BLACK PEPPERCORN AND SEA SALT VENISON TENDERLOIN

Delectable. Delightful. Delicious. Venison tenderloin (backstrap) the way it is supposed to be. Whether there's a hunter in the house or not, a little game can add great variety to your menus. If you can't find venison at a nearby store, such as Whole Foods Market, you can buy excellent venison online. Broken Arrow Ranch is the Texas go-to source.   YIELD: 8 SERVINGS

1 large white onion, diced

3 cups apple cider vinegar: Heinz

3 cups water

2 teaspoons coarse sea salt

1 teaspoon black peppercorns

8 whole cloves

2 large bay leaves

2½ pounds venison tenderloin (steaks or single piece)¾ cup gluten-free flour: Bob's Red Mill White Rice Flour or Pamela's Gluten-free Baking & Pancake Mix

¼ pound bacon, cut into small dice

6 tablespoons butter

2 tablespoons vegetable oil

1 cup sour cream

Combine onion, vinegar, water, salt, peppercorns, cloves, and bay leaves in a zip-top freezer bag. Add venison and marinate in refrigerator for 2 days, turning 2 to 4 times each 24-hour period.

Remove meat, shaking off excess, and reserving marinade. Coat meat well in flour.

In a Dutch oven or Le Creuset, cook bacon until fat is rendered. Remove bacon. Add butter, and melt over medium-high heat.

Add oil. When foam subsides, sauté venison on all sides until golden brown.

Slowly add 2½ cups reserved marinade. Bring to a boil. Reduce heat to medium-low. Cover and simmer 30 minutes to an hour, or until tender. (On an electric stove, you can simmer for 2 hours on setting 2–3 or low.) Remove meat to a warm platter.

Add sour cream to skillet. Stir until thickened and heated thoroughly. Spoon over meat.

Serve immediately.

BACON-WRAPPED VENISON TENDERLOIN WITH BLACK-WALNUT-CHERRY SAUCE

Bill outdid himself on this recipe. It's so good we don't even want to comment. Try it and you'll understand. YIELD: 6 SERVINGS

1 cup brown sugar

1 cup plus 2 tablespoons soy sauce (divided use): Eden Foods Tamari Organic, La Choy, Premier Japan Organic Wheat–free Teriyaki Sauce, or San-J Organic Wheat-free Tamari (Gold Label)

1 teaspoon freshly ground black pepper

½ cup port wine

1 (2-pound) venison tenderloin

10 slices bacon: Boar's Head

4 tablespoons olive oil

1 cup drained, pitted cherries (canned are okay)

½ cup red plum preserves

¼ teaspoon dry mustard: Colman's

¼ cup black walnut pieces

In a bowl, mix brown sugar, 1 cup soy sauce, black pepper, and port until sugar dissolves.

Pour into large zip-top freezer plastic bag. Add venison. Marinate 2 hours in refrigerator.

Remove venison from marinade, shaking off excess.

Lay bacon out on plastic wrap. Add venison on top. Roll. Remove and discard plastic wrap and secure bacon with wooden toothpicks.

Preheat oven to 450 F.

Heat olive oil in large skillet over medium-high heat. Brown venison on all sides, about 2 minutes on each side. Remove venison to a slotted rack with drip pan.

Place in oven. Immediately reduce heat to 350 F. Roast 50 minutes.

Remove meat from oven. Let rest 10 minutes.

While it rests, combine cherries, preserves, remaining 2 tablespoons soy sauce, dry mustard, and black walnuts in a saucepan. Mix well. Heat over medium-low heat until cooked through, approximately 10 minutes. Keep warm.

Slice the venison and serve with the Cherry Sauce.

SERVING SUGGESTION This is great with our Three-Cheese Risotto (see Page 157) and roasted crimini mushrooms. And, of course, a hearty red wine. Then why not have our Buttermilk Toffee Cake with Chocolate Buttercream Frosting (see Page 256) for dessert?

BACON-WRAPPED QUAIL WITH DATES AND JALAPEÑO

We also call this quail *para el rey*—"for the king." Indeed the stuff of royalty. We use Sun Maid Natural California Pitted Dates.   YIELD: 4 SERVINGS

4 quail

1 cup soy sauce: Eden Foods Tamari Organic, La Choy, Premier Japan Organic Wheat-free Teriyaki Sauce, or San-J Organic Wheat-free Tamari (Gold Label)

1 teaspoon sea salt

1 teaspoon freshly ground black pepper

2 tablespoons jalapeño pepper jelly

2 tablespoons melted butter

1 tablespoon water

8 pitted dates: Sun Maid

1 jalapeño pepper, seeded, deveined, and sliced into ⅛-inch matchsticks (see note)

4 cloves garlic, minced

1 tablespoon chopped shallot

8 slices bacon: Boar's Head

Soak quail in soy sauce for 30 minutes. Drain. Pat dry.

Preheat oven to 350 F. Salt and pepper quail. Mix together pepper jelly, butter, and water in a small dish.

Place 2 dates and jalapeño matchstick inside each quail. Sprinkle with garlic and shallot.

Wrap 2 pieces of bacon around each quail.

Place in a baking dish large enough to hold quail in one layer. Pour jalapeno mixture evenly over quail. Roast for 30 minutes.

Increase oven to 425 F and finish at that temperature for 15 minutes.

NOTE: Wear plastic gloves when you handle hot peppers.

SERVING SUGGESTION   This is great with our Havarti, Gouda, and Cheddar Cheese Grits (see Page 158).

THE BEST HOMEMADE CHICKEN STOCK EVER

Real flavor. Real wholesome. Real good. There is just no substitute for real chicken stock. Although there are some good, organic gluten-free chicken stocks on the market these days, there is no substitute for homemade. Fresh vegetables. Controlled salt. We think starting with good-quality, organic chicken is essential. We cube the meat and use it in many of our recipes, such as Indian Ginger-Curry Sauce (see Page 233). YIELD: 10 TO 12 SERVINGS

1 (2-3-pound) chicken, cut up

1 stalk celery, halved

1 carrot, halved

1 medium onion, quartered

1 sprig fresh parsley

1 clove garlic, minced

1 teaspoon sea salt

4 whole black peppercorns

1 bay leaf

Combine all ingredients in large pot. Cover with water and bring to a boil; reduce heat and simmer until meat is tender and falls off bone easily, approximately 1½ hours, stirring occasionally.

Remove chicken, discarding skin, bones, and fat, cube the meat for another use.

Strain remaining mixture through a fine strainer or cheesecloth.

Use immediately, or freeze in 3-cup portions. This classic stock can be stored up to 1 month in the freezer. It will keep only 3 days in the refrigerator.

FISH AND SEAFOOD

Fish and seafood have been a big part of our gluten-free diet for years, and we have created some great recipes. For example, our Potato-Crusted Tilapia with Lime Crème Adobo Sauce is just heavenly. Using potatoes instead of bread crumbs actually tastes much better. The Pecan-Crusted Salmon is so easy to make, yet so incredible. And once you try our Shrimp with Sherry, Garlic, and Bread Crumbs—yes, bread crumbs— you will never want deep-fried shrimp again.

We recommend that you buy only the freshest fish and seafood you can find. Always try to find wild rather than farm-raised. It makes all the difference in the world. If fish smells fishy, don't buy it. Fish is supposed to smell briny, like the ocean. When in doubt, buy frozen, which is quite good these days thanks to flash-freezing techniques on fishing boats. Besides using the freshest fish you can find, the other secret is not to overcook it. Overcooking will make any fish dry.

Kim's brother, Doug, who was born with a fishing rod in his hand and is the real *pescador* of Rockport, Texas, recommends cutting out the red spots in the fillets, as those are the "fishy" tasting spots. He also likes to soak his fish, whether it's salmon, orange roughy, tilapia, or anything else, in cold water for at least five to six hours to get any fishy taste out. It really does work!

LEMON BUTTER SCALLOPS DE CABO SAN LUCAS

Cabo. The place for fresh scallops at the *palapa*, right on the beach. This recipe for Cabo scallops is a rich, lemony, garlicky, and buttery. But that's only if you use high-quality scallops (yes, they're expensive) and don't overcook them. Overcook scallops, and you might just as well eat a golf ball. You can also substitute lime juice for lemon juice.   YIELD: 4 SERVINGS

Nonstick cooking spray

1½ pounds large, fresh scallops, rinsed and patted dry

1 tablespoon chopped garlic

½ teaspoon sea salt

1 chopped red jalapeño pepper, seeded, deveined, and cut into rings

2 tablespoons fresh lemon juice

2 tablespoons unsalted butter, melted

¼ teaspoon cayenne pepper: McCormick or Spice Islands

2 limes, quartered

Spray shallow baking pan with the cooking spray. Spread scallops in the pan.

Sprinkle with garlic, salt, and jalapeno. Drizzle with lemon juice and butter.

Broil 6 to 8 minutes, or until scallops are golden. Serve immediately with lime wedges.

SERVING SUGGESTION   We love this with our Roasted Beet Salad with Goat Cheese and Pecans (see Page 44), fresh corn tortillas, and sliced mangoes.

TORTILLA-CHIP-CRUSTED TACOS DE PESCADO WITH CHILE-MAYO CABBAGE SLAW

We have two recipes for fish tacos, because we couldn't agree on which was better. (It's not the first time we couldn't agree on something.) So you decide. Kim's recipe is crunchy and oh, so full of flavor. The Chile-Mayo Cabbage Slaw puts it over the top. The tacos are great with Mexican martinis or an ice-cold Redbridge beer . . . but what isn't? For entertaining, set up a taco bar. People will love it. We also like to drizzle some La Vaquita Crema Mexicana and Valentina Mexican Salsa Picante on top for the finale.   YIELD: 10 TO 12 TACOS

---

1 pound cod or flounder fillet, cut into 3 x 1-inch strips

¼ teaspoon cayenne pepper: McCormick or Spice Islands

1½ cup finely crushed tortilla chips, broken up in food processor: Tostitos Bite-size Gold, Natural Yellow Corn Tortilla Chips, or Mission Gluten-free Corn Chips

1 teaspoon paprika: McCormick or Spice Islands

1 teaspoon garlic powder

1 teaspoon onion powder

1 teaspoon white pepper: Spice Islands

1 teaspoon ground cumin: McCormick or Spice Islands

1 teaspoon chile powder: McCormick or Spice Islands

1 teaspoon lemon pepper

1 teaspoon sea salt

2 eggs, beaten

1 tablespoon warm water

2 cups peanut oil or vegetable oil

12 to 16 corn tortillas: Mission, El Lago, or Sonoma Organic (see note)

Chile-Mayo Cabbage Slaw (recipe follows)

Optional accompaniments: black beans, corn, avocado slices, red or green salsa, lime wedges

Sprinkle fillets with cayenne and let sit for 10 minutes. Mix tortilla chips with spices and salt in a bowl.

Mix eggs and water in a bowl and dip each fish fillet into the egg mixture. Dip each fish fillet into tortilla-chip mixture and refrigerate for 20 minutes.

Heat oil in large nonstick skillet to 350 F.

Gently fry the fish in batches, turning once until golden brown, approximately 3 to 5 minutes on each side. Drain on paper towels. Wrap the tortillas in foil and heat in a slow oven.

Assemble tacos with warm tortillas, fish, Chile-Mayo Cabbage Slaw, and optional accompaniments you desire.

NOTE: Bill likes to make hard taco shells from scratch. To do this, heat a nonstick skillet. Add 2 tablespoons oil and heat on medium-high until very hot but not smoking. Fry tortillas until they bubble on each side. Gently fold them over for taco shells. Remove and drain on paper towel.

TO BAKE THE FISH: Preheat oven to 350 F. Follow steps above for coating with tortilla-chip crumbs. Gently pat crumbs on fillets to adhere. Refrigerate for 20 minutes. Place on baking sheet, and bake until fish is cooked through, about 14 to 18 minutes, depending on thickness of fish.

CHILE-MAYO CABBAGE

½ cup mayonnaise: Hellmann's, Kraft, or Spectrum

1½ cup La Vaquita Crema Mexicana, organic sour cream, or crème fraîche

2 tablespoons canned chipotle chiles in adobo, puréed

4 tablespoons fresh lime juice

1½ tablespoons chile powder: McCormick or Spice Islands

1 teaspoon ground cumin: McCormick or Spice Islands

¼ teaspoon cayenne pepper: McCormick or Spice Islands

1 tablespoon Dijon mustard: Maille Dijon Originale Mustard or Grey Poupon

⅛ cup Heinz chili sauce

1 teaspoon Worcestershire sauce: Lea & Perrins or French's

½ teaspoon sea salt

½ teaspoon freshly ground black pepper

1 tablespoon chopped fresh parsley

1 tablespoon chopped fresh tarragon

1 teaspoon honey

1 tablespoon Valentina Mexican Salsa Picante

½ to ¾ head of coarsely shredded cabbage

Chopped fresh cilantro (optional)

Mix all ingredients in blender except the cabbage and coarsely blend. In a large mixing bowl, toss with shredded cabbage. Add salt and freshly ground black pepper to taste. Garnish with cilantro.

MIAMI FISH TACOS WITH LIME SAUCE

Miami. Home to the best fish tacos on the planet. We think it is the Cuban influence. Bill says the best fish tacos he ever had were at a small joint not far from Miami International Airport. This recipe most closely approximates those "real" fish tacos. Bill recommends cod, and it must be fried just right. Nothing can be greasy. The sliced cabbage should be crisp. We like to soak it in ice water beforehand.   YIELD: 12 SERVINGS

½ teaspoon freshly ground black pepper

1½ teaspoons sea salt

1 teaspoon garlic powder

1 teaspoon onion powder

¼ teaspoon cayenne pepper: McCormick or Spice Islands

1 teaspoon dry mustard: Colman's

½ teaspoon dried oregano: McCormick or Spice Islands

1 cup gluten-free flour: Bob's Red Mill Biscuit and Baking Mix or Pamela's Baking & Pancake Mix

1 cup plus 2 tablespoons whole milk

Lime Sauce (recipe follows)

Peanut oil

1 pound cod fillets, cut into 3-x-½-inch strips

Bob's Red Mill Biscuit and Baking Mix for dredging

12 taco shells: Ortega

1 cup finely shredded cabbage

Pace Picante Sauce (medium)

Place pepper, 1½ half teaspoons salt, garlic and onion powders, cayenne, dry mustard, oregano, flour, and milk in blender and blend for 20 to 30 seconds. (You could also use an electric mixer.) Pour into glass bowl and cover with plastic wrap. Let sit at room temperature at least 1 hour.

Make Lime Sauce and refrigerate. Preheat oven to 350 F.

In a deep 4-6-quart heavy pot, heat 2 to 3 inches oil to 365 F.

Dip each piece in batter. Let excess batter drip off each strip. Dredge in flour.

Fry cod strips, stirring from time to time, 2 to 4 minutes. Remove with slotted spoon.

Drain on paper towels or paper sack.

Fry remaining fish in batches. Make sure the oil stays at 365 F. Always let it come back up to 365 F before each batch. Add oil as needed to maintain depth.

Place taco shells in oven for 5 minutes or until warm. Remove from oven and keep warm.

Bring oil up to 375 F. Refry fish in batches until golden, 1 to 2 minutes. Drain on paper towels.

Assemble tacos by putting fish in shells. Top with cabbage and drizzle with lime sauce and picante sauce. Serve with lime wedges.

LIME SAUCE

½ teaspoon sea salt

¼ cup mayonnaise: Hellmann's, Kraft, or Spectrum

¼ cup Miracle Whip

¼ cup plain yogurt

¼ cup fresh lime juice

Mix together all ingredients in a small bowl.

SERVING SUGGESTION   We like this with a side of fresh guacamole and cold Redbridge beer.

GRILLED ASIAN MARINATED TUNA STEAKS

Our tuna steaks are definitely a treat. We love to serve these during the summer months. If you can't find excellent-quality tuna steaks, don't make this recipe.   **YIELD: 4 SERVINGS**

¾ cup teriyaki sauce: Premier Japan Organic Wheat-free

2 tablespoons soy sauce: San-J Eden Foods Tamari Organic, or San-J Organic Wheat-free Tamari (Gold Label)

1 tablespoon brown sugar

1 tablespoon sherry

1 tablespoon brown rice vinegar: Eden Foods Organic

4 cloves garlic, minced

1 teaspoon chopped fresh ginger

1 finely chopped scallion (green part only)

⅛ teaspoon hot red pepper flakes: McCormick or Spice Islands

4 (1½-inch thick) tuna steaks

Mix together all ingredients except tuna. Pour over steaks and marinate in refrigerator for 30 to 45 minutes. Remove. Discard the marinade.

Fire up the grill, bringing the temperature to medium-high. Grill in fish grilling basket for 4 minutes on the first side. Turn. Grill for 3 more minutes on the second side.

SERVING SUGGESTION   We like this with wild rice and our Hearts of Palm and Spinach Salad (see Page 37) and our Pineapple Upside-down Cake (see Page 248) for dessert.

SHRIMP WITH SHERRY, GARLIC, AND BREAD CRUMBS

Seafood elegance redefined. It's also one of those "serve immediately" gigs, but so easy to prepare.   YIELD: 3 TO 4 SERVINGS

20 jumbo shrimp, peeled and deveined

1 lemon, quartered

¾ cup butter, softened

¼ cup parsley: McCormick or Spice Islands

1 cup gluten-free bread crumbs made from finely chopped gluten-free bread or Orgran Gluten-free Bread Crumbs

½ cup sherry

6 cloves garlic, minced

1 teaspoon sea salt

½ teaspoon cayenne pepper: McCormick or Spice Islands

½ teaspoon paprika: McCormick or Spice Islands

Preheat oven to 375 F; butter a baking dish that will accommodate shrimp in 1 layer.

Boil shrimp in lightly salted water with the lemon for 2 minutes. Drain and cool. (To cool shrimp down quickly, plunge it into ice water, then drain.)

In a bowl combine butter, parsley, bread crumbs, sherry, garlic, salt, cayenne, and paprika until blended.

Place shrimp in the prepared dish and cover with mixture. Bake until crumbs are golden brown, about 15 minutes. Remove and serve.

SERVING SUGGESTION   We like to serve this with our Pasta with Lemon-Caper Sauce (see Page 75), a crisp white wine, and Kim's Traditional Karrot Kake (see Page 237).

LEMON-PEPPER-BROWN-SUGAR GRILLED SALMON

Your neighbors will line up for this one just from the aroma of the grill. And you will love the combined effect that soy sauce, lemon, ginger and brown sugar bring to this recipe. YIELD: 4 SERVINGS

¾ cup honey

¼ cup soy sauce: Eden Foods Tamari Organic, La Choy, or San-J Organic Wheat-free Tamari (Gold Label)

¼ cup brown sugar

¼ cup pineapple juice

Juice of 1 lemon

1 teaspoon freshly ground black pepper

½ teaspoon cayenne pepper: McCormick or Spice Islands

½ teaspoon paprika: McCormick or Spice Islands

½ teaspoon garlic powder

½ cup olive oil

4 (6-ounce) salmon fillets, skin on

Combine all ingredients except fish in a saucepan and bring just to a boil. Let cool. Reserve about ⅛ to ¼ cup.

Place salmon fillets and remaining sauce in a plastic zip-top freezer bag for 6 to 8 hours.

Fire up the grill, bringing to medium-high heat. Remove salmon, and discard marinade.

Grill salmon 4 to 7 minutes on each side. Serve with reserved sauce on the side.

SERVING SUGGESTION   We like this with our Asparagus Gratin and our Wilted Spinach Salad (see Page 37). How about our Pineapple Upside-down Cake (see Page 248) for dessert?

PECAN-CRUSTED SALMON

Salmon is one of the healthiest proteins that you can eat. The sweet, nutty flavor of the pecans mixes seamlessly with the taste of fresh, wild-caught salmon. The pecans also give the salmon a wonderful crunchy texture. YIELD: 4 SERVINGS

2 tablespoons butter, melted

1 cup finely chopped pecans

2 tablespoons chopped parsley

1 teaspoon sea salt

¼ teaspoon white pepper: Spice Islands

¼ teaspoon cayenne pepper: McCormick or Spice Islands

¼ teaspoon lemon pepper: McCormick or Spice Islands

⅛ teaspoon paprika: McCormick or Spice Islands

⅔ cup gluten-free bread crumbs made from finely chopped gluten-free bread or Orgran Gluten-free Bread Crumbs

4 tablespoons mayonnaise: Hellmann's, Kraft, or Spectrum

1 teaspoon fresh lemon juice

4 (6-ounce) salmon fillets

Preheat oven to 425 F. Grease a baking dish that will hold the fillets in 1 layer.

Combine butter, pecans, parsley, salt, peppers, paprika, and bread crumbs.

Season salmon with sea salt and white pepper. Place salmon skin-side-down in the prepared baking dish.

Mix mayonnaise and lemon juice. Place 1 tablespoon of mayonnaise and lemon juice mixture on each fillet and spread evenly.

Divide bread-crumb-pecan mixture among 4 fillets and press into each. Bake 10 to 13 minutes, or until fish reaches desired doneness.

SERVING SUGGESTION   This is great with our Asparagus and Blue Cheese Risotto (see Page 155). And why not just have a bottle of pink champagne to go with?

MARINATED BROILED SALMON WITH HORSERADISH-CAPER SAUCE

A match made in heaven. The Horseradish-Caper Sauce is a luscious complement to the salmon.

YIELD: 4 SERVINGS

4 (6-ounce) salmon fillets, skin on

1 tablespoon fresh lime juice

3 tablespoons honey

2 tablespoons olive oil

1 tablespoon chopped fresh mint plus more for garnish

Sea salt and freshly ground black pepper to taste

Nonstick cooking spray

2 tablespoons soy sauce: Eden Foods Tamari Organic, La Choy, or San-J Organic Wheat-free Tamari (Gold Label)

2 chopped scallions, green part only

Lemon wedges or quartered limes

Horseradish-Caper Sauce (recipe follows)

Place salmon in a glass or ceramic dish, skin-side down. Combine the lime juice, honey, olive oil, mint, salt, and pepper and pour over salmon. Marinate refrigerated for 1 hour.

Preheat oven to 450 F. Spray a baking dish large enough to hold fillets in 1 layer with nonstick cooking spray.

Remove salmon from marinade. Discard marinade. Paint skinless side of fillet with soy sauce. Lay skinless side down in prepared dish. Bake 15 to 20 minutes, or until thoroughly cooked.

Place salmon under broiler, 6 inches from flame, for 15 minutes. If you don't want the skin to be crispy, turn it over and broil the skinless side instead.

Remove from oven, and garnish with scallions and mint. Serve with lemon wedges or quartered limes and Horseradish Caper Sauce.

SERVING SUGGESTION   We like this with our Wilted Spinach Salad (see Page 37) and Kim's Best Little Coconut Cream Cake in Texas (see Page 239).

HORSERADISH CAPER SAUCE

1 cup sour cream, chilled whipped cream, or crème fraîche

2 tablespoons fresh lemon juice

1 tablespoons grated fresh horseradish or prepared horseradish

2 teaspoons Dijon mustard: Maille Dijon Originale or Grey Poupon

¼ teaspoon sea salt

¼ teaspoon white pepper: Spice Islands

dash of Tabasco sauce

1 tablespoon capers, drained: Mezzetta, Reese, or Star

1 teaspoon chopped fresh parsley

1 teaspoon chopped fresh tarragon

Mix all ingredients together in a small bowl.

POTATO-CRUSTED TILAPIA WITH LIME CREMA ADOBO SAUCE

Potatoes instead of bread crumbs? You bet. Kim grew up making potato patties for her brother and sister . . . and, of course, she always liked to spice them up. Here you have a spicy potato crust on tilapia that makes a fabulous crunchy entrée. YIELD: 4 TO 6 SERVINGS

4 (6-ounce) tilapia fillets

¼ teaspoon cayenne pepper: McCormick or Spice Islands

2 tablespoons gluten-free flour: Bob's Red Mill Biscuit and Baking Mix or Pamela's Baking & Pancake Mix

½ teaspoon paprika: McCormick or Spice Islands

½ teaspoon dried basil: McCormick or Spice Islands

¼ teaspoon freshly ground black pepper

2 teaspoons sea salt

½ teaspoon lemon pepper: McCormick or Spice Islands

¼ teaspoon thyme: McCormick or Spice Islands

½ teaspoon onion powder

½ teaspoon dried oregano: McCormick or Spice Islands

1 tablespoon chopped fresh chives

1 tablespoon minced garlic

3 cups shredded russet potatoes, rinsed, drained, and toweled to remove excess moisture

2 eggs, room temperature, beaten

Peanut or olive oil

Lime Crema Adobo Sauce (see Page 223)

Sprinkle the fillets with cayenne. Let sit for 15 minutes in the refrigerator.

Combine flour, paprika, basil, pepper, salt, lemon pepper, thyme, onion powder, and dried oregano in a medium bowl. Add the chives and garlic and mix. Add the shredded potatoes.

Place eggs in a bowl.

Dip each fillet into the eggs. Pat potato mixture onto both sides of the fillet.

Heat oil to cover the bottom of a large, nonstick skillet to moderately high heat. It is ready when you drop in a potato shred and it starts to sizzle.

Carefully place fillets in the skillet. Cook 9 to 10 minutes on each side, or until crispy brown. Carefully flip fillets and try to cook undisturbed to keep the potatoes in place.

Remove to a plate covered with paper towels, drain, and serve with Lime Crema Adobo Sauce.

SERVING SUGGESTION We like this with our Grilled Peach, Feta, and Spinach Salad with Sherry Balsamic Vinaigrette (see Page 43) and grilled asparagus.

GRILLED TILAPIA WITH VERACRUZ SAUCE

Kim's fave recipe! A fabulous dish for a candlelit evening. We love tilapia. It's a mild fish with many uses. This dish is full of flavor from juicy, red ripe tomatoes, olives, and capers. It also works with redfish.   YIELD: 4 SERVINGS

4 (6-ounce) tilapia fillets

½ teaspoon cayenne pepper: McCormick or Spice Islands

¼ teaspoon garlic powder

¼ teaspoon onion powder

¼ teaspoon chili powder: McCormick or Spice Islands

¼ teaspoon paprika: McCormick or Spice Islands

¼ teaspoon cumin: McCormick or Spice Islands

Veracruz Sauce (recipe follows)

Fire up the grill to medium.

Sprinkle the fillets with cayenne and let sit for 10 minutes.

Mix remaining spices together and rub on each side of fillets. Spray fish basket with cooking spray and place fillets in it.

Place on hot grill and cook 4 to 5 minutes over medium heat, turning only once.

Remove from grill to a warm platter and top with Veracruz Sauce. Serve immediately.

SERVING SUGGESTION   We like this with our Mexican Caesar Salad with Chile Polenta Croutons (see Page 50) and Kim's Famous Over-the-Top Bananas Foster Cake. And, oh, yeah . . . our Homemade Sangria (see Page 96) really complements it.

VERACRUZ SAUCE

1 tablespoon olive oil

1 tablespoon garlic, minced

¼ cup coarsely chopped black olives

¼ cup sliced green olives

1 to 2 tablespoons capers, drained: Mezzetta, Reese, or Star

1 (14.5-ounce) can tomatoes: Hunt's Organic Basil, Garlic, and Oregano Diced Tomatoes or Muir Glen Italian Tomatoes

¼ teaspoon sea salt

¼ teaspoon freshly ground black pepper

¼ teaspoon dried thyme: McCormick or Spice Islands

1 bay leaf

1 cup chicken broth: Health Valley Fat-free, Pacific Natural Foods Organic, or Swanson Natural Goodness

1 tablespoon fresh lime juice

½ teaspoon brown sugar

Dash cayenne pepper: McCormick or Spice Islands

Fresh lime wedges

Heat oil in a medium skillet over medium-high heat. Add garlic, olives, and capers and let sizzle about 2 minutes.

Add tomatoes, salt, pepper, thyme, bay leaf, chicken broth, lime juice, brown sugar, and cayenne pepper. Bring to a boil, reduce heat, and simmer 30 minutes.

JALAPEÑO-PECAN CORNBREAD-CRUSTED TILAPIA

Inspirational. Rich. Delectable. Our recipe for Jalapeño-Pecan Cornbread-Crusted Tilapia is crispy and spicy. What an indulgence. YIELD: 4 SERVINGS

4 (6-ounce) tilapia fillets

¼ teaspoon cayenne pepper: McCormick or Spice Islands

½ cup gluten-free flour: Bob's Red Mill Biscuit and Baking Mix or Pamela's Baking & Pancake Mix

½ cup gluten-free bread crumbs made from finely chopped gluten-free bread or Orgran Gluten-free Bread Crumbs

½ cup cornmeal: Lamb's Stone-Ground Yellow, Albers Yellow, or Arrowhead Mills Organic Yellow

1 teaspoon paprika: McCormick or Spice Islands

1 teaspoon garlic powder

1 teaspoon onion powder

1 teaspoon oregano: McCormick or Spice Islands

1 teaspoon lemon pepper

1 teaspoon sea salt

1 teaspoon thyme: McCormick or Spice Islands

¼ teaspoon white pepper: Spice Islands

¼ teaspoon freshly ground black pepper

¼ cup finely chopped pecans

1 tablespoon jalapeño peppers, seeded, deveined, and finely chopped (see note)

2 eggs, beaten

¾ cup peanut oil

Remoulade Sauce (see Page 21)

Lemon wedges

Sprinkle the fillets with cayenne and let sit for 10 minutes.

Combine bread crumbs, cornmeal, paprika, garlic powder, onion powder, oregano, lemon pepper, sea salt, thyme, peppers, pecans, and jalapeño in a paper bag or bowl.

Place beaten eggs in a separate bowl. Dip each fillet into the egg mixture. Dip each fillet into cornmeal mixture and refrigerate for 20 minutes to set (see note).

Heat oil in large nonstick skillet. Add fillets and cook over medium heat for 2 to 3 minutes per side. Don't crowd fish. Season to taste with salt and pepper.

NOTE: For the best results, breading typically needs a little time to firm up before it is pan-fried. If you bread and fry immediately there is a good chance some of the breading will come loose. This affects the finished texture, and it breaks the oil down more quickly.

Serve with our Remoulade Sauce and lots of lemon wedges.

SERVING SUGGESTION   We love this with our Grilled Peach, Feta, and Spinach Salad with Sherry Balsamic Vinaigrette (see Page 43) and a cold bottle of dry white wine.

VEGETABLES AND SAVORY ACCOMPANIMENTS

W elcome to our world of fresh, nutritious vegetables. Fresh vegetables are an important part of the healthy gluten-free lifestyle. We've learned that there are so many wonderful ways to prepare vegetable dishes. Our Roasted Potatoes with Caramelized Shallots, Blue Cheese and Asparagus tossed with Lemon Vinaigrette is among our favorites, as is Creamed Sweet Corn with Bacon and Jalapeño. And Kim's Balsamic Herb-Roasted Vegetables? So good and so easy.

We've combined many of our vegetables with fruits, cheese, rice, meat, and spices to add variety and excitement. The Roasted Tomato and Goat Cheese Risotto Cakes are phenomenal, and we think Hatch (New Mexico) green chiles add a robust Southwestern flavor to dishes like our Hoochy-Coo Hatch Green Chile Polenta. Another favorite is Havarti, Gouda, and Cheddar Cheese Grits, and we just can't get enough of the Gruyère-Jalapeño Scalloped Potatoes with Caramelized Onions.

By using our delicious recipes, you get the vitamins, minerals, and disease-fighting nutrients found in vegetables. This cookbook reminds you of why vegetables are one of the best and tastiest food groups, as well as so important for good health. We have also provided lots of new ideas to make the gluten-free diet creative, eclectic, and delicious. We like to use organically grown vegetables picked at the peak of perfection and ripeness, grown in soils rich in nutrients and beneficial microorganisms.

It is important to note that corn is a gluten-free-diet staple, so we include fresh corn recipes, especially for the kind of corn you can find at your local farmers' market. Corn and products made from corn, such as cornmeal, grits, polenta, popcorn, corn flour and cornstarch, are gluten-free by nature.

Rice, beans, and their kinfolk, legumes, are also gluten-free staples. Not only are beans affordable, they are rich in protein and a great source of fiber. These are your new life— your nutritious, healthy, and gluten-free new life. Forget the past. Embrace your future.

CREAMED SWEET CORN WITH BACON AND JALAPEÑO

Hot stuff. Fresh creamed corn with a major kick. We make this recipe only when fresh corn is in season. You could substitute frozen corn, but the dish will not be nearly as good. Buy your corn fresh-picked whenever possible. The natural sugars in non-GMO sweet corn start to break down into starch within hours of being picked. We love to buy from our local farmers' market. YIELD: 4 TO 6 SERVINGS

¼ cup diced onion

1 clove garlic, minced

1 tablespoon olive oil

1 teaspoon cornstarch

1 cup half-and-half

3 cups fresh raw corn kernels (sliced off cob)

1 jalapeño pepper, seeded, deveined, and finely chopped (see note)

½ teaspoon sea salt

¼ teaspoon freshly ground black pepper

¼ teaspoon white pepper: Spice Islands

3 slices of bacon, cooked crisp and crumbled

Preheat oven to 350 F.

In a skillet or saucepan, sauté the onion and garlic in the olive oil.

Mix cornstarch and half-and-half until thoroughly blended. Add to mixture. Cook on medium heat for 8 to 10 minutes until it thickens.

Remove from heat and add corn, jalapeño, salt, and pepper.

Pour into baking pie pan. Top with bacon and cover with foil. Bake for 18 to 22 minutes covered. Serve hot.

NOTE: Wear plastic gloves when handling jalapeno or other hot peppers.

SERVING SUGGESTION   We like this with our Marvelous Maple-Mustard Chicken (see Page 121) and our Devil's Devil's Food Cake with Chocolate Fluff Frosting (see Page 244).

ASPARAGUS AND BLUE CHEESE RISOTTO

A savory side dish made with delicate arborio rice fused with the robust flavors of blue cheese and fresh, crisp asparagus. Arborio rice is Italian medium-grain rice grown in the town of Arborio in the Po Valley. The grains are firm, yet creamy and tender when cooked—you can't help but fall in love with this dish. YIELD: 6 TO 8 SERVINGS

1 pound asparagus (stalks lightly peeled, with the tough ends broken off)

3 cups chicken broth: Health Valley Fat-free, Pacific Natural Foods Organic, or Swanson Natural Goodness or vegetable broth: Health Valley Fat-free Vegetable-Flavored Broth or Pacific Natural Vegetable Stock

1 cup uncooked arborio rice

2 cloves garlic, minced

2 tablespoons butter

Dash of Tabasco, or McCormick or Spice Islands cayenne pepper

½ teaspoon freshly ground black pepper

⅔ cup blue cheese: Boar's Head, Kraft, Primo Taglio Crumbled, or Sargento All-natural

Sea salt to taste

In a large saucepan, blanch the asparagus in the broth over high heat for 3 to 4 minutes, or until crisp-tender. Remove. When cool enough to handle, cut into 1½-inch pieces. Set aside.

Bring the broth to a boil. Add rice and garlic. Bring to a boil, then reduce heat to low. Simmer until the liquid is absorbed, about 15 to 18 minutes. Stir during cooking to allow more of the starch to leach into the water, making for a creamier rice dish.

Add butter and Tabasco sauce. Stir in black pepper, asparagus, and blue cheese and serve.

HOOCHY-COO HATCH GREEN CHILE POLENTA

Hatch green chiles are unmatched. The perfect soil conditions along with the dry, high desert air around the town of Hatch, New Mexico, are ideal for growing chiles that burst with flavor. It's the perfect accompaniment for pork, grilled chicken, or grilled fish. YIELD: 10 SERVINGS

---

1 Hatch green chile pepper (see note)

1 tablespoon olive oil

2½ cups chicken broth

½ cup whipping cream

1 cup organic polenta or yellow corn grits

1 cup extra sharp cheddar cheese: Kraft Natural or Boar's Head

½ cup Havarti cheese with jalapeños: Boar's Head

Dash of cayenne pepper: McCormick or Spice Islands

1 tablespoon Valentina Mexican Salsa Picante or Cholula

3 tablespoons butter

1 cup fresh or frozen corn kernels, thawed

½ teaspoon sea salt

¼ teaspoon freshly ground black pepper

Preheat oven to 400 F.

Lightly coat chile pepper with olive oil and place on a baking sheet. Roast for 8 to 10 minutes. Remove and let

cool. When it's cool enough to handle, peel off the skin, seed and chop fine. Set aside.

Bring chicken broth and cream to a boil in a large, heavy saucepan. As it boils, add polenta very, very, slowly, stirring constantly until smooth.

Cover, reduce heat, and cook for 15 to 20 minutes, stirring occasionally until it becomes thick.

Remove from heat and add cheeses, cayenne pepper, hot sauce, butter, corn, salt, pepper, and chopped chile pepper. Let cool to a warm temperature and serve.

NOTE: If Hatch chiles are unavailable, you can substitute a poblano or a couple of Anaheims. It won't be quite the same, but it will still be good. You could also substitute a small can of Hatch chiles, drained.

SERVING SUGGESTION   We like this with grilled chicken and a baby spinach salad with fresh strawberries, blueberries, caramelized walnuts, feta cheese, and our Kim's Fresh Ginger Vinaigrette (see Page 36).

THREE-CHEESE RISOTTO

Here is another "gotta try" recipe. Risotto is so easy to make and so delicious with the flavors of fontina, Asiago, and Havarti cheeses. We've come up with the cheesiest risotto dish of all time. Everyone who tastes this loves it. YIELD: 6 TO 8 SERVINGS

1 small onion, diced

1 tablespoon olive oil

1 clove garlic, finely minced

3 cups chicken broth: Health Valley Fat-free, Pacific Natural Foods Organic, or Swanson Natural Goodness

1 teaspoon butter

1 cup arborio rice

¼ cup heavy cream

1 tablespoon chopped fresh tarragon

¼ cup grated Havarti cheese

½ cup grated fontina cheese

¼ cup grated Asiago cheese

Dash of cayenne pepper: McCormick or Spice Islands

Sea salt and black pepper to taste

In a large saucepan over medium-high heat, sauté the onions in the olive oil until they are translucent. Add the garlic and chicken broth and bring to a boil. Reduce heat to a simmer.

Simmer for 5 minutes; add butter.

Add the rice and simmer for 16 to 18 minutes, stirring occasionally. Rice should become tender and creamy, yet still a little al dente.

Remove from heat and add the cream, tarragon, cheeses, and cayenne. Stir gently until the cheeses are melted. Salt to taste and serve immediately.

SERVING SUGGESTION This is a real treat with roasted chicken and fresh grilled asparagus.

HAVARTI, GOUDA, AND CHEDDAR CHEESE GRITS

Bill spent years perfecting this garlicky, cheesy recipe. These grits are so incredibly good, even a Yankee will love them. Grits are a true gluten-free friend. We think no Southern pantry should be without them. YIELD: 10 TO 12 SERVINGS

5 cups of water or chicken broth (Kim prefers broth)

½ teaspoon sea salt

2 cups quick grits: 3 Minute Brand

1 clove garlic

½ cup Havarti cheese: Boar's Head

1½ cups sharp cheddar cheese: Boar's Head Sharp Vermont

½ cup smoked Gouda cheese

1 stick unsalted butter

½ teaspoon seasoned salt: Lawry's

2 eggs

½ cup half-and-half

½ cup grated Parmesan cheese plus more for topping

Bring water or broth and salt to a rolling boil. Slowly add grits. Reduce heat to medium. Cook 5 to 7 minutes, stirring frequently until grits thicken. Remove from heat.

Chop garlic, cheeses, and butter into small pieces and add to grits. Add seasoned salt. Stir to melt cheese and butter, then let cool.

Preheat oven to 350 F. Butter a shallow 9 x 12 casserole dish.

Mix eggs with half-and-half and stir this into cooled grits. Pour into prepared baking dish.

Top with Parmesan cheese. Bake 35 to 40 minutes, or until Parmesan cheese is bubbly and slightly brown.

Remove from oven. Cool for 5 to 10 minutes, add more Parmesan on top and serve.

SERVING SUGGESTION Grits aren't just for breakfast anymore. These are delicious with our Roasted Pork Loin with Red Currant-Pomegranate Glaze and Portabella Mushrooms (see Page 106).

ROASTED TOMATO AND GOAT CHEESE RISOTTO CAKES

These risotto cakes are among our very favorites, and our family and friends just rave about them. They can be served as an entrée, an appetizer, or savory side dish. This is a phenomenal dish, one of the best and most original recipes Kim has come up with. If you don't want to fry the cakes, simply dust them with Parmesan cheese and bake them.   YIELD: 8 TO 10 SERVINGS

½ cup diced onion

1 clove garlic, minced

2 tablespoons olive oil

1 cup arborio rice

1 tablespoons fresh lemon juice

1 teaspoon sea salt

2½ cups chicken broth: Health Valley Fat-free, Pacific Natural Foods Organic, or Swanson Natural Goodness

1 tablespoon chopped fresh oregano

1 tablespoon finely chopped fresh basil

¼ cup chopped walnuts

¼ cup grated Parmigiano-Reggiano cheese

4 ounces goat cheese, crumbled

¾ cup roasted tomatoes, coarsely chopped (see note)

Cornmeal Mixture (recipe follows)

Olive oil for frying

In a large saucepan, sauté the onion and garlic in the olive oil over medium heat until they are translucent. Add the rice, lemon juice, and salt. Stir thoroughly.

Add chicken broth, oregano, and basil, and bring to a boil; reduce heat and simmer until the rice is tender but still al dente, about 15 to 18 minutes. Stir occasionally. Remove from the stove and let cool.

Stir in the walnuts, cheeses, and tomatoes. Pour risotto into a glass bowl and refrigerate for at least 1 hour and preferably overnight.

Form balls and flatten into patties approximately 2½-inch round. Roll in cornmeal mixture. Pan-fry in olive oil over medium-high heat until they are brown on both sides. Remove and drain on paper towels.

CORNMEAL MIXTURE:

¼ cup Lamb's Stone-ground Yellow Cornmeal, Albers Yellow Cornmeal, or Arrowhead Mills Organic Yellow Cornmeal

½ cup Pamela's Baking & Pancake Mix

½ cup grated Romano cheese.

Mix all ingredients in a flat dish. A pie pan works well.

TO BAKE THE CAKES: Preheat oven to 350 F. Dust each cake with Parmesan cheese and bake for 15 to 20 minutes, or until golden brown.

NOTE: To roast tomatoes, set oven to 185 F (very low). Cut very ripe, garden-fresh tomatoes in half, place on a baking sheet, cut-side-up, and sprinkle with olive oil and a little salt. Leave in the oven 4 to 6 hours.

SERVING SUGGESTION   If you really want to impress your guests, serve these with grilled swordfish and our Hearts of Palm and Spinach Salad (see Page 37). Top it off with our Red Velvet Cupcakes (see Page 255).

BILL'S GARLIC-ROASTED VEGETABLES

This is Bill's version of roasted veggies—simple and to the point.   YIELD: 8 TO 10 SERVINGS

8 ounces white button mushrooms, rinsed and dried

1 onion, cut in 8 pieces

1 red bell pepper, rinsed, seeded, deveined, and cut in 8 pieces

1 green bell pepper, rinsed, seeded, deveined, and cut in 8 pieces

1 pint cherry tomatoes, rinsed

1 bunch asparagus, rinsed well and tough ends snapped off

2 cloves garlic, minced

Extra-virgin olive oil

Preheat oven to 360 F. Toss all ingredients, using just enough olive oil to coat.

Spread in a single layer in a roasting pan and roast uncovered for 40 to 45 minutes.

SERVING SUGGESTION   This is great tossed with gluten-free rigatoni pasta for a healthy, light pasta primavera, or served over brown rice. It's really good during the hot summer months, when fresh vegetables are plentiful at your local farmers' market. We also love to serve this with a strawberry, blueberry, and banana fruit salad with fresh lemon juice.

ROASTED CORN, COTIJA FRESCO CHEESE, AND SUN-DRIED TOMATOES

Viva Mexico. A traditional, south-of-the-border spicy delight. The vibrant flavors of sun-dried tomatoes and cotija fresco make this a scrumptious side dish.   YIELD: 4 SERVINGS

2 cups fresh raw corn sliced off the cob or frozen corn kernels, thawed

2 tablespoons olive oil

1 teaspoon Gloria's Gold Mexican Seasoning (see Page 214)

½ cup sun-dried tomatoes in oil, drained and finely chopped

½ cup sliced black olives

⅛ teaspoon cayenne pepper: McCormick or Spice Islands

Sea salt and freshly ground black pepper to taste

¾ cup crumbled cotija fresco cheese (see note)

1 tablespoon fresh lime juice

Preheat oven to 350 F. Toss corn kernels with olive oil and Mexican seasoning and spread on a baking sheet. Roast for 16 to 20 minutes. Remove and let cool.

Combine with remaining ingredients. It's ready to serve.

NOTE: If you can't get cotija fresco, use ricotta salata or ricotta cheese to which you added some salt.

SERVING SUGGESTION   The perfect side with our Spiced Tequila Chicken (see Page 125).

MONTEREY FRIED RICE

This is the real Mexican rice. We make it in a cast-iron skillet. The real trick is that you have to make Febe's Cocina Mexicana Sauce first (see Page 222). There are no substitutes for Febe's Sauce.   YIELD: 6 TO 8 SERVINGS

1 cup medium-grain white rice

2 tablespoons bacon drippings (see note)

3 tablespoons Febe's Cocina Mexicana Sauce (see Page 222)

2 cups cold water

Sea salt and freshly ground black pepper

Heat cast-iron skillet over medium-high heat until hot. Add bacon drippings. Heat until hot.

Brown rice in bacon drippings until golden, about 3 minutes.

Add Febe's Sauce and cook for 2 minutes. Add water, salt, pepper, and chili powder. Bring to a boil, reduce heat to low, and cover. Do not stir. Do not peek. Cook for 20 minutes, until water is gone.

Check to see whether rice is done; if not, add a few spoonfuls of hot water and turn off heat. Cover, and it will steam a little longer before serving.

NOTE: You can use oil, but it tastes better with bacon drippings. Febe, Bill's piano teacher, used only bacon drippings, and she lived forever.

SERVING SUGGESTION   Great with our Febe's Rockin' Tacos (see Page 104), Cilantro Cream Spinach Enchiladas (see Page 171), or Stuffed Orange Bell Peppers with Homemade Chorizo and Authentic Fresh Pico de Gallo (see Pages 99 and 209).

HARVARD BEETS

Homemade Harvard Beets are a fine Southern food. These keep well for a couple of weeks in the refrigerator. And they just get better with time. **YIELD: 6 SERVINGS**

|||||||||||||||||||||||||||||||||||||||||||||||||||||||||||||||||||||||||||||||||||||||||||||||||||||||

4 medium fresh beets

1 cup sugar

1 cup apple cider vinegar: Heinz

1 cup water

8 cloves

Juice of 1 lemon

Preheat oven to 350 F.

Rinse dirt off beets. Cut tops off. Cut root off about ½ inch from bottom of beet. Wrap each beet in foil and place in a baking dish.

Bake for at least 1½ hours, or until beets are soft to the touch. Remove from oven. When beets are cool enough to handle, slip the skins off. It's easiest to do this under running water.

Cut beets in ¼-inch horizontal slices. Place beets in saucepan over medium heat. Pour sugar over beets. Add vinegar and water in equal parts to cover. (Depending on the size of your beets, you may not need the full 2 cups of vinegar and water. Just be sure the proportion of the liquids is 1:1.)

Cook, stirring, until sugar dissolves. Reduce heat and simmer for an hour—or longer over really low heat.

HATCH GREEN CHILE CHEESE MUFFIN SOUFFLÉS

An encore performance with Hatch chiles at center stage. These are Kim's signature dish. Get ready to stand up and take your own bow, because these are fabulous and so easy. **YIELD: 12 TO 14 MUFFINS**

⅔ cup gluten-free flour: Pamela's Baking & Pancake Mix

¼ cup cornmeal: Lamb's Stone-ground Yellow, Albers Yellow, or Arrowhead Mills Organic Yellow

1 teaspoon xanthan gum

¼ teaspoon ground cumin: McCormick or Spice Islands

⅛ teaspoon cayenne: McCormick or Spice Islands

¼ teaspoon sea salt

2 eggs, room temperature

⅔ cup warm water

6 tablespoons butter, room temperature

¼ cup buttermilk

1 tablespoon finely chopped red peppadew chili pepper, cored and seeded (see note)

¼ cup chopped Hatch green chiles (see note)

½ cup frozen or fresh corn kernels, thawed if frozen

¾ cup grated sharp cheddar cheese: Kraft Natural or Boar's Head

½ cup grated Havarti cheese: Boar's Head

¼ cup finely chopped poblano pepper, cored and seeded (optional)

Preheat oven to 325 F. Grease a 12-muffin pan.

Mix all the dry ingredients together. Mix the eggs, water, butter, and buttermilk together.

Add wet ingredients to dry ingredients and mix until blended.

Fold in the red and green chiles, corn kernels, and cheeses. Fill muffin cups ¾ full. Bake 25 to 30 minutes.

Remove from oven and let set for 20 minutes. Run a knife around the edge of each muffin, lift out, and serve.

NOTE: Wear plastic gloves while handling hot chiles. If you can't find Hatch chiles, substitute poblano or Anaheim, or canned Hatch chiles.

SERVING SUGGESTION They make a great accompaniment to grilled salmon or barbecue chicken, or with breakfast.

ARTICHOKES WITH ROASTED GARLIC AND LEMON-PAPRIKA DIPPING SAUCE

Artichoke lovers will go crazy with this sauce. Serve with steamed artichokes, which are available year-round but best in the spring. Choose only young, firm, and unblemished artichokes that are heavy for their size. Look for tight leaves. Small to medium chokes have the most flavor. Trim off the stem and cut the spiky points off the outside leaves with kitchen scissors. Rinse well under cold water. Cook in sea-salted water approximately 30 to 35 minutes, or until the leaves pull off easily. Savor each leaf with this dipping sauce as you work your way to the scrumptious heart of the artichoke. You will fall in love. YIELD: 1¼ CUPS SAUCE

1 large head garlic, unpeeled

1 cup mayonnaise: Hellmann's, Kraft, or Spectrum

½ teaspoon lemon zest (yellow part only)

2 tablespoons fresh lemon juice

½ teaspoon paprika: McCormick or Spice Islands

¼ teaspoon curry powder: McCormick or Spice Islands

⅛ teaspoon cayenne pepper: McCormick or Spice Islands

Steamed fresh artichokes, 1 per person

Preheat oven to 400 F.

Wrap garlic head in foil. Roast for 45 minutes. Remove from oven and squeeze garlic head free from casings. Place garlic and remaining ingredients except artichokes in blender and blend to combine. Chill.

Serve with fresh steamed or boiled artichokes.

KIM'S BALSAMIC HERB-ROASTED VEGETABLES

So many vegetables are available year-round. Our special Balsamic Herb-Roasted Vegetables include a colorful combination of asparagus, carrots, zucchini, mushrooms, tomatoes, and broccoli flavored with savory spices. Simple ingredients. Simple perfection with lots of color. And remember: The greater the colorful variety of vegetables, the greater the variety of nutrients.   YIELD: 8 TO 10 SERVINGS

¼ bunch asparagus, tough ends snapped off

¼ bunch carrots, peeled and sliced into rounds

1 zucchini squash, sliced into rounds

1 yellow squash, sliced into rounds

¼ bunch broccoli, sliced into smaller pieces

¼ red onion, sliced

¼ pound mushrooms, sliced

3 plum tomatoes, quartered

¼ eggplant, cut into thin ¼-inch slices

2 celery stalks, chopped

¼ cup kalamata olives, coarsely chopped

¼ cup green olives, coarsely chopped

1 tablespoon balsamic vinegar

6 tablespoons olive oil, or just enough to coat the vegetables

1 tablespoon chopped fresh oregano

1 teaspoon chopped fresh thyme

1 clove garlic, minced

Sea salt and freshly ground black pepper to taste

Preheat oven to 400 F. Toss all veggies with olive oil, balsamic vinegar, fresh herbs, garlic, and salt and pepper. Spread on a rimmed baking pan.

Roast 15 to 24 minutes, or until tender and golden brown.

NOTE: Cut the vegetables so that the pieces are approximately the same size. This will help them to cook more evenly.

SERVING SUGGESTION   These are great with wild rice and our Cranberry Waldorf Salad (see Page 36) and, for dessert, our Apple-Cinnamon Sour Cream Kuchen (see Page 245). Add a nice white wine, and you will have a gourmet vegetarian meal. Great tossed with pasta, too.

RED CHILE FRIED GREEN TOMATOES OR TOMATILLOS

You say tomato, I say tomatillo. We present to you a Southern classic. If you've never eaten fried green tomatoes or tomatillos, you have to try these. Tomatillos are relatives of tomatoes, but have a papery outer skin. Sounds kinda twisted, but they are better than you imagine. YIELD: 5 TO 6 SERVINGS

4 large, firm green tomatoes or tomatillos (papery skin removed)

¾ cup Pamela's Baking & Pancake Mix, or as much as needed

¾ cup cornmeal: Lamb's Stone Ground Yellow, Albers Yellow, or Arrowhead Mills Organic Yellow

1 teaspoon sea salt

½ teaspoon freshly ground black pepper

1 teaspoon onion powder

1 teaspoon garlic powder

1 tablespoon chili powder

1 red fresno chili pepper, cored, seeded, and minced (see note)

2 eggs, beaten

¼ cup half-and-half

Olive oil or vegetable oil

Cut tomatoes or tomatillos into ½-inch-thick slices.

In a bowl, mix dry ingredients. Add the fresno pepper. In another bowl, mix eggs and half-and-half.

Dip tomato slices in liquid, then dredge slices in dry mixture.

In a heavy skillet, heat oil, ¼-inch deep, to 365 F. Fry slices in oil until browned, being careful not to crowd them. Always bring temperature back up to 365 F with each new batch.

Remove. Drain on paper towels. Salt to taste while still hot.

NOTE: Wear plastic gloves when handling hot peppers.

SERVING SUGGESTION   Our Buttermilk Romano Herb Dressing (see Page 31) or Remoulade Sauce (see Page 21) go great with these. We also like to serve these alongside our Walnut Dill Chicken Salad (see Page 39) on an organic Bibb lettuce leaf.

CILANTRO CREAM SPINACH ENCHILADAS

Enchiladas *fabulosos*. Tex-Mex for a greater tomorrow. Even if you don't like spinach enchiladas, you'll love these. Honest.   YIELD: 6 SERVINGS

1 (10-ounce) package frozen chopped spinach, thawed and squeezed dry

1 (10¾-ounce) can cream of chicken soup: Health Valley Organic, undiluted

1 cup sour cream

3 tablespoons minced green onion

1 (4-ounce) can chopped green chiles, drained

1 tablespoon chopped fresh cilantro

4 cups shredded Monterey Jack or Pepper Jack cheese (divided use): Boar's Head

¾ cup diced white onion

12 corn tortillas: Mission, El Lago, or Sonoma Organic

Olive oil

Preheat oven to 325 F. Lightly grease a 12 x 9-inch baking dish.

In a blender, combine spinach, soup, sour cream, green onion, chiles, and cilantro. Process until smooth.

In ¼ inch hot oil in a skillet, cook tortillas for 5 seconds on each side, or just until softened. Drain tortillas well on paper towels. Keep warm.

Spoon 1 tablespoon of cheese and 1 tablespoon of onion on each tortilla; roll up tightly. Place rolled-up tortillas, seam side down and touching each other, in the prepared baking dish. Spoon spinach mixture over tortillas. Top with remaining cheese.

Bake uncovered 30 to 45 minutes. Serve immediately.

SERVING SUGGESTION   This is great with our Monterey Fried Rice (see Page 164), Authentic Fresh Pico de Gallo (see Page 209), and fresh fruit.

HERB-ROASTED SWEET POTATOES

Herb-Roasted Sweet Potatoes with rosemary are delicious and unusual. For purposes of this recipe, we make no distinction between sweet potatoes and yams. They are also festive served at dinner parties. YIELD: 6 TO 8 SERVINGS

Nonstick cooking spray

4 medium sweet potatoes

3 tablespoons unsalted butter, melted

1 tablespoon finely chopped fresh rosemary

1 teaspoon tarragon: McCormick or Spice Islands

⅛ teaspoon sage: McCormick or Spice Islands

½ teaspoon oregano: McCormick or Spice Islands

½ teaspoon coarse sea salt

Preheat oven to 400 F. Spray a shallow baking dish with cooking spray.

Peel sweet potatoes. Cut into ½-inch-thick slices.

Bring large pot of salted water to a boil. Boil potato slices for 5 minutes. Remove from water and drain on paper towels. Pat dry.

In bowl, toss potatoes with remaining ingredients. Spread evenly in prepared dish. Roast 20 minutes. Turn potatoes over. Roast another 20 minutes.

Remove. Salt. Serve.

SERVING SUGGESTION   These are great with pork dishes, such as our Cajun-style Balsamic Roasted Pork Loin (see Page 105). They also go well with a vegetarian meal of steamed vegetables and a fresh fruit salad.

GRUYÈRE-JALAPEÑO SCALLOPED POTATOES WITH CARAMELIZED ONIONS

It's the Mexican crema, gruyère, and jalapeño jack cheeses, plus caramelized onions and bold spices, that put the pizzazz in these scalloped potatoes. YIELD: 8 REGULAR PEOPLE OR 4 FOR THOSE WHO CAN'T GET ENOUGH!

1 tablespoon butter

1 tablespoon olive oil

1 onion, thinly sliced

1 teaspoon brown sugar

2 teaspoons sea salt plus a dash for onions (divided use)

Nonstick cooking spray

1 cup La Vaquita Crema Mexicana

½ cup half-and-half

½ cup plus 2 tablespoons whole milk

½ teaspoon freshly ground black pepper

4 cups peeled, thinly sliced russet potatoes (about 3 large potatoes)

1 cup grated Gruyère cheese

1 cup grated Monterey Jack cheese

1 jalapeño pepper, seeded, deveined, and finely chopped (see note)

In a thick-bottomed sauté pan or skillet, melt the butter. Add olive oil, brown sugar, and a dash of salt. Add onions and cook on medium-low heat for 30 minutes. Be careful not to stir too much, as this will ruin the caramelization process.

Preheat oven to 350 F. Spray 9 x 13-inch baking pan with cooking spray.

In a medium bowl, mix crema, half-and-half, milk, 2 teaspoons salt, and pepper. Spread ¼ of cream mixture on bottom of prepared pan.

Arrange ¼ of the sliced potatoes over that and top with ¼ cheeses. Sprinkle with ¼ jalapeño pepper. Repeat layers three times.

Top with caramelized onions. Cover and bake for 50 minutes. Remove cover and bake uncovered for 15 minutes more. Let set for 10 minutes and serve.

NOTE: Wear plastic gloves when handling hot peppers.

SERVING SUGGESTION Instead of traditional potato salad with barbecue chicken, try these fabulous scalloped potatoes.

ROSEMARY ROASTED RED POTATOES

Elegant, easy, engaging, . . . You just can't go wrong. And we love to grow our own rosemary.   YIELD: 6 SERVINGS

Nonstick cooking spray

2 pounds red potatoes, scrubbed and halved or quartered

3 tablespoons extra-virgin olive oil

1 tablespoon finely chopped fresh rosemary

1 teaspoon sea salt

Preheat oven to 375 F. Spray a rimmed baking pan that will hold the potatoes in 1 layer with cooking spray.

In large bowl, toss remaining ingredients well. Spread in an even layer in prepared pan.

Bake for 50 to 60 minutes. Shake pan occasionally during roasting.

SERVING SUGGESTION   We like these with a mixed green salad with our *Sauce Vinaigrette* (French Vinaigrette, see Page 35), our Marinated Broiled Salmon with Horseradish-Caper Sauce (see Page 148) and a fresh fruit salad. They are also excellent with pork dishes. And as kooky as it sounds, they are great leftovers for breakfast. If there are any leftovers.

PERFECT ROASTED POTATOES WITH CARAMELIZED SHALLOT, BLUE CHEESE, AND ASPARAGUS TOSSED WITH LEMON VINAGIRETTE

Perfect potatoes. The name speaks for itself. These versatile potatoes are ideal to dress up a plate for that special dinner, or just as a nice, easy side to the backyard barbecue. We love to use the little red potatoes and leave the skins on. The caramelized shallot adds a distinct richness. Shallots are somewhere between an onion and garlic, but not overpowering. YIELD: 8 SERVINGS

---

1 tablespoon butter

1 tablespoon olive oil

6 tablespoons minced shallot

1 teaspoon sugar

7 to 8 medium red potatoes, scrubbed and quartered

10 tablespoons Lemon Vinaigrette (divided use, recipe follows)

1 teaspoon sea salt

½ bunch asparagus, rinsed, tough ends snapped off, cut into 2 or 3 pieces each

¾ cup blue cheese: Boar's Head, Kraft, Primo Taglio, or Sargento All Natural

Freshly ground black pepper

Preheat oven to 350 F.

Heat butter and oil in a small skillet over medium-high heat; add shallot. Sprinkle with sugar.

Brown shallot until caramelized, about 3 to 5 minutes.

In large bowl, toss potatoes with 8 tablespoons of Lemon Vinaigrette, shallots, and salt. Mix well and spread potatoes in even layer on a rimmed baking pan. Roast in oven for 25 minutes. Shake pan occasionally during roasting.

Toss asparagus with remaining 2 tablespoons Lemon Vinaigrette. Remove potatoes and shallots from oven and add asparagus. Increase heat to 450 F. Bake an additional 10 to 12 minutes. Shake pan occasionally.

Remove from oven and toss with blue cheese and additional Lemon Vinaigrette to taste.

LEMON VINAIGRETTE

¼ cup fresh lemon juice

2 teaspoons Dijon mustard: Grey Poupon

2 teaspoons thyme: McCormick or Spice Islands

½ teaspoon oregano: McCormick or Spice Islands

2 minced cloves garlic

1 teaspoon sea salt

½ cup olive oil

Whisk vinaigrette ingredients together until well blended.

SERVING SUGGESTION   This is great served with our Cajun-style Balsamic Roasted Pork Loin (see Page 105). They are also a vegetarian's delight.

POTATO PANCAKES WITH SHALLOT

You will write home about these incredible latkes. Two secrets here: One, squeeze all the water out of the grated potato. Two, make sure your oil is frying hot, but not too hot.   YIELD: 6 SERVINGS

3 cups grated raw peeled russet potatoes, liquid pressed out with paper towels

3 tablespoons grated onion

1 clove garlic, minced

1 tablespoon chopped shallot

¼ teaspoon celery powder: McCormick or Spice Islands

2 eggs, beaten

½ teaspoon sea salt

½ teaspoon pepper

¾ cup oil

1 tablespoon of butter

In a mixing bowl, combine all ingredients except oil and butter. Mix well. (Kim likes to add ¾ cup sharp cheddar or Havarti cheese to the mixture.) Mold into ½-inch-thick pancakes; pat dry.

In a deep-sided skillet or pan, bring oil and butter to 350 F.

Fry each pancake until golden brown. Turn. Fry other side until golden brown.

Serve immediately.

SERVING SUGGESTION   Kim loves these for breakfast. They are also great with our Marinated Broiled Salmon with Horseradish-Caper Sauce. Then top it off with our Apple-Cinnamon Sour Cream Kuchen (see Page 245).

GOLDEN BROWN BELGIAN POTATO PATTIES WITH CHIVES

An all-time family favorite that's great served sizzling hot. We love the color and flavor chives add. Great for brunch, dinner, or in between. Your guests will be so impressed.   YIELD: 12 TO 14 (4-INCH) PATTIES

1 cup water

½ cup olive oil (divided use)

1 cup gluten-free flour: Bob's Red Mill Biscuit and Baking Mix or Pamela's Baking & Pancake Mix

4 eggs

3 cups mashed russet potatoes (no faux . . . use only real potatoes)

¼ teaspoon sea salt

¼ teaspoon freshly ground black pepper

Milk as needed

3 tablespoons grated white onion

1 teaspoon celery powder: McCormick or Spice Islands

1 tablespoon finely chopped chives

1 cup vegetable oil

In a large saucepan, bring water to a boil. Add ¼ cup oil and return to a boil. Stir in flour, mix thoroughly. Remove from stove and allow to cool.

Add eggs, 1 at a time, beating constantly into mixture. Add mashed potatoes, mix well. Add salt and pepper.

Add just enough milk so that mixture will mash—nothing more. Mix well. You want the potatoes to be fairly stiff. Add onion, celery powder, and chives. Mix well.

Using a cake decorator (squeeze bag) or cookie dough press, squeeze into 3-inch patties ¼-inch thick.

Heat oil in a deep-sided pot to 350 F. Cook patties until golden brown. Don't crowd and do not overcook. Drain on paper towels.

SERVING SUGGESTION   We like these with our Maple-Glazed Barbecue Ribs (see Page 94) and our Italian Crema Cake (see Page 252).

FRIJOLES RANCHEROS CON CHORIZO

A good-ol'-boy classic. A gluten-freed cowboy's staple. These ranch-style beans made with chorizo are hearty and tasty. Obviously, you must use gluten-free chorizo. And you must use Mexican (as opposed to Spanish) chorizo in this recipe. This is also great with homemade tortillas. YIELD: 10 SERVINGS

|||||||||||||||||||||||||||||||||||||||||||||||||||||||||||||||||||||||||||||||||||||||||||||||||||||||||||||||||||||

1 cup chorizo: Johnsonville chorizo, removed from casings, crumbled, or our East Austin Trailer Park Spicy Homemade Chorizo (see Page 103)

1 tablespoon bacon drippings

1 large onion, diced

3 cloves garlic, minced

1 large green pepper, chopped

2 fresh ripe tomatoes, chopped

1 (53-ounce) can Bush's Best Pinto Beans (frijoles pintos)

¼ teaspoon freshly ground black pepper

½ teaspoon chili powder: McCormick or Spice Islands

Sea salt to taste

2 chopped pickled jalapenos (optional)

In a large skillet over medium-high heat, cook the crumbled chorizo in bacon drippings. Add the onion and garlic, and cook until onion is wilted.

Add the remaining ingredients and simmer for 30 minutes. If you prefer your beans spicy, add the pickled jalapenos. Serve in small individual bowls.

BROWN SUGAR, BACON, AND JALAPEÑO BAKED BEANS

These are not your mama's baked beans. These are Bill's baked beans. So many commercial brands of baked beans contain gluten or MSG, so we decided to pick the brands that don't and own it. We love these beans. People are always asking for this recipe. YIELD: 8 TO 10 SERVINGS

Nonstick cooking spray

1 (28-ounce) can Bush's Original Baked Beans

1 (28-ounce) can Bush's Country-style Baked Beans

¼ medium white onion, diced

2 large cloves garlic, finely minced

3 strips thick bacon, cooked crisp and crumbled

1 jalapeño pepper, seeded, deveined, and finely chopped (see note)

1 tablespoon ketchup: Heinz

1 teaspoon red wine vinegar: Heinz or Regina

4 tablespoons brown sugar

2 tablespoons yellow mustard: French's Prepared Classic

Preheat oven to 350 F. Spray a large baking dish with nonstick cooking spray.

Mix remaining ingredients and pour into prepared baking dish. Bake 30 to 45 minutes, or until top is a little browned and crispy.

NOTE: Wear plastic glove when handling hot peppers.

SERVING SUGGESTION We like these beans with our Texas Oven-Style Barbecue Brisket (see Page 80) and potato salad.

BREADS

Bread is so elemental to life that it really was hard to imagine living without it. We've eaten some lousy gluten-free breads, and a cheeseburger on a corn tortilla is, well, a cheeseburger on a corn tortilla. No more. We love bread. No longer will you have to go without sandwiches, biscuits, your favorite Thanksgiving dressing, blueberry crumb muffins, cheese biscuits, pumpkin walnut bread, or buttermilk pancakes. They're all here. Kim's the baker and she adores pizza. Her last meal would be pizza. Our recipe for Pizza Crust is crispy and divine. You would never guess it's gluten-free. Our recipes are creative and comforting, and they don't taste like the side of a milk carton.

Remember, recipes that call for flour, bleached white flour, whole wheat, cracked wheat, barley, semolina, spelt, faro, kamut, triticale, or vital wheat gluten are not gluten-free. Don't even think about eating those ingredients. Also remember that prepackaged bread crumbs, croutons, flour tortillas, pizza crust, piecrust, pretzels, wraps, pita bread, crackers, flatbread, and muffins are not gluten-free unless labeled as such. Our recipes really do allow you not only to maintain a gluten-free diet, but to enjoy it. We offer you one of the most important gifts in a gluten-free life: extraordinarily good-tasting gluten-free breads.

SOME GLUTEN-FREE STARCH BASICS

THICKENERS: It's a different ballgame when you can't use wheat flour. For thickening most things, we use cornstarch or arrowroot starch. We mix it with a little cold water first before adding it to the recipe. You can also use tapioca starch or potato starch. Any of these are interchangeable. You can even use white rice flour. Kim likes cornstarch, and Bill prefers white rice flour. Bill says cornstarch sometimes goes gooey and gluey when it's overcooked. Freezing cornstarch also changes its consistency.

For gravies, use arrowroot starch in a 1-to-2 ratio, such as 1 tablespoon of arrowroot to 2 tablespoons water. Potato starch is also a nice thickener. Tapioca starch should be added at the end of cooking. Just keep in mind that it will thicken rather fast, so be sure to stir often. Potato flour, cooked mashed potatoes, or mashed sweet potatoes can be used as thickeners. We sometimes use egg yolks to thicken certain sauces, such as hollandaise or béarnaise. If we are using egg yolks, we heat the sauce more slowly and blend it with a whisk (so the eggs don't curdle).

Once you start working with the different kinds of thickening agents, you will get the hang of them and your preferences.

THE GLUE/THE HOLDER TOGETHER: Gluten-free flours can be somewhat crumbly. In order to make them stretchier and more elastic, we generally add xanthan gum. It is derived from corn, so anyone who is sensitive to corn products might try guar gum instead, which comes from legumes. If you prefer not to use any type of binding gum, gluten-free starches are another alternative, but they're not as effective. You can always try a tablespoon of potato starch, tapioca starch, or arrowroot, but be sure to whisk them with a warm liquid. Keep in mind that a little bit of honey will also add some moistness and a slight binding effect to your recipe.

FOR PIECRUST: We recommend using organic shortening or butter. If you find the shortening flavorless, add vanilla, cinnamon, rum, or almond extract.

YEAST AND RISING AGENTS: Gluten-free flours don't rise like traditional flours, so we use yeast. A teaspoon of lemon juice or sugar will help activate its rising ability. Baking powder and baking soda are also alternatives—just make sure they are gluten-free and aluminum free.

BATTER UP: Gluten-free flours are just different from traditional flours. Depending on what you use, they can become stretchier, stiffer, or ooey-gooey stickier. Sometimes when you are beating them, they have a tendency to climb the beater. When that happens, just turn the speed down a notch and put the batter back in its place—in the bowl. If you are baking cookies and looking for a sugar substitute, we do not recommend honey, especially if you prefer a crisp cookie. Honey tends to make cookies softer and chewier.

THE OVEN WATCH: Ovens vary, and gluten-free flours tend to burn more quickly than traditional flours. You will want to keep a close eye on your recipe when baking.

PASTA: As a rule, do not overcook your pasta. You want it to be al dente, as it will continue to cook in the sauce and to absorb the sauce.

IS IT GLUTEN-FREE?

Here's a list of grains, flours, starches, and thickening agents that contain no gluten.

Corn, cornmeal, grits, polenta

Quinoa, quinoa cereal flakes, and quinoa flour

Rice—white, brown, basmati, jasmine, risotto

Amaranth and amaranth flour

Rice flour—white rice, brown rice

Millet and millet flour

Sorghum flour

Coconut flour

Corn flour

Teff flour

Nut meals and flours—almond, cashew, chestnut, pecan

Chickpea (garbanzo), soy (soya), and bean flour

Tapioca and tapioca starch (manioc)

Potato flour and starch

Sweet potato and sweet potato flour

Arrowroot starch

Cornstarch

NOTE: Kim's favorite gluten-free mix for bread is Pamela's Baking & Pancake Mix or Arrowhead Mills Gluten Free All Purpose Baking Flour. Bill really likes Bob's Red Mill. And while we agree to disagree, we obviously know who is right.

THIN AND CRISPY SICILIAN PIZZA DOUGH

Pizza. There was a time when living gluten-free meant going without. Sure, people concocted some crazy stuff to try to sate their pizza cravings. But the results almost always tasted disgusting and would fall apart. With Kim's recipe for Thin and Crispy Sicilian Pizza Dough in your mitt, you can make all the pizzas your heart desires. Gluten-free flours tend to burn much more quickly and can become mushy, so we cook our dough for a few minutes before putting on the toppings. YIELD: 1 (12-INCH) PIZZA CRUST

1¼ cup Bisquick Gluten Free Pancake and Baking Mix

½ teaspoon sea salt

1 tablespoon Italian herb seasoning: Spice Islands

3 tablespoons grated Parmesan cheese

⅓ cup water

⅓ cup olive oil

2 eggs, beaten

1 to 2 tablespoons cornmeal: Lamb's Stone Ground Yellow, Albers Yellow, or Arrowhead Mills Organic Yellow

1 cup pizza sauce: Contadina or Enrico's

Mix flour, salt, Italian seasoning, and Parmesan. Add the water, olive oil, and eggs. Mix well.

Preheat oven to 425 F. Generously grease pizza pan with olive oil. Sprinkle cornmeal evenly over the oil.

Pour dough into pan and flatten dough with oiled hands. Bake 12–14 minutes. Remove from oven.

Add sauce and desired toppings from our Pizza "Put-Ons" list. Bake for 12–14 minutes longer, or until crust is brown and cheese is melted.

PIZZA "PUT-ONS"

Feta cheese

Black olives

Green olives

Kalamata olives

Cooked crumbled spicy Italian sausage

Organic mushrooms

Baby fresh mozzarella

Romano cheese

Parmesan cheese

Grilled eggplant

Canadian bacon

Cheddar cheese

Fresh chopped basil

Grilled shrimp

Caramelized onion

Hot peppers

Sweet peppers

Roasted tomatoes

Goat cheese

Sun-dried tomatoes

Boar's Head pepperoni

Veggie chorizo

SAVORY MEXICAN PIZZA WITH POLENTA CRUST

My sister Kerri is the hippie of the family. I'm the drugstore, Johnny-come-lately hippie. Kerri is always having epiphanies. She loves the earth and the soil. She was green before it was cool. She ate healthy, unprocessed food before everyone did, and she made delicious, creative, healthy meals for her three children. This is her recipe. YIELD: 1 (12-INCH) PIZZA

¼ cup gluten-free flour: Bob's Red Mill Biscuit and Baking Mix or Pamela's Baking & Pancake Mix

1 tablespoon xanthan gum

½ teaspoon sea salt

1 teaspoon yeast: Red Star or Fleischmann's Active Dry

1½ cups water

1 cup fine-ground polenta

¼ cup grated Romano cheese

1 jalapeño pepper, seeded, deveined and finely chopped (see note)

¼ cup chopped poblano pepper

2 tablespoons extra virgin olive oil

½ pound ground beef

2 tablespoons Gloria's Gold Mexican Seasoning (see Page 214)

¾ cup tomato sauce: Contadina, Del Monte Organic, or Hunt's

¼ cup picante sauce: Pace Organic Mild

¾ cup grated sharp cheddar cheese: Kraft Natural or Boar's Head

¼ cup sliced black olives

Sliced mushrooms, chopped bell peppers, sliced green olives (optional)

Preheat oven to 350 F.

In a large mixing bowl, combine flour, xanthan gum, salt, and yeast. Set aside.

Bring the water to a boil in a small saucepan and add the polenta. Whisk vigorously and cook on medium heat for 4 to 5 minutes. Add cheese, reduce heat to low and continue to stir for 3 to 4 minutes. Add jalapeño and poblano peppers. Let cool.

Preheat oven to 350 F. Add polenta and olive oil to the flour mixture and form a ball.

With oiled hands, knead the dough until it is shiny and smooth, adding more flour if needed, but as little as possible. Press into a pizza pan with oiled hands and bake for 15 minutes.

For topping, brown ground beef in a small pan with 2 tablespoons Mexican Seasoning. Drain.

Mix tomato sauce with picante sauce and spread on top of polenta. Top with browned ground beef, cheese, olives, and any additional optional toppings.

Bake 14 to 18 minutes longer, or until crispy.

NOTE: This pizza has a Mexican theme, but you can use any topping combination you like on this polenta crust. It's also great with marinara sauce, fresh mozzarella, gorgonzola, and chicken or roasted veggies.

TUSCAN FOUR-CHEESE PIZZA

The pizza might sound weird, with two different kinds of olives, but it works. In fact, when you make it, double the recipe. One won't be enough.   YIELD: 1 (12-INCH) PIZZA

½ cup grated Romano cheese

½ cup grated sharp cheddar cheese: Kraft Natural or Boar's Head

½ cup grated Havarti: Boar's Head

½ cup feta cheese

¼ cup pitted and chopped green olives

¼ cup pitted and chopped kalamata olives

¼ cup olive oil

2 cloves garlic, minced

1 tablespoon chopped fresh basil

½ cup chopped roasted or sun-dried tomatoes

Thin and Crispy Sicilian Pizza Dough, omitting the Parmesan and Italian seasoning (see Page 185)

Preheat oven to 325 F.

Mix cheeses, olives, olive oil, garlic, basil, and sun-dried tomatoes and set aside.

Prepare Thin and Crispy Sicilian Pizza Dough, omitting the Parmesan cheese and Italian seasoning.

Lightly grease pizza pan or pizza stone with olive oil. With oiled hands, flatten dough into round, flat disk and sprinkle with cornmeal. Flatten further and press dough into pan.

Bake for 6 to 8 minutes. Remove from oven. Add prepared cheese topping.

Increase oven temperature to 350 F, and bake 8 to 14 minutes longer, or until crust is brown and cheese is melted.

Switch to broil, and broil the pizza for a few seconds until bubbly and golden brown.

BILL'S BEST BUTTERMILK CORNBREAD

Good old Southern cornbread. Life just wouldn't be the same without it. This is a staple for the gluten-freed lifestyle. This makes the most awesome cornbread stuffing or dressing you can imagine.   YIELD: 6 SERVINGS

Vegetable oil

2 eggs

1 cup buttermilk

4 tablespoons butter, melted

1¼ cup cornmeal: Lamb's Stone-ground Yellow, Albers Yellow, or Arrowhead Mills Organic Yellow

¾ cup Pamela's Baking & Pancake Mix

2 tablespoons sugar

1 teaspoon sea salt

Preheat oven to 375 F. Pour enough oil in cast-iron skillet to lightly coat bottom. Place skillet in oven for 10 minutes so that the oil can heat. This will yield a nice crust on the bottom of the cornbread.

Beat eggs and buttermilk in a bowl. Add the melted butter and beat. (Let butter cool a little before you pour it in, because you don't want to cook the eggs.)

Add remaining ingredients, but don't overmix. Pour mixture into prepared skillet. Bake 20 minutes or until done.

Remove from oven, loosen cornbread and turn onto a cooling rack. Let rest 5 minutes and serve.

NEW ORLEANS RED CHILE, HAVARTI, AND BUTTERMILK CORNBREAD

Classic Southern cornbread . . . all jazzed up. This is Kim's take on cornbread, defined by fresh-cut corn, savory cheeses, and chile peppers. The chiles add great flavor, but if you're heat-shy, taste your raw pepper before you begin cooking, as they can have varying degrees of heat. The longer, thinner, and redder the pepper, the hotter it usually is. If you want to turn down the heat, cut out the seeds and pithy ribs.   YIELD: 6 SERVINGS

3 eggs

1¼ cup buttermilk

6 tablespoons butter, melted

1¾ cup cornmeal: Lamb's Stone-ground Yellow, Albers Yellow, or Arrowhead Mills Organic Yellow

1½ cup Pamela's Baking & Pancake Mix

1 teaspoon honey

1 teaspoon sea salt

Kernels cut from 3 ears of corn

1½ cup grated white cheddar cheese

1½ cup grated extra-sharp cheddar cheese

¾ cup grated Havarti-and-red-pepper cheese

2 jalapeño peppers, seeded, deveined and finely chopped (see note)

1 small red fresno chile pepper, seeded, deveined, and finely chopped (see note)

Preheat oven to 350 F. Grease a 13 x 9-inch pan. Set aside.

In a large mixing bowl, beat eggs and buttermilk. Add the melted butter and beat. (Let butter cool a little before you pour it in, because you don't want to cook the eggs.)

Fold in remaining ingredients. Pour mixture into prepared pan. Bake 20 to 24 minutes, or until done. Let rest 5 minutes and serve.

NOTE: Wear plastic gloves when handling hot peppers.

APPLE SAUSAGE THANKSGIVING DRESSING

Oh, yeah, finally dressing—yes, dressing for the turkey, made with Bill's Best Buttermilk Cornbread and gluten-free bread. For food safety, we never advise stuffing the turkey with dressing. Serve it as a side dish. That said, this makes a lot of dressing! You can easily cut it in half or freeze some for a rainy day.   YIELD: 7 QUARTS

1 pound chorizo: J. C. Potter Regular Pork Sausage, or Johnsonville Sausage, or our East Austin Trailer Park Spicy Homemade Chorizo (see Page 103)

1 cup diced onion

1 quart celery, diced

2 green apples, cored and diced

4 cups cornbread, broken into small pieces (see recipe for Bill's Best Buttermilk Cornbread)

4 cups bread, torn into bite-size pieces: Kinnikinnick Italian White Tapioca Rice Bread or Udi's White Sandwich Bread

1 tablespoon sea salt

½ teaspoon pepper

1 teaspoon poultry seasoning: Spice Island or Paul Prudhomme Poultry Magic

2 cups chicken broth: Health Valley Fat-free, Pacific Natural Foods Organic, or Swanson Natural Goodness

Preheat oven to 400 F. Grease a 9 x 13-inch baking dish or pan.

In a skillet over medium-high heat, brown the sausage, breaking it into small pieces. Add onion and celery. Reduce heat to low and cook until celery and onion are soft, but not browned. Add the apples.

Transfer to a large mixing bowl and add the cornbread and gluten-free bread. Toss to blend.

Add the salt, pepper, and poultry seasoning to the chicken broth. Pour broth mixture over all ingredients and blend. Adjust seasoning as desired. Pour into prepared dish or pan.

Bake about 30 minutes, or until browned on top.

SOUTHWESTERN CORNBREAD

A new Texican favorite, this hearty cornbread can be a meal in itself. It also makes great leftovers for a couple of days. But it won't last that long.   YIELD: 6 SERVINGS

1 cup cornmeal: Lamb's Stone-ground Yellow, Albers Yellow, or Arrowhead Mills Organic Yellow

1 cup milk

2 tablespoons sugar

2 eggs

¾ teaspoon sea salt

½ teaspoon baking soda: Arm & Hammer

1 (17-ounce) can cream-style corn: Del Monte or Safeway store brand

¼ cup bacon drippings

1 pound ground beef (½ pound sirloin, ½ pound chuck)

1 cup diced onion

Vegetable oil

½ pound Monterey Jack cheese, shredded: Boar's Head

½ pound cheddar cheese, shredded: Boar's Head

½ cup canned chopped green chiles

2 to 4 jalapeño peppers, seeded, deveined, and finely chopped (see note)

Preheat oven to 350 F.

In a large bowl, combine cornmeal, milk, sugar, eggs, salt, baking soda, creamed corn, and bacon drippings. Mix well; set aside.

In a 10-inch or larger skillet, brown the beef and onion over medium-high heat. Drain off excess fat. Remove beef and onion to a bowl.

Wipe skillet clean and grease with oil. Pour half the cornbread batter in the skillet. Layer the beef mixture on top. Add the cheeses and peppers on top of that. Top with remaining cornbread mixture.

Bake 55 minutes, or until browned on top.

NOTE: Wear gloves when handling hot chiles.

GRUYÈRE AND ASIAGO CHEESE BISCUITS

Gooey, chewy, crispy, cheesy, peppery . . . say no more. These rich and cheesy crispy biscuits are sure to put a smile on everyone's face. You can also use pepper jack and sharp cheddar cheese. For an even zestier biscuit, try Havarti with jalapeño and extra-sharp white cheddar. The flavors happily play off one another. YIELD: 18 TO 20 BISCUITS

2 cups gluten-free flour: Pamela's Baking & Pancake Mix

¼ teaspoons xanthan gum

1½ teaspoons sea salt

1 teaspoon freshly ground black pepper

½ teaspoon white pepper: Spice Islands

½ teaspoon paprika: McCormick or Spice Islands

Dash of cayenne pepper: McCormick or Spice Islands

6 tablespoons nonhydrogenated vegetable shortening

⅔ cup buttermilk

1 teaspoon honey

1 cup grated Gruyère cheese

1 cup grated Asiago cheese

Preheat oven to 300 F. Lightly grease a baking sheet.

In a large bowl, mix together the flour, xanthan gum, salt, peppers, paprika, and cayenne. Cut the shortening into the dry ingredients with a pastry cutter, or use a stand mixer with dough hook for 3 minutes.

Stir in the buttermilk and honey. Add cheeses, mix, and form a ball.

Lightly dust wax paper and fingers with some gluten-free flour or olive oil to keep from sticking. Spread dough ½-inch thick.

With biscuit cutter (2½-inch round), cut into biscuits. Place on prepared baking sheet.

Bake, checking after 7 minutes. If they are browning on the bottom, turn them over. Total baking time will be 12 to 16 minutes. Remove from oven.

FETA, OLIVE, AND SUN-DRIED TOMATO LOAF

A true work of art in the world of gluten-free breads, this loaf has a Mediterranean flair and is bursting with flavor.   YIELD: 1 (6½ X 10½-INCH) LOAF

2¼ teaspoons yeast: Fleischmann's or Red Star Active Dry

1 teaspoon sugar

½ cup warm water

1½ cups gluten-free flour: Pamela's Baking & Pancake Mix

1 cup polenta

¼ teaspoon sea salt

1 teaspoon baking powder: Clabber Girl, Hain, or Rumford

2 teaspoons xanthan gum

1 tablespoon chopped fresh oregano

1 tablespoon chopped fresh basil

3 eggs, beaten

¾ cup crumbled feta cheese

½ cup coarsely chopped sun-dried tomatoes packed oil

½ cup sliced kalamata olives

Olive oil

Mix yeast, sugar, and warm water. Let sit for 10 minutes. Grease and flour a 6½ x 10½-inch loaf pan.

In a large bowl, combine the flour, polenta, salt, baking powder, and xanthan gum, mixing well. Add oregano, basil, eggs, and yeast water. Mix well.

If you have a stand mixer, knead using the dough hook for about 4 minutes. If not, knead the dough for 2 to 3 minutes with oiled hands.

Add feta cheese, tomatoes, and olives. Mix well. Place in the prepared loaf pan. In a warm place, cover and let rise for 1½ hour.

Preheat oven to 350 F. Mark it (cut a thin slit down the middle of the top) if you like and brush top with olive oil—this will help prevent cracking.

Bake 35 to 45 minutes. Remove from oven and let cool. It contains no preservatives, so it will stay fresh only a couple of days. If you are not going to freeze it, it must be refrigerated. We like to store it in the freezer and use as needed.

SERVING SUGGESTION   This is a great accompaniment to our Creamy Tomato Basil Soup (see Page 56).

ROMANO AND OREGANO CRISPS

Our answer to cheese crackers. Serve these flavorful crisp wafers on the side of a plate of pasta or leafy green salad. They make a snappy accompaniment to an appetizer platter with fresh seasonal sliced fruit, assorted cheeses, and olives. For more kick, you can also use sharp cheddar cheese and jalapeños instead of Romano cheese and oregano. YIELD: 20 TO 24 CRISPS

⅔ cup gluten-free flour: Pamela's Baking & Pancake Mix

3 tablespoons polenta

½ teaspoon baking powder: Arm & Hammer, Calumet, or Clabber Girl

Sea salt to taste

½ teaspoon paprika: McCormick or Spice Islands

⅛ teaspoon cayenne pepper: McCormick or Spice Islands

2 eggs, beaten

6 tablespoons butter, room temperature

¾ cup grated Romano cheese

1 tablespoon chopped fresh oregano

Place all dry ingredients in bowl and mix thoroughly. Add egg and butter and mix again.

Add Romano cheese and oregano and mix well.

Gather dough into a cylinder, approximately 7x 1 ¾-ish inches (like a cucumber). Wrap in plastic wrap or wax paper. Refrigerate for 1 hour.

Preheat oven to 325 F. Grease a baking sheet.

Place dough on floured surface and slice into 20 to 24 rounds. Lay on prepared baking sheet. Bake for 8 minutes, or until golden brown. Remove from oven and turn over. Bake for 4 to 5 minutes longer.

SPICED PUMPKIN WALNUT BREAD

This is great for breakfast with a fresh cup of hot tea and the rising sun. There are no rules, though, so feel free to take a slice for lunch or savor for a bedtime snack.   YIELD: 1 (10 X 6-INCH) LOAF

1¾ cups gluten-free flour: Pamela's Baking & Pancake Mix

½ cup buttermilk

1½ teaspoons pumpkin pie spice: Spice Island

2½ teaspoons nutmeg: McCormick or Spice Islands

1 teaspoon cinnamon

½ teaspoon allspice

¼ teaspoon sea salt

¾ cup granulated sugar

¼ brown sugar

⅓ cup oil

2 large eggs

1 cup canned pumpkin filling: Libby

1 tablespoon fresh lemon juice

2 tablespoons butter, room temperature

1 cup chopped walnuts

Preheat oven to 350 F. Generously grease a 10 x 6-inch nonstick loaf pan and dust with flour.

In a bowl, mix all ingredients together except walnuts and beat with an electric mixer on high for 2 minutes.

Fold in walnuts and pour in loaf pan. Bake 45 to 55 minutes, remove from oven and let cool.

MR. FLUFFY PEPPER JACK AND AGED CHEDDAR BISCUITS

Thanks to Mr. Fluffy ... your *gluten free sliders have finally arrived!*

This is *huge* 'cuz Mr. Fluffy puts sliders back in the game! The gluten-freed society can now have their version of sliders.! These amazingly light morsels are so good, and so versatile.

You will be in heaven when you eat them fresh out of the oven, all hot and smushy. We use them for turkey sliders, hamburger sliders, ham sliders...you name it. Did you ever think you would hear the words hot and smushy and gluten-free in the same sentence?   YIELD: 2 DOZEN (3½-INCH) BISCUITS

1 cup gluten-free baking mix: Pamela's Baking & Pancake Mix

1 cup cornstarch

2 tablespoons xanthan gum

3 tablespoons baking Powder: Clabber Girl, Hain, or Rumford

1 teaspoon sea salt

¼ teaspoon white pepper: Spice Islands

¼ teaspoon freshly ground black pepper

⅛ teaspoon cayenne pepper: McCormick or Spice Islands

1 cup non-hydrogenated shortening

⅔ cup buttermilk

2 eggs, well beaten

1 teaspoon honey

1½ cups grated aged cheddar cheese

1 cup grated pepper jack cheese

1 jalapeño, seeded, deveined and finely chopped (optional, see note)

Preheat oven to 325 F. Lightly grease a baking sheet.

In a large bowl, mix the dry ingredients and spices together. Cut the shortening into the dry ingredients with a pastry cutter. Or use a stand mixer with dough hook for 3 minutes. Add buttermilk, eggs, and honey and stir.

Add cheeses and jalapeño and mix well. Cover and let rise in a warm place for 1 hour.

Spread flour on wax paper. Gather a scoop, about ¼ cup, with oiled hands, roll into a ball, and place on prepared sheet. Mash ball into a round biscuit about ½-inch thick. Repeat with remaining dough.

Bake 10 to 14 minutes, or until lightly brown on bottom. Let sit in the pan for 5 minutes.

NOTE: Wear gloves to handle hot peppers.

SERVING SUGGESTION   Try these with leftover baked ham and our Horseradish-Caper Sauce (see Page 148). Good to have on hand during the holidays. You can also refrigerate or freeze the dough balls so when you are having a dinner party, all you have to do is take out what you need and bake them.

BLUEBERRY CRUMB MUFFINS

Finally . . . blueberry muffins for breakfast that are worth getting out of bed for. There is no better accompaniment to a cup of hot coffee than a light, fluffy blueberry muffin. You will be astonished at how great they taste—without conventional flour. Be daring: Try substituting fresh blackberries, cranberries, or raspberries and add a few walnuts. YIELD: 12 MUFFINS

1½ cups gluten-free flour: Pamela's Baking & Pancake Mix

½ cup plus 2 tablespoons sugar

¼ cup oil

⅔ cup buttermilk

1 egg

¼ cup water, room temperature

½ teaspoon lemon zest

1 cup fresh or frozen blueberries or more to taste

Crumb Topping (recipe follows)

Preheat oven to 325 F. Lightly grease a nonstick muffin tin.

In a large bowl, combine the baking mix, sugar, oil, buttermilk, egg, water, and lemon zest. Beat with an electric mixer on high for 2 minutes. Fold in the blueberries.

Fill muffin tins ½ full with batter. Gently sprinkle crumb topping over batter and bake for 20 minutes. Let cool about 10 minutes.

CRUMB TOPPING:

2 tablespoons brown sugar

Pinch of sea salt

1 tablespoon gluten-free flour: Pamela's Baking & Pancake Mix

½ tablespoon butter, room temperature

Combine dry ingredients and then cut in butter with a fork until crumbly.

SAVORY TARRAGON BISCUITS

Here's our Academy Award winner—so much more than just a biscuit. Gluten-freed folk can use these for little sandwiches, canapés, paninis, hors d'oeuvres or just to snack on. Another alternative to bread, they're so much more nutritious and easier to digest. They're big. They're bad. They're the best gluten-freed biscuits you've ever tasted. YIELD: 18 TO 24 BISCUITS

2¼ teaspoons yeast: Fleischmann's or Red Star Active Dry

1 teaspoon sugar

⅛ cup warm water

1 cup gluten-free flour: Bob's Red Mill Biscuit and Baking Mix or Pamela's Baking & Pancake Mix

1 cup cornstarch

2 tablespoons xanthan gum

2 tablespoons baking powder: Clabber Girl, Hain, or Rumford

1 teaspoon sea salt

¼ teaspoon white pepper: Spice Islands

½ teaspoon chopped fresh tarragon

¼ teaspoon freshly ground black pepper

⅛ teaspoon cayenne pepper: McCormick or Spice Islands

1 cup non-hydrogenated shortening

⅔ cup buttermilk

2 eggs, room temperature and beaten

Dissolve yeast and sugar in warm water and let stand for 5 minutes.

In a large bowl, mix the dry ingredients, herbs, and spices together. Cut in the shortening with a pastry cutter or use a stand mixer with dough hook for 3 minutes.

Add buttermilk, eggs, and yeast-sugar blend and mix well. Cover and let rise in a warm spot for 1½ hours.

Preheat oven to 325 F. Lightly grease a baking sheet.

With oiled hands, gather a scoop, about ¼ cup, roll into a ball and place on cookie sheet. Mash ball into a round biscuit about ¾-inch thick. Repeat with remaining dough.

Bake 11 to 16 minutes. Remove from oven.

SERVING SUGGESTION(S)   These biscuits are so versatile. Cut them in half and spread with our Horseradish Caper Sauce (see Page 148) to make prime rib or chicken sandwiches. They're also great for breakfast or brunch with hot scrambled eggs and sausage. Kim's favorite is to stuff them with our Smoked Gouda-Cheddar Pimento Cheese Spread (see Page 11). But oh, we forgot. We also love them with blue cheese and sliced beef tenderloin with a little cayenne mayo. Oh, but wait, honey ham and Brie with some cranberry chutney . . . our Spiced Egg Salad, or better yet . . . they're incredible right out of the oven with our French Farmer Pâté (see Page 14), apple slices, and champagne. You get the idea.

RELISHES AND SALSAS

Relishes and salsas add so much zing to so many dishes. We've included some of our favorites, ranging from Authentic Fresh Pico de Gallo, a traditional Mexican table sauce, to the incredibly exotic Feta, Roasted Tomato, and Pine Nut Mediterranean Salsa. Healthy and gluten-free, relishes and salsas spice up almost any meal. And don't forget: The better your ingredients, the better the flavor, so use fresh, high-quality fruits and vegetables. We love to prowl the farmers' markets in season. You will want your entrée to tango with these. Cha-cha-cha.

FETA, ROASTED TOMATO, AND PINE NUT MEDITERREAN SALSA

This is a Greek masterpiece with the many flavors of Mediterranean cuisine rolled into one mouthwatering salsa. It is wonderfully satisfying with grilled fish. It is also great on toasted bread or your favorite gluten-free cracker. And with a glass of red wine, of course.   YIELD: 2 CUPS

½ cup feta cheese, crumbled

1 cup chopped roasted tomatoes (see recipe Page 41)

3 tablespoons toasted pine nuts (see note)

¼ cup kalamata olives, pitted and sliced

¼ cup green olives, pitted and sliced

¼ teaspoon lemon zest (yellow part only)

1 tablespoon fresh lemon juice

4 tablespoons extra-virgin olive oil

1 teaspoon chopped fresh basil

1 teaspoon chopped fresh oregano

½ teaspoon freshly ground black pepper

1 finely minced garlic clove (optional)

Blend all ingredients in a mixing bowl. Refrigerate.

NOTE: To toast pine nuts, place in a small skillet over medium-high heat and shake occasionally. Don't let them burn. Immediately remove from skillet.

ROASTED CORN, TOMATO, AND BLACK BEAN SALSA

The perfect all-occasion salsa . . . or side dish.   YIELD: 4 CUPS

2 cups fresh or frozen corn kernels, thawed if frozen

¼ cup Anaheim chile, seeded and finely chopped (see note)

2 tablespoons olive oil

4 to 5 very ripe Roma tomatoes, diced

½ cup chopped green chiles

1 clove garlic, minced

2 tablespoons fresh lime juice

1 tablespoon sea salt

1 (15-ounce) can black beans: Bush's or Progresso

1 to 2 tablespoons chili powder: McCormick or Spice Island

Preheat oven to 400 F. Mix corn and Anaheim chile together with olive oil. Place them in roasting pan and roast for 10 to 12 minutes. Let cool. Mix with remaining ingredients and serve at room temperature.

NOTE: You can also use a jalapeño pepper, if you prefer a spicier flavor. Wear plastic gloves to seed, devein and finely chop the chile.

SERVING SUGGESTION   Not only is this great at parties, but it's a flavorful accompaniment to scrambled eggs served with refried beans and warm corn tortillas, sided with a fruit salad of blueberries, strawberries, and sliced bananas.

PINEAPPLE-JALAPEÑO RELISH

Delight in the fresh flavors of the Caribbean. This fantastic Pineapple-Jalapeño Relish goes well with grilled fish, especially mahi mahi. Use only fresh pineapple with this recipe.   YIELD: 1¼ CUPS

1 cup chopped fresh pineapple

1 tablespoon orange marmalade

1 teaspoon chopped fresh cilantro

1 tablespoon finely chopped jalapeño, seeded and deveined (see note)

2 teaspoons fresh lime juice

¼ teaspoon sea salt

1 teaspoon diced red onion

Combine all ingredients in a bowl. Refrigerate.

NOTE: Wear gloves when handling hot peppers.

CILANTRO-MANGO ORANGE SALSA

Inspired by the fresh and earthy cuisine of Jamaica, our Cilantro-Mango Orange Salsa is absolutely delicious and bursting with flavors both sweet and hot. Kim taught Bill to pair Mediterranean and Mexican cuisine. Of course, he was against it. Now he understands the vision, likes it, and is embracing the fusion madness.   YIELD: 2 CUPS

3 ripe mangoes, peeled and chopped into cubes (see note)

1 tablespoon orange marmalade

1 teaspoon chopped fresh cilantro

1 tablespoon finely chopped jalapeño

2 tablespoons fresh orange juice

1 tablespoon apple cider vinegar: Heinz

¼ cup diced red onion

¼ teaspoon sea salt

Combine ingredients in a bowl. Chill and serve.

NOTE: If you have never cut a mango before, here's how. Cut off both ends. Peel. A mango has a pithy core that is not eaten. Slice mango from top to bottom outside and parallel to core. Make one slice down four sides of the mango. Then dice into uniform pieces.

SERVING SUGGESTION   This is good with grilled fish and our Roasted Tomato and Goat Cheese Risotto Cakes (see Page 161).

ORANGE-CHILE CHUTNEY

Orange Chile Chutney is a "bang" of flavor. But remember, some like it hot and others, not. We start with half an average jalapeño. You can always add more. Or less.   YIELD: 1½ CUP

¼ cup finely diced red onion

1 cup chopped mandarin orange slices

1 tablespoon water

1 tablespoon fresh lime juice

2 tablespoons fresh orange juice

1 teaspoon orange zest (orange part only)

1 tablespoon sugar

¼ teaspoon sea salt

½ jalapeño pepper, seeded, deveined, and finely chopped (see note)

Mix well in a bowl. Refrigerate.

NOTE: Wear gloves when handling hot peppers.

SERVING SUGGESTION   This is great with our Lemon Butter Scallops de Cabo San Lucas (see Page 138), poultry or fish.

RED BELL PEPPER RELISH

This relish is gonna ring your bell. It has a most distinctive flavor and pairs well with so many different dishes.

YIELD: ABOUT 4 CUPS

2 cups chopped red bell peppers

½ cup diced white onion

½ cup diced red onion

1 cup apple cider vinegar: Heinz

½ cup sugar

½ teaspoon mustard seeds

½ teaspoon celery seeds: McCormick or Spice Islands

Dash sea salt

¼ teaspoon red pepper flakes: McCormick or Spice Islands

Combine ingredients in a heavy saucepan over medium-high heat. Reduce heat to medium-low and simmer about 1 hour.

SERVING SUGGESTION   A teaspoon of Red Bell Pepper Relish on top of grilled fish is just divine coupled with our Three-Cheese Risotto (see Page 157) and a salad of sliced mangoes drizzled with local honey and fresh lime juice . . . and icy cold champagne, of course.

AUTHENTIC FRESH PICO DE GALLO

A Mexican Classic. Although this is a simple dish to make, the finished product is rich and complex. This does not keep well so make it right before you serve it. Great for parties. This stuff packs a flavor punch.

As always, adjust the amount of jalapeño for taste or your tolerance for heat.   YIELD: 10 SERVINGS

1 white or yellow onion

1 tomato

1 cucumber, cut lengthwise and seeds removed

1 green bell pepper

1 jalapeño, seeded and deveined

1 mild pepper (poblano or Serrano), seeded

3 tablespoons chopped fresh cilantro

1 lime

Chop ingredients (excluding cilantro and lime) into very fine pieces. Do not use a blender. All pieces need to be approximately the same size. Put into serving bowl. Add cilantro. Mix well. Squeeze lime over it: thoroughly mix again gently.

MARINADES, SEASONINGS, AND SAUCES

We love bold taste. We think the most important part of any dish is the seasoning. Not only do spices make a dish piquant and intriguing, but so many of the herbs and spices we commonly use have marvelous medicinal and healing properties. We use a wide variety in our recipes, and that goes for our mouthwatering marinades and zesty sauces, too. Our marinade for chicken, beef, and lamb, and our sparerib seasoning will have your family coming back for seconds. Our recipes for New Orleans Peach-Bourbon Basting Sauce and our Asian Ginger-Plum Dipping Sauce are always crowd-pleasers.

We recommend making your own sauces and marinades whenever possible. You would not believe how many of the sauces, marinades, and seasonings on the supermarket shelves have gluten in them. Even basic, simple items, like ketchup, soy sauce and other Asian sauces, barbecue sauce, and mustard often contain gluten, though you'd never know it by reading the label.

MAGIC PORK SPARERIB SEASONING

Magical. Mystifying. Magnificent. Magic Pork Sparerib Seasoning has only four ingredients, but together they create pork sparerib magic. Also try this seasoning on unsliced pork bacon.   YIELD: 1¼ CUP

1 cup brown sugar

½ cup fine sea salt

2 tablespoons paprika: McCormick or Spice Islands

2 tablespoons cayenne pepper: McCormick or Spice Islands

Mix ingredients well. Rub a big slab of baby back ribs with this seasoning, then wrap the meat in plastic wrap and refrigerate overnight. It is best not to grill these ribs. Once you unwrap them, either cook in a Brinkmann smoker (follow the manufacturer's directions), or in a 325-degree oven wrapped in foil.

AUTHENTIC ATCHAFALAYA BLACKENED CAJUN SPICE

So authentically Cajun . . . so extraordinarily good . . . so fabulously hot. Use it as a blackening seasoning, or just to spice up some chicken or pork chops. Add a little lemon pepper to those pork chops, and you just won't believe it. I love this seasoning for both blackened and grilled fish. It is also a fabulous shrimp-boil seasoning.   YIELD: 1 ½ CUP

½ cup sea salt

¼ cup cayenne pepper: McCormick or Spice Islands

2 tablespoons white pepper: Spice Islands

2 tablespoons freshly ground black pepper

2 tablespoons paprika: McCormick or Spice Islands

2 tablespoons onion powder

2 tablespoons garlic powder

1 teaspoon dry mustard: Colman's

1 teaspoon oregano: McCormick or Spice Islands

1 teaspoon chili powder: McCormick or Spice Islands

Combine all ingredients and mix well.

NORTH TEXAS BARBECUE BEEF BRISKET RUB

True Texas Grit . . . now we are talking barbecue. This blend makes the best beef brisket in the world.

YIELD: ¼ CUP

2½ tablespoons brown sugar

2 tablespoons paprika: McCormick or Spice Islands

2 teaspoons dry mustard: Colman's

2 teaspoons onion powder

1 tablespoon garlic powder

1½ teaspoons basil: McCormick or Spice Islands

1 bay leaf: McCormick or Spice Islands

¾ teaspoon coriander: McCormick or Spice Islands

¾ teaspoon ground savory: McCormick or Spice Islands

¾ teaspoon thyme: McCormick or Spice Islands

¾ teaspoon white pepper: Spice Islands

⅛ teaspoon ground cumin: McCormick or Spice Islands

⅛ teaspoon allspice: McCormick or Spice Islands

1 tablespoon sea salt

¾ teaspoon freshly ground black pepper

Combine all ingredients and mix well. If using on a brisket, rub all over and wrap airtight in plastic. Refrigerate overnight. Follow directions with your smoker to smoke it about 3 hours. Preheat oven to 325 F. Wrap in foil and slow-roast another 5 hours. Remove foil. Continue roasting for 1 more hour.

GLORIA'S GOLD MEXICAN SEASONING

A splendid spicy Mexican blend that is worth its weight in gold. Great for fish tacos, grilled beef fajita meat, grilled chicken, beef tacos—anything that calls for a Mexican seasoning. We use it in everything (almost!).   YIELD: ¼ CUP

4 tablespoons paprika: McCormick or Spice Islands

3 tablespoons sea salt

2 tablespoons garlic powder

2 tablespoons onion powder

3 tablespoons chile powder: McCormick or Spice Islands

1 tablespoon oregano: McCormick or Spice Islands

¼ teaspoon white pepper: Spice Islands

1 tablespoon cumin: McCormick or Spice Islands

1 teaspoon red pepper flakes: McCormick or Spice Islands

Dash of cayenne pepper: McCormick or Spice Islands

1 teaspoon Paul Prudhomme Ground Dried Magic Chile—New Mexico (optional)

Mix all ingredients. Keep in airtight container in refrigerator for up to 3 months.

MOROCCAN DRY RUB

Rich, exotic, and inspiring. Our Moroccan Dry Rub is an exotic blend of herbs and spices perfect for a leg of lamb. You will think twice about ever buying a bottled Moroccan rub again. But you can buy a tagine and learn a new art of cookery.   YIELD: ½ CUP

½ teaspoon ground cumin: McCormick or Spice Islands

½ teaspoon ginger: McCormick or Spice Islands

½ teaspoon sea salt

½ teaspoon freshly ground black pepper

¼ teaspoon cinnamon: McCormick or Spice Islands

½ teaspoon coriander seeds: McCormick or Spice Islands

½ teaspoon cayenne pepper: McCormick or Spice Islands

¼ teaspoon allspice: McCormick or Spice Islands

¼ teaspoon cloves: McCormick or Spice Islands

Combine all ingredients and mix well.

AUSTIN STEAK MARINADE

Marinated steak is always a big hit. Bill fiddled with this recipe for a long time before getting it right. You haven't had steak like this. This stuff is righteous.   YIELD: 1 CUP

5 large cloves garlic, finely minced

1 teaspoon sea salt

½ cup Chianti or other dry red wine

¼ cup balsamic vinegar

1 teaspoon soy sauce: Eden Foods Tamari Organic, La Choy, or San-J Organic Wheat-free Tamari (Gold Label)

1 tablespoon honey

Mash garlic with salt to make a paste. Add to blender with remaining ingredients and whirl to blend. To marinate steaks, place in a bowl, pour marinade over, and refrigerate 1 to 2 hours. Grill steaks as desired.

NOTE: We like to buy a whole beef tenderloin and slice our own steaks.

LEMON-TAMARI-BROWN-SUGAR MARINADE FOR GRILLED CHICKEN

This marinade for grilled chicken sounds so easy and tastes so good. There will not be any leftover grilled chicken. That's because everybody loves chicken cooked this way.   YIELD: 2 CUPS

⅛ cup soy sauce: Eden Foods Tamari Organic, La Choy, or San-J Organic Wheat-free Tamari (Gold Label)

1 ounce apple cider vinegar: Heinz

¼ cup brown sugar

1 cup fresh lemon juice

2 large cloves garlic, finely minced

1 tablespoon Worcestershire Sauce: Lea & Perrins or French's

1 tablespoon chopped fresh parsley

¼ teaspoon freshly ground black pepper

½ cup olive oil

Combine all ingredients. To marinate chicken, add to a zip-top plastic freeze bag with cut-up chicken. Refrigerate 2 to 4 hours. Then you're ready to discard the marinade and fire up the grill.

LEMON-SAGE MARINADE FOR LAMB AND GRILLED PORK CHOPS

The sage makes this one sassy. The marinade is a distinctive mix of herbs and spices that will have dinner guests asking what your secret is.   YIELD: ¼ CUP

¼ cup oil

4 tablespoons balsamic vinegar

1 teaspoon sage: McCormick or Spice Islands

1 tablespoon grated lemon zest

1 tablespoon minced dried onion

1 tablespoon dry mustard: Colman's

1 teaspoon ground cloves: McCormick or Spice Islands

¼ teaspoon allspice: McCormick or Spice Islands

1 teaspoon cayenne pepper: McCormick or Spice Islands

1 teaspoon sea salt

1 teaspoon freshly ground black pepper

Mix all ingredients well. To marinate meat, cover with marinade in a covered glass bowl for 2 to 4 hours refrigerated. Remove meat and grill or bake. Brush leftover marinade on pork chops during grilling. Lamb should be baked, medium-rare to medium, and served hot on preheated plates.

SERVING SUGGESTION   Serve chops with our Gruyère-Jalapeño Scalloped Potatoes with Caramelized Onions (see Page 173) and a fresh, leafy green salad, and you have a great meal that everyone will love.

CANTONESE MARINADE

Bring an Asian accent to the table. This delicious marinade works for baby back ribs, beef, pork, or chicken and is great for shish kebabs. It is also exceptional on grilled salmon. Enjoy.   YIELD: 2½ CUPS

½ cup soy sauce: Eden Foods Tamari Organic, La Choy, or San-J Organic Wheat-free Tamari (Gold Label)

½ cup ketchup: Heinz

½ cup dry sherry

½ cup brown sugar

½-inch piece fresh ginger, peeled and minced

3 cloves garlic, crushed and minced

Juice from 3 lemons

Combine all ingredients. Marinate meat or salmon 2 hours.

NEW ORLEANS PEACH-BOURBON BASTING SAUCE

Hallelujah. The saints come marching in. With its bold and unique taste, New Orleans Peach Bourbon Basting Sauce produces incredible pork tenderloin or baked chicken. This is Kim's favorite.   YIELD: ABOUT 2 CUPS

½ cup bourbon: Maker's Mark

½ cup peach preserves

½ cup Ever-So-Easy Honey Dijon Mustard (see Page 220)

1 tablespoon onion flakes

1 tablespoon onion salt

1 tablespoon powdered garlic

1 teaspoon grated fresh ginger

1 tablespoon fresh lemon juice

1 tablespoon ketchup: Heinz

¼ cup water or white wine

1 teaspoon liquid smoke: Colgin or Wright's

In saucepan over medium-high heat, combine all ingredients, except liquid smoke, and bring to a boil. Reduce heat and simmer about 5 minutes, stirring occasionally.

Remove from heat. Add liquid smoke. Simmer 5 minutes longer. Cool.

Baste your pork or chicken every 25 minutes while it roasts in the oven.

BILL'S FINEST BRISKET BASTING SAUCE

This always hits a home run right outta the ballpark. Barbecue cooks know that basting keeps the meat from drying out, especially on a grill or smoker. Basting sauce is for what the name says: basting. It is not barbecue sauce. If you have a brisket on the smoker, you have to use this stuff. It's shockingly good.   YIELD: 3½ CUPS

1 cup butter

4 tablespoons fresh lemon juice

1 tablespoon Worcestershire sauce: Lea & Perrins or French's

1 tablespoon soy sauce: Eden Foods Tamari Organic, La Choy, or San-J Organic Wheat-free Tamari (Gold Label)

1 teaspoon sea salt

½ teaspoon freshly ground black pepper

1 teaspoon garlic powder

1 teaspoon onion powder

½ teaspoon celery powder: McCormick or Spice Islands

1 teaspoon chili powder: McCormick or Spice Islands

2 cups boiling water

In heavy saucepan over low heat, combine butter, lemon juice, Worcestershire sauce, soy sauce, salt, pepper, garlic powder, onion powder, and celery powder. Stir occasionally while butter melts.

Mix chili powder with boiling water and add to mixture. Bring to a boil, reduce heat to medium and cook 5 to 10 minutes.

For big meats like brisket, baste every 25 to 30 minutes. Baste smaller cuts, fish and vegetables (yes, it tastes so good on them) more frequently.

KANSAS CITY JALAPEÑO-BROWN-SUGAR BARBECUE SAUCE

The sweetest of the sweet. Great on baby back ribs, brisket, chicken, or pork.   YIELD: 2½ CUPS

2 cups ketchup: Heinz

1½ cups tomato sauce: Contadina, Del Monte Organic, or Hunt's

¾ cup brown sugar

¾ cups red wine vinegar: Heinz or Regina

½ cup molasses

4 tablespoons liquid smoke: Wright's or Colgin's

3 tablespoons pickled jalapeño juice

2 tablespoons butter

1 teaspoon garlic powder

1 teaspoon onion powder

1 teaspoon paprika: McCormick or Spice Islands

½ teaspoon celery seed

⅛ teaspoon cinnamon

1 teaspoon cayenne pepper: McCormick or Spice Islands

1 teaspoon sea salt

1 teaspoon freshly ground black pepper

Combine all ingredients in a nonstick saucepan and bring to low boil. Reduce heat to medium-low. Simmer for 40 minutes, stirring often. Remove from heat, ready to use.

BILL'S BETTER BOURBON BARBECUE SAUCE

Hoochy-'cue. Bill's Better is the best barbecue sauce west of the Mississippi. This sauce makes some sweet "Q" . . . and we mean barbecue. This very easy recipe calls for a couple of brand-name sauces that do not contain gluten that are liquored and spiced up. You won't have to worry about leftovers. It's the sauce . . . *the* sauce. YIELD: 3 CUPS

2 cups barbecue sauce: Cattleman's Original, Heinz Original, or Kraft Original

1 tablespoon soy sauce: Eden Foods Tamari Organic, La Choy, or San-J Organic Wheat-free Tamari (Gold Label)

1 tablespoon Worcestershire sauce: Lea & Perrins or French's

½ cup brown sugar

⅔ cup bourbon: Maker's Mark

1 heaping tablespoon coarse Dijon mustard: Grey Poupon

Juice of 1 lemon

3 tablespoons maple syrup

¼ teaspoon sea salt

¼ teaspoon red pepper flakes: McCormick or Spice Islands

4 shakes Louisiana Hot Sauce

Combine all ingredients and mix well.

NOTE: For grilled chicken, paint it with sauce 10 minutes before it comes off the grill.

EVER-SO-EASY HONEY DIJON MUSTARD

Simply delicious. YIELD: 6 TABLESPOONS

2 tablespoons coarse Dijon mustard: Grey Poupon

2 tablespoons regular Dijon mustard: Grey Poupon

2 tablespoons honey, preferably local

Mix all ingredients.

Works great on turkey sandwiches or any sandwich for that matter or dipping sauce!

RICO SUAVE RED CHILI ENCHILADA SAUCE

Big taste. Bold Southwestern flavor. For the Southwestern palate, this recipe has authentic Mexican flavors and will rival any Mexican restaurant sauce. Use it for the sauce in any enchilada recipe. Olé.   YIELD: 3½ CUPS

1 (28-ounce) can chicken broth: Health Valley Fat-free, Pacific Natural Foods Organic, or Swanson Natural Goodness

4 tablespoons butter (divided use)

¼ cup diced onion

1 clove garlic, minced

2 tablespoons chili powder: Spice Islands

¼ cup white rice flour

1½ teaspoons sea salt

¼ teaspoon freshly ground black pepper

¾ teaspoon ground cumin: McCormick or Spice Islands

1 (6-ounce) can tomato paste: Del Monte Organic, Hunt's, or Muir Glen

1½ cups of water for thinning at the end

In a saucepan over medium-high heat, bring chicken broth to a boil.

Melt 2 tablespoons butter in a medium nonstick skillet over medium-high heat. Sauté onion and garlic until translucent. Add to boiling chicken broth.

Add 2 more tablespoons butter to a skillet over medium heat. Stir in the chili powder, rice flour, salt, pepper, cumin, and tomato paste and make a paste. Lightly brown but don't burn, cooking about 1 to 2 minutes.

Slowly add a ladle of the broth to the skillet to thin the paste. Stir constantly. Keep adding ladles of broth to the mixture until well mixed and transformed to a sauce.

Simmer over low heat 20 minutes.

SERVING SUGGESTION   Tangle this with your favorite enchilada, our Monterey Fried Rice and then bring out the Warm Chocolate Pudding Cake with Kahlua Whipped Cream! Macho mixed with sassy!

FEBE'S COCINA MEXICANA SAUCE

This recipe was taught to Bill by his piano teacher, Febe Garcia, and we use it in a number of Mexican dishes. It is great on our recipe for huevos rancheros, but it must be cooked first. Simple, delicious, and healthy, this is a "fundamental" sauce. You will want to keep it on hand in the refrigerator because it is so versatile and integral to authentic Mexican cooking. **YIELD: 2 CUPS**

1 (16-ounce) tomato sauce: Contadina, Del Monte Organic, or Hunt's

1 large white onion, diced

1 large green bell pepper, seeded and diced

4 cloves garlic, minced

1 teaspoon freshly ground black pepper

½ teaspoon sea salt

½ teaspoon chopped fresh cilantro

¼ teaspoon ground cumin: McCormick or Spice Islands

Blend all ingredients in blender or food processor. Store in mason jars or plastic containers in the refrigerator, where it will last about 1 week. It also freezes well in zip-top plastic freezer bags.

LIME CREMA ADOBO SAUCE

This recipe uses chipotles in adobo sauce, a condiment in which smoked jalapeño peppers are stewed in a sauce with tomatoes, garlic, vinegar, salt, and spices. They can be found in the Hispanic canned foods section of many grocery stores.   YIELD: 1¼ CUP SAUCE

1 shallot, finely minced

2 cloves garlic, minced

2 tablespoons butter

½ cup white wine

½ cup chicken broth: Health Valley Fat-free, Pacific Natural
    Foods Organic, or Swanson Natural Goodness

1 cup whipping cream

1 tablespoon tomato paste: Del Monte, Hunt's, or Muir Glen

½ teaspoon chopped fresh oregano

1 tablespoon fresh lime juice

½ teaspoon cornstarch dissolved in 2 tablespoons water

1 teaspoon canned chipotle chilies in adobo, puréed

Sea salt

Freshly ground black pepper

In a medium saucepan over medium-high heat, sauté shallots and garlic in butter for 2 to 3 minutes. Add wine and chicken broth. Bring to a boil, reduce to slow simmer until volume is reduced by half.

Add whipping cream, tomato paste, oregano, and lime juice and simmer for 6 to 8 minutes.

Add cornstarch mixture. Simmer, stirring constantly, for 1 minute. Add adobo sauce. Mix thoroughly.

NOTE: For thickening, we use cornstarch or arrowroot starch. We mix it with a little cold water first before adding it to a recipe. Keep in mind you can also use tapioca starch or potato starch. These are all interchangeable.

SERVING SUGGESTION   This is a mouthwatering accompaniment for our Potato-Crusted Tilapia (see Page 149). End of story.

NUT-CASE PESTO

This is our take on traditional pesto. The walnuts give it a special nutty taste. Pesto is excellent on toast or pasta, and as a topping for some meats and fish. We like to harvest basil out of the herb garden before the first freeze of the year and make a big batch of this. You can freeze it in small containers or zip-top plastic freezer bags, and it lasts several months. Be daring: try it with sage and jalapeño! Kim's favorite!   YIELD: 2 CUPS

1 cup basil leaves, stems removed, packed tightly

3 cloves garlic

⅛ cup walnuts

¼ cup pine nuts

¼ cup extra-virgin olive oil

½ teaspoon sea salt

¼ cup grated Parmigiano-Reggiano cheese

2 tablespoons unsalted butter, room temperature

⅛ teaspoon white pepper: Spice Islands

Place basil, garlic, walnuts, pine nuts, oil, and sea salt in a blender or food processor and blend to a paste. Be careful not to overblend.

Add cheese; blend a little more to combine. Add butter, blend a little more, and add pepper. Blend just until mixed in.

BELLAGIO PUTTANESCA SAUCE

A bold yet elegant Italian tradition, this is a zesty Italian sauce like none other. Don't be afraid of the anchovies.   YIELD: 5 ½ CUPS

2 anchovy fillets, chopped

1 tablespoon extra-virgin olive oil

2 small cloves garlic, minced

2 tablespoons chopped shallots

2 cups jarred marinara: Newman's Own Organic

1 (29-ounce) tomato sauce: Hunt's 100% Natural

Sea salt to taste

Freshly ground black pepper to taste

1 tablespoon chopped fresh oregano

1 tablespoon capers, drained: Mezzetta, Reese, or Star

¼ cup chopped kalamata olives

⅛ teaspoon red pepper flakes, or to taste: McCormick or Spice Islands

In a large saucepan over low heat, sauté anchovies in olive oil until they disintegrate. Add garlic and shallots and sauté about 1 minute.

Add remaining ingredients and bring to a boil. Reduce heat and simmer 15 to 20 minutes. Adjust salt and pepper to taste.

SERVING SUGGESTION   Serve over hot spaghetti. We like Mrs. Leeper's organic corn spaghetti pasta. Great with our Mexican Caesar Salad with Chile Polenta Croutons (see Page 50).

BASIL-BLACK-PEPPER ITALIAN TOMATO SAUCE

Not your ordinary marinara sauce, this is a must-have for every kitchen. If you had an Italian grandmother, she would cook something like this. From this very basic, healthy sauce come many Italian dishes, such as lasagna and spaghetti and meatballs. Why would you ever buy prepared tomato sauce when you can make something this good? Try it.   YIELD: 10 CUPS

Extra-virgin olive oil

1 diced yellow or sweet onion

3 cloves garlic, minced

2 stalks celery with leaves, chopped

1 carrot, diced

2 bay leaves

1 teaspoon sugar

1 heaping teaspoon sea salt

¼ teaspoon freshly ground black pepper

1 teaspoon chopped fresh basil

1 teaspoon chopped fresh thyme

1 teaspoon chopped fresh oregano

1 teaspoon Italian flat-leaf parsley

3 (28-ounce) cans of Pastene San Marzano Italian Plum Tomatoes with Basil or other San Marzano tomatoes

Drizzle a little olive oil into a large, medium-hot pan or pot, such as a 7-quart Duthc oven or Le Creuset. Sauté onion. Add garlic, celery, carrot, and bay leaves, and sauté until softened.

Add sugar, salt, pepper, fresh herbs, and tomatoes. Bring to low boil. Reduce heat; simmer uncovered on low heat for 1 hour. Remove bay leaves and serve.

This freezes well, up to two months. We freeze it in 2-cup portions in good-quality 1-gallon zip-top freezer bags.

FRENCH GOURMET BROWN SAUCE

An absolute classic, and among the most elegant sauces in the world. This is Bill's recipe, the ultimate expression of his French gourmet culinary expertise. We're both very proud of it. It is especially good on our beef tenderloin steaks or with roast beef. It freezes well, too, for up to two months. You owe it to yourself to make it at least once. YIELD: 2 QUARTS

2 pounds veal bones

2 pounds beef bones

1 large onion, quartered

4 carrots, peeled and quartered

2 stalks celery with leaves, coarsely chopped

½ teaspoon thyme: McCormick or Spice Islands

1 teaspoon black peppercorns

3 bay leaves

1 tablespoon coarse sea salt

½ cup rice flour

2 quarts water (divided use)

1 (750ml) bottle dry white wine

1¼ cups tomato paste: Del Monte Organic, Hunt's, or Muir Glen

3 sprigs parsley

Preheat oven to 475 F.

Combine bones, onion, carrots, celery, thyme, peppercorns, bay leaves, and salt in a large roasting pan.

Place in oven and roast for 45 minutes. Reduce heat to 425 F if bones begin to burn.

Remove from oven. Sprinkle with rice flour. Roast 15 minutes longer.

Transfer solid ingredients to a large stockpot.

Place roasting pan over 2 stove burners over medium-low. Add 1 quart water. Stir, scraping browned bits from bottom of roasting pan.

Pour the liquid from the roasting pan into the stock pot. Add remaining water, wine, tomato paste, and parsley. Bring to a rapid boil, reduce heat, and simmer 2 hours.

Add more water if necessary. Skim off fat and foam as it rises to surface. Cool and strain.

BASIC BROWN BEEF GRAVY

No, don't you dare open up a mix packet chock-full of sodium, MSG, and some form of gluten. Make this the old-fashioned way—without any of those things. We've got the how-to. This works with the drippings of any roast beef recipe.　YIELD: ¾ CUP

---

2 tablespoons butter

2 tablespoons Bob's Red Mill White Rice Flour

½ cup cold water

Roast beef drippings and pan scrapings

Sea salt and pepper to taste

Melt butter in a skillet over medium heat. Remove pan from stove. Add flour and mix well. Add cold water and stir until smooth.

Return skillet to stove over medium heat. Stir constantly until it thickens. Add the juice from homemade roast beef as well as scrapings from the bottom of the roasting pan. Stir well.

Bring to a slow, rolling boil. Reduce heat. Cook, stirring occasionally, until it reaches desired consistency.

SERVING SUGGESTION　Pour in a sauceboat and serve along with roast beef, mashed potatoes, and a cold iceberg lettuce salad with our Better-Than-a-French-Kiss French Dressing (see Page 34). Cap it off with our Pineapple Upside-down Cake (see Page 248). Now that's a Sunday dinner.

GARLIC-SESAME-GINGER STIR-FRY SAUCE

This brings stir-fry up a notch. You will never look at stir-fry the same way again! YIELD: 2¾ CUP

‖‖

½ cup chopped garlic

½ cup chopped fresh ginger

¼ teaspoon sea salt

¼ teaspoon freshly ground black pepper

½ cup finely chopped scallions

1 cup rice wine vinegar

½ cup soy sauce (divided use): Eden Foods Tamari Organic, La Choy, or San-J Organic Wheat-free Tamari (Gold Label)

4 cups chicken broth: Health Valley Fat-free, Pacific Natural Foods Organic, or Swanson Natural Goodness

2 tablespoons sesame oil: Eden Foods Toasted, House of Tsang, or Lee Kum Kee

Place garlic, ginger, salt, pepper, scallions, rice wine vinegar, and ¼ cup soy sauce in saucepan over medium-high heat. Cook until reduced by half.

Add chicken broth and remaining ¼ cup soy sauce. Cook until reduced by 25 percent.

Remove from heat and cool. Pour into a blender or food processor. Add sesame oil and blend until smooth.

STIR-FRY

2 tablespoons canola oil

½ cup thinly sliced carrot rounds

½ cup chopped onion

½ pound peeled, deveined, and cooked shrimp (about 31 count size)

2 tablespoons stir-fry sauce

Heat wok over high heat. Add oil and heat until shimmering but not smoking. Add carrots and onion. Stir fry until onion is translucent. Remove. Add shrimp and stir-fry while you count to 45. Return veggies to wok. Mix well with the shrimp. Remove wok from heat and stir in sauce. Don't overcook.

BILL'S WOK WONKISMS: A word about woks and cooking. Buy a heavy one. Don't buy an electric one. Never use olive oil. You need an oil that can get very hot without smoking. Invest in some high quality wok tools. Read books on wok technique, or at least one. I've cooked in the same wok for 40 years.

SERVING SUGGESTION   We like using this sauce to stir-fry shrimp or chicken. Serve with basmati rice and Indian raita.

ASIAN GINGER-PLUM DIPPING SAUCE

This thick, rich sauce bursting with Asian flavors is great for dipping pot stickers, spring rolls, wontons—or even just fresh-cut vegetables. It also makes an excellent glaze for baked chicken, chicken wings, or pork ribs. This can also be your "go-to" for our Sesame Chicken.   YIELD: 1 CUP

¼ cup soy sauce: Eden Foods Tamari Organic or San-J Organic Wheat-free Tamari (Gold Label)

2 tablespoons water

½ teaspoon sesame oil: Kame Eden Foods Toasted, House of Tsang, or Lee Kum Kee

1 large clove garlic, finely minced

2 green onions, minced

3 tablespoons hoisin sauce: Kame, Dynasty, Le Kum Kee, or Premier Japan

½ teaspoon grated fresh ginger

1 teaspoon plum sauce: Dynasty or Le Kum Kee Gold Label

1 teaspoon granulated sugar

Dash of red chile flakes: McCormick or Spice Islands

Mix all ingredients well; cover and refrigerate 2 hours. Serve at room temperature.

COCONUT CURRY SAUCE

A bold and delectable favorite from southern India. Just add pieces of boiled chicken, and violà: You have delicious chicken curry. Of course, you could also do this with shrimp, tofu, or vegetables. It's the fresh coconut that makes this dish.   YIELD: 5 CUPS

Meat of 1 fresh coconut, grated

1 quart milk, scalded

2 tablespoons butter

1 medium onion, diced onion

1 (1½-inch) piece fresh ginger, finely chopped

2 cloves garlic, minced

2 tablespoons curry powder: Spice Islands

½ teaspoon brown sugar

2 tablespoons plus 2 teaspoons Bob's Red Mill White Rice Flour

Sea salt to taste

Mix coconut meat and scalded milk together; let stand 1 hour. Strain through a cheesecloth and squeeze until coconut meat is dry. Reserve milk.

Melt butter in double boiler. Sauté onion, ginger, and garlic until lightly browned. Do not burn. Stir in curry powder and sugar.

Mix well; add flour slowly, stirring. Gradually stir in strained coconut milk. Do not add salt until time to serve.

INDIAN GINGER-CURRY SAUCE

It may not be authentic Indian, but boy, is it good. We love to add cut-up pieces of chicken to this sauce. The accompaniments are the beauty of this dish. Long ago in India, each accompaniment was held by a boy. The accompaniments, collectively, were referred to as "boys." We suggest that you serve all the listed accompaniments. Use your imagination; the list is endless.   YIELD: 4½ CUPS

½ cup butter

3 tablespoons diced onion

1 clove garlic, minced

½ teaspoon chopped fresh ginger

1 tablespoon curry powder: Spice Islands

½ cup Bob's Red Mill White Rice Flour

1 cup chicken stock: our Homemade Chicken Stock on page 134, or Kitchen Basics Natural or, Full Flavor Foods Gluten-free Chicken Soup Stock

2 cups milk

1 cup cream

1 tablespoon sherry

¼ teaspoon sea salt

Melt butter in double boiler. Add onion, garlic, and ginger, and cook about 5 minutes over low to medium heat.

Add curry powder and mix thoroughly about 1 minute. Add flour; mix thoroughly.

Stir in chicken stock and milk. Slowly stir in cream. Stir briskly and mix well. Heat on medium.

Before serving, add sherry and salt. Mix well.

We like to serve the accompaniments in separate bowls or "boys," as they are called in India. Chop the following and pass at the table or serve buffet style.

ACCOMPANIMENTS

Sweet pickles
Bacon (crisp and crumbled)
Hard-cooked eggs, chopped
Coconut
Black or green olives
Green onions
Fresh pineapple
Diced smoked ham
Spiced peaches/red apple rings

SERVING SUGGESTION   Serve with basmati rice and Indian raita.

DESSERTS

L ife is too short. Eat dessert first. The end of the meal is Kim's favorite time: sitting around the table with a cup of freshly brewed coffee and sharing a grand-finale dessert with family or friends.

Previously, gluten-free desserts were like eating raw corn grits with sugar baked on them, then set out in the sun for a couple of days and, of course, freeze-dried for a couple of months. They were dry as concrete, tasteless, and so different from regular desserts.

Finally, we have gluten-free desserts that are simple to make and so incredibly rich and moist they melt in your mouth.

Gluten-free flours, while opening the door to divine gluten-free desserts, are more challenging to bake with than traditional white flour. Figuring out the exact measurements for rice, potato, or corn flour can get very complicated because you cannot just substitute one cup of gluten-free flour for one cup of traditional wheat flour. Moreover, gluten-free flours do not rise like wheat flours; indeed, they tend to flop. Kim has spent many hours covered in gluten-free flour to perfect these recipes that we are pleased to offer. They are shockingly moist. And they're so good, you'll forget they're gluten-free.

As for Bill, he doesn't eat desserts, or at least eats them rarely. His idea of dessert is Cognac and a Partaga cigar. Many of the recipes are from Kim's mother, Irene, which Kim de-glutenized. All are winners, so enjoy.

ABOUT BAKING GLUTEN-FREE

· Gluten-free flours tend to burn quicker, so be sure to closely watch your cakes, cookies, bread, biscuits, etc. We also use lower temperatures to cook than with traditional flours.

· We advise beating the batters for the recommended time, as this incorporates air into them—and they need all the lift they can get.

· We recommend nonstick pans for all of the desserts. Also, most of the cakes turn out better if you use three (9-inch) pans.

· Do not overfill your cake pans. Oven temperatures will vary—adjust yours accordingly.

· We like to line the bottom of the cake pans with parchment paper or wax paper to prevent sticking. This makes clean-up faster, too.

· Gluten-free cakes tend to rise in the oven, but fall back down. Cake batters will also be thicker.

· Gluten-free baked goods freeze well. Kim prefers hers slightly chilled or at room temperature.

LEMON-SOUR-CREAM POUND CAKE

Our recipe is a classic and a dear friend to the gluten-free diet. It's perfectly satisfying served warm at the breakfast table with a cup of hot tea or coffee. It's also a great addition to a nice lunch or dinner. YIELD: 1 (10 X 6-INCH) POUND CAKE

1 cup granulated sugar

½ cup non-hydrogenated shortening

3 eggs

2 teaspoons lemon zest

4 tablespoons fresh lemon juice

1¾ cups Pamela's Baking & Pancake Mix

¼ teaspoon sea salt

⅛ cup water

¼ cup buttermilk

¼ cup sour cream

Preheat oven to 325 F. Grease and flour (gluten free) a 10 x 6-inch loaf pan.

In a medium bowl, cream sugar and shortening. Add eggs, 1 at a time. Add lemon zest and juice.

Add baking mix, salt, water, buttermilk, and sour cream. Using an electric mixer, beat on high for 2 minutes.

Pour into prepared pan. Bake 25 minutes. Remove from oven and let cool.

KIM'S TRADITIONAL KARROT KAKE

Here's your old-fashioned carrot cake, which Bill calls a vegetable casserole. Kim calls it the best carrot cake ever. It's so rich, you won't believe it's gluten-free. Carrots add color, texture, and flavor. Plus they are rich in vitamins C, E, B$_6$, and K and betacarotene.   YIELD: 1 (9-INCH) TRIPLE-LAYER CAKE

3 eggs

½ cup buttermilk

½ cup oil

1 teaspoon vanilla extract: McCormick or Adams Pure

¼ cup water

1½ cups granulated sugar

1 teaspoon sea salt

2 cups Pamela's Baking & Pancake Mix

1 tablespoon ground nutmeg: McCormick or Spice Islands

2 tablespoons ground cinnamon: McCormick or Spice Islands

1 tablespoon allspice: McCormick or Spice Islands

1 cup chopped pecans or walnuts

2 cups shredded carrots

1 cup chopped pineapple chunks (optional)

Cream Cheese Icing (recipe follows)

Preheat oven to 350 F. Lightly grease and flour (gluten-free) or line with parchment paper 3 (9-inch) round cake pans.

In a mixing bowl, combine the eggs, buttermilk, oil, vanilla, water, sugar, salt, baking mix, nutmeg, cinnamon, and allspice. Using an electric mixer, beat on high for 2 minutes.

Fold in the walnuts, carrots, and pineapple, if using. Pour batter into the prepared baking pans. Do not overfill.

Bake 22 to 28 minutes. Watch carefully; do not overcook. Remove from oven and let cool completely.

To frost, place 1 cake layer on a cake platter and spread ¼ of icing on the top. Add the second layer and repeat. Top cake with final layer, ice the top and down the sides of the entire cake.

CREAM CHEESE ICING

2 (8-ounce) packages cream cheese, softened

6 tablespoons butter, at room temperature

3 cups powdered sugar

1 teaspoon vanilla extract: McCormick or Adams Pure

2 tablespoons fresh lemon juice

Place cream cheese and butter in a large mixing bowl. Mix on low speed until combined. Add powdered sugar, a little bit at a time, blending with mixer on low speed until the sugar is well incorporated, about 1 minute. Add vanilla extract and lemon juice. Increase mixer speed to medium and blend until the frosting is fluffy, about 1 more minute.

THE BEST LITTLE COCONUT CREAM CAKE IN TEXAS

This cake is very seductive . . . and suddenly nothing in the world matters but you and the night and a slice of Coconut Cream Cake. This is Kim's most requested cake. And for the finale, Kim likes to serve it with pink champagne. Does anybody really need a recipe for pink champagne? Cheers.   YIELD: 1 (9-INCH) TRIPLE-LAYER CAKE

4 eggs

¾ cup buttermilk

½ cup oil

1 teaspoon vanilla: McCormick or Adams Pure

¼ cup water

½ cup sour cream

1½ cups granulated sugar

¾ teaspoon sea salt

2½ cups Pamela's Baking & Pancake Mix

Whipped Cream Icing (recipe follows)

½ cup grated coconut (fresh or frozen is best)

Preheat oven to 350 F. Lightly grease and flour (gluten-free) or line with parchment paper 3 (9-inch) round cake pans (see note).

In a mixing bowl, combine the eggs, buttermilk, oil, vanilla, water, sour cream, sugar, salt, and baking mix. Using an electric mixer, beat on high for 2 minutes.

Pour batter into baking pans. Do not overfill. Bake 22 to 28 minutes. Watch carefully; do not overcook. Remove from oven and let cool completely.

To frost, place 1 cake layer on a cake platter and spread ¼ of icing on the top. Sprinkle with coconut. Add the second layer and repeat. Top cake with final layer, ice the top and, if you want, down the sides of the entire cake. Sprinkle with coconut.

Refrigerate 4 hours and serve. This cake can be made a day ahead of time, as it is so refreshing after a day in the refrigerator. It freezes well, too. This is also great with fresh sliced pineapple in the middle of the layers.

WHIPPED CREAM ICING

2 cups heavy whipping cream

1¼ cups powdered sugar, or more to taste

2 tablespoons sour cream

1 (8-ounce) package cream cheese, softened

Beat whipping cream until it reaches the consistency of butter. Add powdered sugar, sour cream, and cream cheese. Beat just until smooth, only a few seconds. Do not overbeat, or it will lose its consistency.

NOTE: You can make this cake using 2 (10-inch) pans. The cooking time for 2 pans is 26 to 30 minutes.

CHOCOLATE-CHIP PECAN COOKIES

These are so good, only licensed physicians should be allowed to dispense them.   YIELD: 2 DOZEN COOKIES

2 cups Pamela's (gluten-free) Baking & Pancake Mix

½ cup cornstarch

1 tablespoon baking powder: Clabber Girl, Hain, or Rumford

½ teaspoon sea salt

1 teaspoon cream of tartar: McCormick or Spice Islands

½ cup plus 2 tablespoons soft butter, room temperature (see note)

½ cup plus 2 tablespoons brown sugar

½ cup plus 2 tablespoons granulated sugar

2 beaten eggs, room temperature

2 tablespoons vanilla: McCormick or Adams Pure

1¼ cup semisweet chocolate chips: Nestlé Toll House

1 cup coarsely chopped pecans or walnuts

Preheat oven to 325 F. Line a baking sheet with parchment paper.

Combine baking mix, cornstarch, baking powder, salt, and cream of tartar in a medium mixing bowl. Set aside.

In another mixing bowl, cream butter and sugars with an electric mixer. Add eggs and vanilla. Add flour mixture. Beat on high for 2 minutes. Fold in chocolate chips and pecans.

Drop rounded teaspoons of cookie dough about 2 inches apart on the prepared baking sheet. Bake for 8 to 11 minutes. (If you prefer a softer cookie, take them out a minute or 2 earlier, as they will continue to bake.)

Remove from oven and let cool. Remove cookies from baking sheets.

NOTE: For a fluffier cookie, use ½ cup plus only1 tablespoon of butter

WARM CHOCOLATE PUDDING CAKE WITH KAHLUA WHIPPED CREAM

Chewy, crunchy, chocolaty—you won't be able to put this cake down. This recipe is unique in that you mix dry ingredients together with the buttermilk, oil, and vanilla. Then you mix the icing ingredients, pour them on top, and bake all together. Violà. And so easy.   YIELD: 10 TO 12 BARS

5 tablespoons cocoa powder (divided use): Nestlé or Ghirardelli Unsweetened

1 cup Pamela's Baking & Pancake Mix

⅔ plus ⅛ cup granulated sugar (divided use)

½ teaspoon sea salt

½ cup buttermilk

½ cup oil

1 egg

1 tablespoon vanilla: McCormick or Adams Pure

¾ cup walnuts plus more for garnish

½ cup semisweet chocolate chips: Nestlé Toll House

⅛ cup brown sugar

½ cup boiling water

Kahlua Whipped Cream (recipe follows)

2 to 3 sliced bananas

Preheat oven to 350 F.

In a large mixing bowl, combine 4 tablespoons cocoa powder, baking mix, and ⅔ cup sugar. Add the buttermilk, oil, egg, and vanilla. Stir well. Add walnuts and chocolate chips.

Pour into a nonstick 8 x 8 x 2-inch pan.

Combine remaining 1 tablespoon cocoa, ⅛ cup granulated sugar, and ⅛ cup brown sugar and mix well. Sprinkle mixture evenly over cake batter. Pour boiling water over all.

Bake 20 to 23 minutes. Remove from oven and let cool 5 minutes. Cut around the edges and scoop into bowls. Add banana slices, additional chopped walnuts, and Kahlua Whipped Cream.

KAHLUA WHIPPED CREAM

1 cup heavy whipping cream

¼ to ½ cup granulated sugar or to taste

1 tablespoon Kahlua or to taste

Whip cream to the consistency of butter. Add sugar and Kahlua. Mix well.

DEVIL'S DEVIL'S FOOD CAKE WITH CHOCOLATE FLUFF FROSTING

Sinful. Decadent. Outrageous. This is a chocolate lover's dream. Go to confession . . . and lie about this deep, rich, chocolaty, velvety cake. You get absolved, right?   YIELD: 1 (9-INCH) TRIPLE-LAYER CAKE

4 eggs

¾ cup buttermilk

½ cup oil

1 teaspoon vanilla: McCormick or Adams Pure

¼ cup water

½ cup sour cream

1¾ cups granulated sugar

2½ cups Pamela's Baking & Pancake Mix

1 teaspoon sea salt

7 tablespoons cocoa powder: Ghirardelli Unsweetened or Nestlé

Chocolate Fluff Frosting (recipe follows)

Preheat oven to 350 F. Lightly grease and flour (gluten-free) or line with parchment paper 3 (9-inch) round cake pans or 2 (10-inch) pans.

In a large mixing bowl, combine the eggs, buttermilk, oil, vanilla, water, sour cream, sugar, baking mix, salt, and cocoa powder. Using an electric mixer, beat on high for 2 minutes.

Pour batter into cake pans and bake for 22 to 28 minutes. Watch carefully; do not overcook.

Remove from oven and let cool.

To frost, place 1 cake layer on a cake platter and spread ¼ of icing on the top. Add the second layer and repeat. Top cake with final layer, ice the top and down the sides of the entire cake.

CHOCOLATE FLUFF FROSTING

8 tablespoons butter, softened

1 (8-ounce) package cream cheese, softened

⅛ teaspoon sea salt

⅔ cup cocoa powder: Nestlé or Ghirardelli Unsweetened

3 cups powdered sugar

¼ cup whole milk

1 tablespoon vanilla: McCormick or Adams Pure

Place butter, cream cheese, salt, and cocoa in a large mixing bowl. Beat with electric mixer on low speed until blended.

Add powdered sugar, milk, and vanilla to the bowl and beat on low speed until the frosting lightens and is fluffy, about 2 to 3 minutes. If frosting is too thick, add a little more whole milk.

APPLE-CINNAMON SOUR CREAM KUCHEN

Bill says that if he is going to eat a dessert, this is the one. A moist, rich, and buttery cake, this dessert is always a party hit. Served warm and sprinkled with cinnamon, it is especially rich and wicked. Be sure to hide some if you want leftovers.   YIELD: 1 (7 X 11-INCH) CAKE

2 eggs

¼ cup buttermilk

¼ cup oil

8 tablespoons butter, softened (divided use)

1 teaspoon vanilla: McCormick or Adams Pure

¾ cup sour cream (divided use, reserve 3 tablespoons for topping)

2 tablespoons lemon juice

1 cup granulated sugar

1 teaspoon sea salt

2 cups Pamela's Baking & Pancake Mix

2 cups peeled, cored, and sliced cooking apples, such as Granny Smith or Red Delicious (¼-inch thick slices from 3 large or 4 small apples)

1 tablespoon fresh lemon juice

½ cup brown sugar

Pinch of sea salt

1 teaspoon ground cinnamon: McCormick or Spice Islands

½ teaspoon nutmeg: McCormick or Spice Islands

Preheat oven to 350 F. Lightly grease and flour (gluten-free) or line with parchment paper a 9 x 13-inch cake pan.

In a bowl, combine the eggs, buttermilk, oil, 4 tablespoons butter, vanilla, ¾ cup sour cream, lemon juice, sugar, salt, and baking mix. Using an electric mixer, beat on high for 2 minutes.

Pour batter into prepared baking pan.

Meanwhile, toss the apple slices with the lemon juice in a large mixing bowl.

Place the brown sugar, pinch of salt, cinnamon, and nutmeg in a small mixing bowl and stir until well combined.

Arrange the apples in rows across the top of the batter. Sprinkle the sugar mixture evenly over the apples.

Drizzle the remaining 4 tablespoons melted butter over the apples and sugar mixture. Drizzle the remaining 3 tablespoons sour cream over the apples and sugar mixture.

Bake for 40 to 48 minutes, or until cake is golden brown and a toothpick inserted in the center comes out clean. Test before removing from oven. Watch carefully; do not overcook.

Remove from oven and allow to cool. Sprinkle with additional cinnamon, if you like.

OOEY-GOOEY CHOCOLATE BROWNIES

Finally, ooey-gooey, fresh and chewy. A chocolate lover's dream—but gluten-free this time. They are a real indulgence and, no surprise, a big hit with children. **YIELD: 2 DOZEN**

2 cups granulated sugar

2 cups Pamela's Baking & Pancake Mix

1 tablespoon cinnamon: McCormick or Spice Islands

½ teaspoon salt

½ cup buttermilk

2 eggs, beaten

1 tablespoon vanilla: McCormick or Adams Pure

½ cup butter, softened

½ cup oil

½ cup cocoa powder: Ghirardelli Unsweetened or Nestlé

¾ cup hot water

¾ cup semisweet chocolate chips: Nestlé or Ghirardelli

Chocolate Frosting (recipe follows)

Preheat oven to 350 F. Grease and flour (gluten free) a 9½ x 14-inch cake pan.

Mix together sugar, baking mix, cinnamon, salt, buttermilk, eggs, vanilla, butter, oil, and cocoa powder in a large mixing bowl. Slowly add water and, with an electric mixer, beat on medium for 2 minutes.

Stir in chocolate chips. Pour into prepared pan. Bake for 32 to 36 minutes.

Start making chocolate frosting about 5 minutes before brownies are done.

Spread on the hot brownies while still in the pan. (Spread icing on the edges first and then the middle.) Let cool before cutting.

CHOCOLATE FROSTING

6 tablespoons butter

¼ cup milk

¼ cup cocoa powder: Nestlé or Ghirardelli Unsweetened

3 cups powdered sugar

¼ teaspoon cinnamon: McCormick or Spice Islands

1 teaspoon vanilla: McCormick or Adams Extract Pure

1 cup chopped pecans

Combine butter, milk, and cocoa powder in a saucepan and bring to a boil, stirring constantly. Gradually stir in powdered sugar and cinnamon. Stir in vanilla and chopped pecans.

MEXICAN BROWNIES   For an added twist, add ⅛ teaspoon cayenne pepper and 1 extra teaspoon of cinnamon to the batter.

SOUTHERN BELLE PEACH PIE

This Southern peach pie will certainly ring your bell. You won't believe how delish it is, and with a flaky—yes, flaky—crust. And yes, we prefer fresh ingredients, but must admit, using canned peaches in this recipe is shockingly good and does the trick.   YIELD: 1 (9-INCH) PIE

7 tablespoons melted butter

¾ cup granulated sugar

⅛ cup plus 2 tablespoons cornstarch

4 to 5 tablespoons fresh lemon juice

2 tablespoons cinnamon: McCormick or Spice Islands

1½ teaspoons vanilla: McCormick or Adams Pure

1 (29-ounce) can peaches in juice, with ¾ cup juice reserved

Flaky Piecrust (recipe follows)

Make the piecrust. (We prefer to use a tall pie dish to keep the juices from overflowing.) Roll the dough out thin enough to make several piecrust strips for the top. Set aside.

Preheat oven to 350 F. Combine butter, sugar, cornstarch, lemon juice, cinnamon, vanilla, and reserved peach juice in a microwave-proof bowl. Mix well. Microwave on high (100 percent power) for 3 minutes, stirring occasionally. Make sure the cornstarch is dissolved.

Remove from microwave and add peaches. Pour peach filling mixture into prepared crust and top with remaining piecrust strips. Bake 35 to 45 minutes.

Remove from oven. Let pie cool at least 20 minutes before serving as this will help the juices to thicken.

FLAKY PIECRUST

We don't have to pass on mom's apple pie—or any other pie, for that matter. This piecrust is good as it gets in the world of gluten-freed living. Admittedly, it doesn't have the same taste or texture as traditional piecrust, but it's such an improvement over the usual gluten-free crust that you won't want to leave it on your plate. When making a piecrust, add a teaspoon of cinnamon to enhance the flavor of the gluten-free flours. And don't forget: Gluten-free flours tend to burn faster than traditional flours. Protect the crust with a pie shield or strips of aluminum foil to prevent it from browning too much.   YIELD: 1 (9- OR 10-INCH) ROUND PIECRUST

2 cups gluten-free flour: Bob's Red Mill Biscuit and Baking Mix

½ cup plus 2 tablespoons butter

¼ cup plus 2 tablespoons cold water

In a mixing bowl, blend together flour and butter with a pastry cutter, or in a food processor, until well cut. Add water and knead well until it forms a ball.

With oiled hands, place ball on a sheet of wax paper. (Also rub oil on the rolling pin.) Roll to fit pie plate.

Fill with desired pie filling and bake according to pie recipe directions.

PINEAPPLE UPSIDE-DOWN CAKE

Buttery. Crunchy. Caramel-y. Pineapple-y. What more can you ask for? Kim grew up watching her mother, Irene, turn this sensational cake upside down. The buttery yellow skillet cake has a crunchy, caramelized brown-sugar topping fused with golden brown pineapple. It is absolutely delicious—a classic for any occasion.   YIELD: 1 (11-INCH) ROUND CAKE

4 large eggs

2 cups Pamela's Baking & Pancake Mix

1 teaspoon sea salt

1¼ cups granulated sugar

½ cup plus 2 tablespoons oil

½ cup buttermilk

¼ cup water

1½ teaspoon vanilla: McCormick or Adams Pure

½ cup plus 2 tablespoons butter

2 cups brown sugar

⅛ cup rum: Captain Morgan

1 (20-ounce) can sliced pineapple, drained

Preheat oven to 325 F.

In a bowl, add the eggs, baking mix, salt, sugar, oil, buttermilk, water, and vanilla.

Using an electric mixer, beat on high for 2 minutes.

In a large, cast-iron skillet, melt butter and add brown sugar. Stir constantly while cooking, until butter and brown sugar are slightly bubbly, from 1 to 3 minutes.

Remove from heat and arrange pineapple slices on brown sugar-butter mixture. (Kim likes to add raspberries or blueberries in the middle of the pineapple circles.) Slowly and very gently pour cake batter over brown sugar and butter-pineapple.

Bake for 28 to 38 minutes, or until cake is golden all over and springs back when lightly tapped. Remove from oven and let cool for 1 hour.

Slide knife around sides to loosen the brown sugar. Place a round platter, top side down, on top of the skillet. Turn the whole thing over to loosen the cake from the skillet. You may also need to scoop some of the brown sugar-butter from pan and fill in holes on cake.

Let cool for 20 minutes without covering before serving. If—if—there should be any leftovers, you will need to cover this cake to store it.

LIMONCELLO CUSTARD

So light and lemony, so elegant and Italian. This desert is reminiscent of a French crème brûlée. Kim likes to drizzle Limoncello liqueur on top. It makes a nice complement to a luncheon or light dinner. YIELD: 4 (6-OUNCE) SERVINGS

¾ cup granulated sugar

1½ tablespoons butter plus more for buttering ramekins

2 teaspoons grated lemon zest

3 egg yolks, beaten

3 tablespoons rice flour

¼ cup fresh lemon juice

1 cup whole milk

3 egg whites, stiffly beaten

1 tablespoon Caravella Limoncello Originale d'Italia

Whipped cream (optional)

Preheat oven to 350 F. Butter 4 (6-ounce) custard cups.

In a medium bowl, combine sugar, butter, and lemon zest and beat well. Add beaten egg yolks. Stir in rice flour, lemon juice, and milk.

Gently fold in beaten egg whites and mix. Gently fold in limoncello. Pour into prepared custard cups. Set cups in a pan large enough to hold all, surrounded by 1 inch of water.

Bake for 45 minutes. Immediately remove cups from hot water.

Serve with a dollop of whipped cream and a drizzle of Caravella Limoncello Originale d'Italia, if desired.

SERVING SUGGESTION These are also good finished with a little crème de menthe and fresh mint leaves.

KIM'S FAMOUS OVER-THE-TOP BANANAS FOSTER CAKE

If you make only one dessert, this is it. You will absolutely think you have died and gone to heaven the first time you try this. There will not be one morsel, not one itty-bitty spoonful left of this. Nada. None. You will love it.

YIELD: 1 (9 X 13-INCH) CAKE

4 large eggs

2½ cups Pamela's Baking & Pancake Mix

1 teaspoon sea salt

1½ cups granulated sugar

1 tablespoon ground cinnamon: McCormick or Spice Islands

1 tablespoon dark rum or McCormick rum extract

1 tablespoon banana liqueur

½ cup plus 2 tablespoons oil

¾ cup buttermilk

1½ teaspoon vanilla: McCormick or Adams Pure

2 tablespoons fresh lemon juice

½ cup sour cream

¼ cup water

4 bananas, sliced lengthwise

Bananas Foster Sauce

Preheat oven to 325 F.

In a large bowl, combine the eggs, baking mix, salt, sugar, cinnamon, rum, banana liqueur, oil, buttermilk, vanilla, lemon juice, sour cream, and water. With an electric mixer, beat on high for 2 minutes.

Pour into a lightly greased 9 x 13-inch baking dish. Bake for 30 to 38 minutes. Check after 15 minutes. You may need to add a piece of foil on top to keep cake from burning because oven temperatures vary.

Remove from oven and let cake cool before serving. The cake can be made a day before.

Place bananas on top of cake and drizzle Bananas Foster Sauce over cake and bananas.

BANANAS FOSTER SAUCE

2 cups brown sugar

¾ cup butter

1 tablespoon cinnamon: McCormick or Spice Islands

¼ cup banana liqueur

⅛ cup dark rum

Combine brown sugar, butter, and cinnamon in a large skillet. Cook over low to medium heat, stirring constantly, until bubbly, about 5 to 7 minutes. Add banana liqueur and dark rum. Stir constantly until all butter and liquid are mixed into the brown sugar, about 1 to 3 minutes.

SERVING SUGGESTION   Add whipped cream, vanilla ice cream, or cinnamon ice cream.

ITALIAN CREMA CAKE

Not even a Fourth of July fireworks display would pull your guests away from this dessert. Even people who don't like sweets ask for seconds. Dessert junkies go into a drug-like realm of bliss when they get their fix of this. Otherwise good, decent, hardworking people quit their jobs and quit bathing once they get hooked on this cake. Powerful stuff.   YIELD: 1 (9-INCH) TRIPLE-LAYER CAKE

4 eggs

¼ cup butter, room temperature

½ cup sour cream

2 cups granulated sugar

½ cup oil

¾ cup buttermilk

¼ cup water

2 cups Pamela's Baking & Pancake Mix

¼ teaspoon sea salt

1 teaspoon vanilla: McCormick or Adams Pure

½ cup chopped pecans or walnuts

⅓ cup grated coconut (fresh or frozen is best)

Icing (recipe follows)

Preheat oven to 325 F. Grease and flour (gluten-free) 3 (9-inch) cake pans.

In a large bowl, combine the eggs, butter, sour cream, sugar, oil, buttermilk, water, baking mix, salt, and vanilla. Using an electric mixer, beat on high for 2 minutes.

Fold in pecans and grated coconut.

Pour batter into prepared pans. Bake for 22 to 28 minutes.

Remove from oven and let cool.

ICING

2 (8-ounce) packages softened cream cheese

6 tablespoons butter

3½ cups powdered sugar

1 teaspoon vanilla: McCormick or Adams Pure

¼ teaspoon fresh lemon juice

½ cup chopped pecans or walnuts

⅓ cup grated coconut (fresh or frozen is best,)

Combine cream cheese, butter, powdered sugar, vanilla, and lemon juice.

Using an electric mixer, beat on high for 1 minute. Fold in pecans and coconut.

To frost, place 1 cake layer on a cake platter and spread ¼ of icing on the top. Add the second layer and repeat. Top cake with final layer; ice the top and down the sides of the entire cake.

CRANBERRY PECAN CAKE

Tart cranberries, buttermilk, and crunchy pecans . . . this cake is just bursting with flavor, and it's always a favorite. So simple to make, and incredibly delicious.   YIELD: 1 (9-INCH) BUNDT OR 1 (6 X 10-INCH) RECTANGLE CAKE

2 tablespoons butter, room temperature

1½ cup granulated sugar

2 cups Pamela's Baking & Pancake Mix

½ cup oil

½ teaspoon sea salt

2 eggs, beaten

¼ cup fresh lemon juice

½ cup buttermilk

¼ cup water

1 cup sweetened dried cranberries

1 cup chopped pecans

Preheat oven to 325 F. Grease and flour (gluten free) a 9-inch Bundt pan or a 6x10-inch cake pan.

In a large bowl, cream butter and sugar. Add baking mix, oil, salt, eggs, lemon juice, buttermilk, and water. Using an electric mixer, beat on high for 2 minutes. Gently stir in the pecans and cranberries.

Pour into prepared pan. Bake 42 to 48 minutes. You may need to place a piece of foil on top after 20 minutes to keep it from getting too brown. Remove from oven and let cool.

RED VELVET CUPCAKES

Unbelievable. Unforgettable. These are so moist and decadent that they deserve a standing ovation. YIELD: 36 TO 40 CUPCAKES, OR 1 (9-INCH) TRIPLE-LAYER CAKE

4 eggs

¾ cup buttermilk

½ cup oil

¼ cup water

½ cup sour cream

1¾ cups granulated sugar

2½ cups Pamela's Baking & Pancake Mix

1 teaspoon salt

4 tablespoons cocoa powder: Ghirardelli Unsweetened or Nestlé

2 tablespoons red food color: Betty Crocker red gel or McCormick

Cream Cheese Icing (see Page 237)

Preheat oven to 325 F. Place cupcake liners in a cupcake tray. Or, grease and flour (gluten free) 3 (9-inch) round cake pans.

In a large bowl, combine eggs, buttermilk, oil, water, sour cream, sugar, baking mix, salt, cocoa powder, and food color. Using an electric mixer, beat on High for 2 minutes.

Fill cupcake liners about ¾ full. Or, pour batter into prepared cake pans.

Bake cupcakes for 10 to 12 minutes, or until a toothpick comes out clean. You may need to rotate the pan after the first 8 minutes to ensure even baking. Watch closely. Do not overcook. For the cake, bake 22 to 24 minutes.

Remove from oven, let cool and top with Cream Cheese Icing.

NOTE: The cupcakes tend to pull away from the cupcake liners. Kim suggests serving them without the cups. They make a very elegant little cupcake.

BUTTERMILK TOFFEE CAKE WITH CHOCOLATE BUTTERCREAM FROSTING

Rich. Rich. Rich. Anything else you want to know? This is gluten-freedom society's answer to the traditional yellow cake with chocolate frosting. Only so much better.   YIELD: 1 (10 X 13-INCH) CAKE

2 cups Pamela's Baking & Pancake Mix

1¼ cups granulated sugar

½ teaspoon sea salt

½ cup oil

4 eggs

¾ cup buttermilk

¼ cup water

1 tablespoon vanilla: McCormick or Adams Pure

1 cup toffee bits: Heath Bits O Brickle or Skor English Toffee bits (divided use)

Chocolate Buttercream Frosting (recipe follows)

Preheat oven to 325 degrees. Lightly grease a 10 x 13-inch baking dish.

In a large mixing bowl, combine baking mix, sugar, salt, oil, eggs, buttermilk, water, and vanilla. Using an electric mixer, beat on medium-high for 2 minutes.

Pour into prepared baking dish. Sprinkle with ½ of the toffee bits and bake for 22 to 28 minutes. Check cake after 15 minutes. You may need to put a piece of foil on top to keep the cake from burning.

Remove from oven and let cake cool. Spread frosting on cake. Sprinkle remaining toffee bits on top.

CHOCOLATE BUTTERCREAM FROSTING

6 tablespoons butter

3 cups powdered sugar

⅜ cup cocoa powder: Ghirardelli Unsweetened or Nestlé

4 tablespoons sour cream

¼ cup half-and-half

1 teaspoon vanilla: McCormick Vanilla Extract or Adams Pure Vanilla Extract

In a medium bowl, cream butter and powdered sugar. Add cocoa powder and mix. Add sour cream and half-and-half. Using an electric mixer, beat for 1 minute on high. Add vanilla and beat 1 minute more until creamy.

PANTRY LIST

Here's your guide to what we use and what we have found that works after years of research and trial and error. The products and ingredients that contain gluten are mind-boggling. Do you have any idea how many ingredients have gluten in them? Who would have thought that some brands of corn chips contain gluten? Your favorite barbecue sauce? Spaghetti sauce? Ranch dressing? Salad dressing? Seasoning? Marinade? Soy sauce? Potato chips? Ice cream? Mustard? And on the ingredient label, gluten might be disguised in these as well: brown rice syrup, fillers, artificial flavors and natural flavors, seasonings and spice blends, stabilizers, starch, and some yeasts. There are times you just want to throw your hands in the air and say, "Just give me a banana."

The new Food and Drug Administration rule about "gluten free" on labels is going to help a lot. With it, any food labeled "gluten free," "without gluten," "free of gluten" or "no gluten" will be limited to less than 20 ppm (parts per million) of gluten. The rule goes into effect in August 2014, and it's in line with international standards.

Many foods that are gluten-free will display this proudly on their labels. But there will be others that don't. It won't be a big enough deal for them. So you still have to be a sleuth. What sets this cookbook apart is we take the hassle out of finding brands and ingredients that are gluten-free, whether it says so on the label or not. In each recipe, we specify brand names for the ingredients that can be found at your local grocery store, which means you no longer have to check labels to decifer if a product is gluten free. We do rely on the truthfulness of manufacturers and what they list on the food ingredient food label. But manufacturers can change their ingredients and manufacturing processes. So we can't give you a list of every gluten-free brand

and ingredient available today, but we've also come up with an everyday pantry list that includes our favorite products, and we give you enough brands and ingredients to cook what you want.

Our goal is to tell you about brands and ingredients that regular people use in kitchens. Real stuff that's in our pantries and refrigerators from local grocery stores, such as Randall's, Albertsons, HEB, Kroger, Central Market, Whole Foods Market, Sun Harvest, Winn Dixie, Publix, A&P, Hannaford, ShopRite, Wegmans, and Safeway, to name a bunch. This list will instantly make your life easier and make grocery shopping a snap, because you won't have to spend hours analyzing ingredients.

We especially like Kraft and McCormick products. Their labels tell us what we need to know. We applaud their labeling. We also really like Newman's Own products. Not only are they good, but we both love his movies. The fact that profits go to charities is a major "plus" with us. Vaya con Dios, Señor Newman.

Some grocery stores provide lists of gluten-free foods that they sell. Ask the store manager to see whether your store does.

How do you know if an item is gluten-free? An item is generally gluten-free if the label shows that it does not contain: gluten, monosodium glutamate (MSG), barley, bulgur, couscous, wheat, graham, semolina, spelt, durum, einkorn, kamut, matza, matzo, matzah, oats, oat bran, oat fiber, oat gum, rye, faro, seitan wheat, triticale wheat berry, wheat germ, wheat grass, wheat gluten, wheat nut, wheat starch, hydrolyzed vegetable protein (HVP), texturized vegetable protein (TVP), hydrolyzed plant protein (HPP), modified starch, modified food starch, vegetable gum, or gliadin. Organic labeling does not necessarily mean gluten-free or MSG-free. (Also, check with your doctor or pharmacist, as medications and vitamins contain fillers. Make sure that you are taking gluten-free medications and vitamins.)

For further information, we highly recommend contacting the Celiac Sprue Association (www.csaceliacs.org) and ordering their CSA Gluten-free Product Listing book—more than 400 pages of information you absolutely must have.

Truth is, even with the product listing, new labels, this cookbook and Internet research, you will have to read labels the rest of your life. Why? Products change. Ingredients change. Manufacturing processes change. But it's getting easier all the time, and here's our contribution to help you along:

APPLESAUCE, CANNED

Eden Organic Apple Sauce

Langers Unsweetened Apple Sauce

Mott's Applesauce, Natural Applesauce

ANCHOVIES

Crown Prince Flat Fillets Anchovies, Anchovy Paste

Reese Flat Fillets of Anchovies

ARTICHOKES, JARRED OR CANNED

California Girl Artichoke Hearts

Gelson's Finest Artichoke Hearts

Maria: Quartered Artichokes, Artichoke Hearts

Reese: Artichoke Bottoms, Artichoke Hearts

ASIAN SAUCES

A Taste of Thai: Fish Sauce, Garlic Chili Pepper Sauce,
    Pad Thai Sauce, Peanut Satay Sauce, Peanut Sauce
    Mix, Sweet Red Chili Sauce

Lee Kum Kee Sriracha Chili Sauce

Thai Kitchen: Original Pad Thai Sauce, Peanut Satay
    Sauce, Premium Fish Sauce, Sweet Red Chili Sauce

BAKING MIXES (see flours and baking mixes)

BAKING POWDER

Calumet Baking Powder

Clabber Girl Baking Powder

Ener G Baking Powder

Hain Featherweight Baking Powder

Rumford Baking Powder

BAKING SODA

Albertson's Brand 100% Baking Soda

Arm & Hammer Pure Baking Soda

Bob's Red Mill Pure Baking Soda

Ener G Baking Soda

BEEF BROTH

Imagine Organic Beef Flavored Broth

Pacific Organic Beef Broth

BEEF STOCK

Emeril's

Kitchen Basics

Swanson's

BUTTER

Land O' Lakes Butter: Salted, Unsalted, Light

BREAD CRUMBS

Aleia's: Italian Bread Crumbs, Plain Bread Crumbs

Glutino Gluten Free Bread Crumbs

Katz Gluten Free Bread Crumbs

Orgran: All Purpose Rice Crumbs, Corn Crispy Crumbs

CAPERS

Delicias Capers

Mezzetta Non-pareil Capers

Reese Non-pareil Capers

Star Capers

CEREALS

General Mills Chex Cereal: Chocolate, Cinnamon,
Corn, Honey Nut, Rice, Vanilla

Nature's Path Honey'd Corn Flakes

CHEESES

Alouette: Crème de Brie, Blue Cheese Crumbled

Boar's Head: American Cheese (Yellow and White),
Canadian Cheddar Cheese, Cream Havarti, Cream
Havarti with Jalapeno, Cream Havarti with Dill,
Lacey Swiss Cheese, Longhorn Colby Cheese,
Monterey Jack Cheese, Mozzarella Cheese (Whole
Milk, low moisture), Vermont Cheddar (yellow or
white)

Boursin Cheese (all varieties)

Cracker Barrel: Baby Swiss, Aged Reserved, Extra
Sharp Cheddar, Extra Sharp White Cheddar, Sharp
Cheddar, Sharp White Cheddar, Vermont Sharp
White Cheddar

Crystal Farms Fresh Accents: Crumbled Blue Cheese,
Wisconsin Crumbled Gorgonzola Cup

DiGiorno Parmesan Cheese Wedge

Ile de France Goat Cheese

Kerry Gold: All Kerry Gold products except Kerry
Gold Dubliner with Irish Stout

Kraft: Aged Swiss, Natural Cheddar and Monterey,
Colby Jack, Extra Sharp Cheddar, Havarti,
Mexican Four Cheese, Mild Cheddar, Monterey
Jack, Mozzarella, Pizza Four Cheese, Pizza
Mozzarella Cheddar

Kraft Shredded Cheese: Parmesan, Parmesan
Romano and Asiago

Kraft Grated Cheese: Parmesan, Parmesan &
Romano, Romano

La Vaquita: Crema Hondurena, Crema Mexicana,
Crema Salvadorena, Panela, Queso Fresco,
Quesadilla

Primo Taglio: Crumbled Danish Blue Cheese, Lacy
Swiss, American Cheddar, Danish Havarti,
Provolone, Shredded Asiago, Hot Pepper Jack

Publix: Blue Cheese Crumbled, Crumbled Goat,
Grated Parmesan, Shredded Parmesan

Sargento: All Sargento natural cheeses except blue
cheese

Tillamook: All cheese, yogurt, sour cream, and butter
products

Winn-Dixie: All forms—block, shredded, cubed or
sliced

CHERRIES, CANNED

Oregon Fruit Red Tart Cherries

CHICKEN, FRESH

Bell and Evans Chicken Breast Nuggets

Boar's Head: Hickory Smoked Chicken Breast,
  Rotisserie Seasoned Roasted Chicken Breast,
  Maple Glazed Roasted Chicken Breast

Jennie-O Oven Roasted Chicken Breast

Organic Prairie Whole Chicken

Perdue Farms Individually Frozen Chicken Breasts

Perdue Farms Individually Frozen Chicken
  Tenderloins

Perdue Farms Individually Frozen Chicken Wings

CHICKEN BROTH

Hain Organic Chicken Broth

Health Valley No Salt Added Chicken Broth

Imagine Organic Free-Range Chicken Broth

Pacific All Natural Foods Free Range Chicken Broth

Pacific Natural Foods Organic Free-Range Chicken
  Broth

Progresso 100% Natural Chicken Broth

Safeway Chicken Broth

Shelton's Chicken Broth

Swanson Natural Goodness Chicken Broth

Swanson Organic Chicken Broth

Wolfgang Puck Organic Free-Range Roasted Chicken
  Broth

CHICKEN STOCK

Kitchen Basics Original

Swanson Chicken Stock

CHILE PASTE

Thai Kitchen Roasted Red Chili Paste

CHILE PEPPERS, CANNED

Heinz, all varieties

CHILI SAUCE

Heinz Chili Sauce

CHIPS

Doritos Toasted Corn Tortilla Chips

Fritos Corn Chips: Original, Scoops

Kettle Chips

Lay's: Classic Potato Chips, Natural Sea Salt Flavored
  Thick Cut Potato Chips

Ruffles Potato Chips: Original, Reduced Fat

Terra Chips: Yukon Gold Original, Yukon Gold Salt &
  Pepper

Tostitos: Simply Natural Blue Corn Tortilla Chips,
  Simply Natural Yellow Corn Tortilla Chips, Baked
  Tostito Scoops Tortilla Chips

Xochitl Totopos de Maiz

CHOCOLATE

Baker's Baking Chocolate: Semi-sweet Baking Chocolate Bar, Sweet Baking Chocolate Bar, Unsweetened Baking Chocolate Bar

Ghirardelli: 100% Unsweetened Cocoa, Sweet Ground Cocoa, Double Chocolate Bittersweet Baking Chips

Hershey's: Semi-sweet Chocolate Chips, Special Dark Chips, Cocoa, Special Dark Cocoa

Hy-Vee Baking Cocoa

Nestle: Cocoa Powder, Toll House Semi-Sweet Morsels, Toll House Dark Chocolate Morsels, Toll House Milk Chocolate Morsels, Toll House Chocolate Chunks

Trader Joe's Organic Conacado Powder

Watkins Baking Cocoa

COCKTAIL SAUCE

Heinz Original Cocktail Sauce

Ken's Steakhouse Cocktail Sauce

COCONUT

Baker's: Angel Flake Coconut (bag and can)

Safeway Sweetened Shredded Coconut

CORNMEAL

Arrowhead Mills: Organic Yellow Cornmeal, Blue Cornmeal

Albers: Yellow, White Cornmeal

Bob's Red Mill Gluten-free Medium Stone-ground Cornmeal

El Peto Cornmeal

Hodgson Mill White All Natural Cornmeal, All Natural Yellow, and Organic Yellow

Lamb's Stone-Ground Yellow Cornmeal

CORN STARCH

Argo Corn Starch

Hodgson Mill 100% Pure Corn Starch

Kingsford Corn Starch

Safeway Brand

CRACKERS

Back to Nature Gluten Free Rice Thins

Blue Diamond Nut Thins

Ener G Foods: Seattle Crackers, Flax Crackers

Glutino Crackers

Mary's Gone Crackers

Mr. Krispers Baked Rice Snack Products

Sesmark Crackers

CRANBERRY SAUCE

Ocean Spray Cranberry Sauce

R. W. Knudsen Natural Cranberry Sauce

CREAM CHEESE

Albertson's Brand Cream Cheese

Organic Valley Cream Cheese

Philadelphia Cream Cheese

Safeway Brand Cream Cheese

Winn-Dixie Brand Cream Cheese

CURRY PASTE

A Taste of Thai: Green, Red or Yellow Curry

Thai Kitchen: Green Curry and Red Curry

ENCHILADA SAUCE, RED

Las Palmas: Red Enchilada Sauce, Red Chile Sauce,
   Crushed Red Tomatoes

EXTRACTS

McCormick (all extracts)

FISH SAUCE

A Taste of Thai Fish Sauce

FLOURS AND BAKING MIXES

Arrowhead Mills All Purpose Gluten Free Baking Mix

Arrowhead Mills Organic White Rice Flour

Arrowhead Mills Pancake and Baking Mix

Bisquick Gluten-free Pancake & Baking Mix

Bob's Red Mill Gluten Free All Purpose Baking
   Flour, Biscuit and Baking Mix, Brown Rice Flour,
   Cornbread Mix, Potato Flour, White Rice Flour,
   Tapioca Flour

Pamela's Baking & Pancake Mix

FRUIT, CANNED

Del Monte

FRUITS, DRIED

Sun-Maid Raisins

GARLIC-CHILE PEPPER SAUCE

Taste of Thai Garlic Chili Pepper Sauce

Taste of Thai Sweet Red Chili Sauce

GRITS

Arrowhead Mills Yellow Corn Grits

Three Minute Brand Quick Grits

HAM

Boar's Head Smoked Virginia Ham

Jennie-O Turkey Ham

Primrose Black Forest Ham

HAM, DEVILED

Underwood's Deviled Ham

HOT SAUCE

Cholula Hot Sauce

Emeril's Kick It Up Red Pepper Sauce

Frank's: Red Hot Sauce Original, XTRA Hot, Buffalo
   Wings Sauce

Louisiana Hot Sauce

Pickapeppa Original Sauce

Tabasco Sauce: Green Pepper, Original

Trappy's Louisiana Hot Sauce

HOISIN SAUCE

Dynasty

Kame

Lee Kum Kee

Premier Japan Organic Hoisin Sauce

HORSERADISH SAUCE

Boar's Head Horseradish Sauce

Heinz Horseradish

ICE CREAM

Blue Bell: Chocolate Chip, Homemade Vanilla, Mint
  Chocolate Chip, Natural Vanilla Bean, Tin Roof

Häagen-Dazs: Chocolate Peanut Butter, Coffee, Rocky
  Road, Vanilla

JAMS, JELLIES, PRESERVES

Braswell's Green Pepper Jelly

Polaner (all jellies, jams, and preserves)

Safeway Brand jams and jellies

Select Brand jams and jellies

Winn-Dixie Brand jams, jellies, marmalades, and
  preserves

Bonne Mamam: All jams and preserves

Smuckers: All jams, jellies, and preserves

JUICES

Campbell: Cranberry, Tomato Juice

Mott's 100% Apple Juice

Ocean Spray: Cranberry, Cran-Apple, Ruby Tangerine

Odwalla: Apple, Carrot, Orange

POM Pomegranate Juice

Smart Juice Organic Juice

Tropicana Cranberry Cocktail, Grape, Orchard Style
  Apple Juice

V8 Vegetable Juice

KETCHUP

Annie's Organic Ketchup

Heinz Regular Ketchup, Organic

Organicville

LIQUID SMOKE

Colgin's

Wright's Liquid Smoke: Hickory, Mesquite

MARSHMALLOWS

Kraft

MAYONNAISE

Best Foods Real Mayonnaise

Cain's All-natural Mayonnaise

Hellmann's Mayonnaise: Regular and Light

Heinz Mayonnaise

Kraft Mayonnaise

Miracle Whip

Spectrum Mayonnaise

MILK, CONDENSED

Eagle Brand Sweetened Condensed Milk

MIXES, BAKING (see flours and baking mixes)

MOLASSES

Grandma's

Plantation Blackstrap

MUSHROOMS, CANNED

Brandywine Sliced Mushrooms

Green Giant: Whole or Sliced Mushrooms

MUSTARD

Annie's: Organic Dijon, Organic Honey Mustard, Organic Horseradish, and Organic Yellow

Boar's Head Delicatessen Style

Colman's: Dry Mustard

Eden Foods Brown Mustard

Emeril's Dijon Mustard, Horseradish Mustard, NY Deli Style Mustard

French's: Classic Yellow Mustard, Spicy Brown Mustard, Honey Dijon Mustard, Dijon, Honey Mustard Dipping Sauce

Grey Poupon: Classic Dijon Mustard, Country Dijon

Heinz: all varieties

Hellman's: Dijonnaise Creamy, Dijon Mustard

Maille Dijon Originale Mustard

Organicville: Stone Ground Mustard, Yellow Mustard, Dijon Mustard

Zatarain's Creole Mustard

MUSTARD, HONEY

Amy's Organic Honey Mustard

Boar's Head Honey Mustard

Di Lusso Cranberry Honey Mustard

Emeril's Smooth Honey Mustard

French's Honey Mustard

NUTRITION BARS

Bakery on Main Granola Bars

Enjoy Life Foods Chewy Bars, Decadent Soft Baked Bars

Glutino Breakfast Bars

KIND bars

Larabar

SoyJoy Bars

NUTS

Blue Diamond: Roasted Salted Almonds, Smokehouse Almonds, Barbeque Almonds, Honey Roasted Almonds

Frito Lay: Cashews, Salted, Roasted Almonds, Sunflower Seeds

Hy-Vee English Walnut Pieces

Nature Valley: Roasted Nut Crunch Bars, Almond
 Crunch

OIL, COOKING

Crisco: Canola, Vegetable Oil

Newman's Own Organics Extra-Virgin Olive Oil

Pam: Original, Butter, and Olive Oil

OLIVES

Albertson's brand

Early California

Mt. Olives

Safeway Brand Manzilla

Winn Dixie Brand (green, ripe)

OLIVES, KALAMATA

Albertson's Brand

Divina Organic

Mezzetta Colossal Queen Olives

Peloponnese Pitted Kalamata

Winn Dixie Brand: Green olives (all varieties), ripe
 olives (all varieties)

OYSTER SAUCE

Kikkoman Red Label Oyster Sauce

Panda Brand Green Label Oyster Sauce

PASTA

Bionature: Gluten-free pasta (many varieties)

De Boles: Gluten-free pasta (many varieties)

Ener-G Foods: Rice Spaghetti, Vermicelli, White Rice
 Lasagna, White Rice Macaroni, Small Shells

Glutano Gluten-free Pasta (many varieties)

Lundberg Family Farms: Gluten-free pasta (many
 varieties)

Mrs. Leeper's: Brown Rice Penne, Spaghetti, Corn
 Elbows, Rice Veggie Twists, Rice Spaghetti

Orgran Rice and Corn Gluten-free pasta (many
 varieties)

Tinkyada Gluten-free Rice Pasta (many varieties)

PASTA SAUCES

Albertson's Brand Pasta Sauce (not spaghetti sauce)

Amy's: Organic Pasta Sauce, Family Marinara,
 Tomato Basil

Classico (many varieties)

Contadina Garlic and Onion Tomato Sauce

Del Monte (many varieties)

Emeril's: Homestyle Marinara Pasta Sauce, Kicked Up
 Tomato, Gaaahlic Pasta Sauce, Roasted Red Pepper
 Pasta Sauce

Great Value (WalMart traditional pasta sauce)

Heinz Classico Red Pasta Sauces

Newman's Own Sauce (many varieties)

Prego Extra: All organic varieties

Ragu: Traditional Organic (many varieties)

Safeway Brand: All Verdi Pasta/Marinara

Winn-Dixie Brand: Classic Marinara (many varieties)

PEACHES, CANNED

Del Monte Lite Peaches

Del Monte Yellow Cling Peaches

PEPPERONI

Hormel Pepperoni

PICANTE SAUCES (see salsas)

PINEAPPLE, CANNED

Dole Pineapple Slices in Juice or in Syrup

PIZZA CRUST

Arrowhead Mills Pizza Crust Mix

Ener-G Foods Rice Pizza Shells

Glutino Premium Pizza Crust

Kinnikinnick Foods 7- and 10-inch Pizza Crusts

PIZZA SAUCE

Contadina Pizza Sauce: all types

Ragu Pizza Sauce

PLUM SAUCE

Dynasty

Lee Kum Kee Gold Label

POLENTA

Bob's Red Mill Gluten Free Corn Grits

San Gennaro: Traditional, Garlic Basil

POTATOES, INSTANT MASHED

Betty Crocker Potato Buds

Hungry Jack Potato Flakes

POTATOES, PROCESSED

Ore-Ida: French Fries, Golden Crinkles, Southern
Style Hash Browns, Extra Crispy French Fries

PRETZELS

Ener-G Crisp Pretzels

Glutino Pretzel Twists

Mary's Gone Crackers Sticks & Twigs

Snyder's of Hanover: Gluten-free Mini Pretzels, Hot
Buffalo Wing Pretzels, Honey Mustard and Onion
Sticks

PUMPKIN, CANNED

Libby Pumpkin

RELISH

Heinz: all types

RICE

Albertson's Brand Instant White or Brown Rice

Kraft Minute Brand Instant Enriched Long-grain
White Rice

Kraft Minute Brand Instant Enriched Premium Long-grain White Rice

Kraft Minute Brand Instant Boil-in-Bag Long-grain White Rice

Rice Select Organic Texmati Brown Rice, White Rice

Safeway Select Brand: Basmati Rice, White, Long Grain, Enriched Calrose

Taste of Thai Jasmine Rice

Uncle Ben's: Arborio, Basmati, Jasmine

Uncle Ben's: Long Grain Boil-in-Bag Rice, Whole Grain Boil-in-Bag Rice

Uncle Ben's Instant Brown Rice

Uncle Ben's Instant Rice Enriched Long-grain Rice

Uncle Ben's Natural Whole-grain Brown Rice

Uncle Ben's Long Grain Brand Rice

RICE VINEGAR

Kikkoman Rice Vinegar

Mirin Rice Vinegar

Marukan Genuine Brewed Rice Vinegar

Regina: all vineyards and all cooking wines

Safeway Brand Seasoned Rice Vinegar (all vinegar except malt vinegar)

RISOTTO

Lindberg White Arborio Rice

Rice Select Arborio Rice

Uncle Ben's Arborio Rice

ROAST BEEF

Applegate Farms Roast Beef

Boar's Head Roast Beef

SALAD DRESSINGS

Annie's Naturals: Organic French, Balsamic Organic Vinaigrette, Organic Homegrown Cowgirl Ranch, Organic Buttermilk, Organic Green Goddess

Emeril's: Caesar Dressing, Vinaigrette, House Vinaigrette, Italian Vinaigrette, Raspberry Balsamic Vinaigrette, Balsamic Vinaigrette

Ken's: Zesty Italian, Fat-Free Raspberry Pecan Herb, Creamy Italian, Fat-free Sun-dried Tomato, Buttermilk Ranch, Lite Caesar, Lite Russian, Thousand Island

Kraft: Golden Italian, Zesty Italian, French Caesar, Thousand Island

Litehouse: Bacon Bleu Cheese, Balsamic Vinaigrette, Bleu Cheese, Buttermilk Ranch, Caesar, Coleslaw Dressing, Salsa Ranch, Thousand Island, Zesty Italian Vinaigrette

Newman's Own: Creamy Caesar, Lite Italian, Parmesan and Roasted Garlic, Lite Balsamic Vinaigrette, Ranch

Safeway Brand Zesty Italian (Lite and Regular)

Wishbone Russian Dressing

SALAMI

Applegate Farms Salami

Boar's Head Beef Salami, Genoa Salami (natural casing), Hard Salami

Gallo Salami

Louis Rich Honeysuckle White Hickory Smoked Cooked Turkey Salami

SALSA/PICANTE SAUCE

Albertson's Brand Picante Sauce

Clint's Texas Hot Sauce

Emeril's Original Recipe Salsa

Green Mountain Gringo: Hot, Mild, Medium Salsa

Heinz TGI Fridays Salsas (all)

Herdez Mild Salsa Verde

La Victoria: Salsa Brava, Hot Sauce

Mrs. Renfro's: Hot, Mild Salsa

Newman's Own Bandito Salsa: Hot, Medium, Mild

Newman's Own: Mild, Medium, Hot, Roasted Garlic, Peach, Pineapple, Tequila Lime

Ortega: Black Bean & Corn, Original, Garden, Picante

Tostitos All Natural Medium (mild) Chunky Salsa

SAUSAGE

Boar's Head: Kielbasa, Smoked Sausage

Hatfield: Jumbo Country Links, Classic Country Sausage Roll, Classic Country Links

J. C. Potter Pork: Regular, Hot, Sage, Lite, Italian Style, Taco Seasoned

Jennie-O: Breakfast Lover's Turkey Sausage, Hot Italian Sausage

Johnsonville Chorizo Breakfast Sausage

Johnsonville Original Breakfast Sausage: Original, Vermont Maple, Hickory Smoked

Jones All-natural Pork Sausage (many varieties)

Safeway Select Brand: Smoked Beef, Italian, Turkey, Chicken Parmesan Basil

SEAFOOD STOCK

Kitchen Basics

SESAME OIL

Eden Foods Organic Sesame Oil: Extra Virgin, Toasted

House of Tsang Pure Sesame Oil

Lee Kum Kee Sesame Oil

Sun Luck Pure Sesame Oil

SHERBET AND SORBET

Bluebell Sherbet: Lemon, Orange, Pineapple

Häagan-Dazs Sorbet: Coconut, Mango, Orchard Peach, Raspberry, Strawberry, Zesty Lemon

SHORTENING

Crisco: all products (except No Stick Spray with Flour)

Spectrum Organic All-vegetable Nonhyrodgenated
    Shortening

SOFT DRINKS

Canada Dry Ginger Ale

Coca-Cola: regular and Diet

Diet Rite

Dr Pepper (all flavors)

Fresca

Schweppes (all flavors)

7UP

Sprite (and diet)

SOUP

Pacific Natural Foods Broth

SOUP, CHICKEN

Health Valley Cream of Chicken Soup

Pacific Chicken and Wild Rice

Pacific Chicken Pho

Pacific Cream of Chicken Condensed Soup

Progresso: Traditional Chicken Rice with Vegetable,
    Traditional Chicken Cheese Enchilada Flavor, High
    Fiber Chicken, Tuscany

SOUP, CREAM OF CELERY

Imagine Cream of Celery Soup

SOUP, FRENCH ONION

Progresso Vegetable Classics French Onion

SOUP, MUSHROOM

Amy's Organic Cream of Mushroom Soup

Imagine Organic Creamy Portabello Mushroom Soup

Progresso Vegetable Classics Creamy Mushroom
    Soup

SOY SAUCE

Eden Foods Tamari Organic Soy Sauce

Kikkoman: Soy Sauce, Teriyaki Marinade and Sauce

La Choy Soy Sauce

Premier Japan Organic Gluten-free Teriyaki Sauce

San-J Organic Gluten-free Tamari Soy Sauce (Gold
    Label)

San-J Organic Gluten-free Reduced-sodium Tamari
    Soy Sauce (Platinum Label)

SPICES, HERBS AND SEASONINGS

Dynasty Five-Spice Powder: Not certified but website
    says it's 5 ground spices only

Eden Foods Sea Salt

Emeril's Essence: Original, Italian, Bayou Blast

Grandma Ferdon's spices: All, including sea salt

Lawry's: Seasoned Salt, Garlic Salt, Lemon Pepper

McCormick: All single-ingredient spices, all extracts

McCormick Taco Seasoning

Old Bay Seasoning

Paul Prudhomme: All items except Breading Magic and Gumbo Gravy Mix

Safeway Brand: All pure spices

Spice Hunter: Spices and spice blends do not contain gluten with the exception of Grill Shakers Rib Seasoning

Spice Islands: All single-ingredient spices

Texjoy All-purpose Cajun Seasoning

Wick Fowler's 2-alarm Chili Mix

STEAK SAUCE

A-1 Steak Sauce

Heinz Jack Daniel's Steak Sauce

SYRUP

Karo: All syrups

TACO AND TOSTADA SHELLS

Mission: Corn Tortillas, Taco Shells, Tostadas and Corn Gorditas

Ortega: White Corn Taco Shells, Yellow Corn Taco Shells

Ortega Tostado Shells

TERIYAKI SAUCE

Heinz Jack Daniels EZ Marinader, Teriyaki variety

Kikkoman

Premier Japan: Organic Wheat-free Teriyaki Sauce

TOFFEE BITS

Heath Bits o' Brickle

Skor English Toffee Bits

TOMATOES, CANNED

Contadina: All crushed tomatoes, diced tomatoes, stewed tomatoes, and whole tomatoes

Del Monte: Whole tomatoes and tomato products

Eden Food Diced Tomatoes with Green Chilies, Organic

Hunt's: All tomatoes and Diced Tomatoes with Basil, Garlic and Oregano

Hy-Vee Brand Diced Tomatoes and Green Chilies, Mexican Lime and Cilantro

Muir Glen Organic: Whole Tomatoes, Crushed Tomatoes with Basil

Pastene San Marzano Italian Plum Tomatoes with Basil Leaf

Pomi: Strained Italian Tomatoes, Chopped Tomatoes

Ro-Tel Diced Tomatoes and Green Chilies: Mild, Original

Safeway Brand: All canned tomatoes, tomato sauce, tomato paste

TOMATO PASTE

Del Monte Organic Tomato Paste

Hunt's Tomato Paste

Muir Glen Organic Tomato Paste

TOMATO SAUCE

365 Organic (Whole Foods store brand)

Contadina: All Contadina tomato and tomato products are gluten free except Contadina Tomato Paste with Italian Seasoning

Del Monte: All tomatoes and tomato products

Hunt's Tomato Sauce

Muir Glen Organic Tomato Sauce

TORTILLAS

El Lago Tortillas

Food for Life Wheat- and Gluten-free Brown Rice Tortillas

La Tortilla Factory Wheat- and Gluten-free Soft Wraps

Mission Foods: Corn Tortillas, Corn Tortilla Chips, Taco Shells

Trader Joe's: Brown Rice Tortillas, Corn Tortillas

Winn-Dixie Brand Corn Tortillas

TURKEY

Applegate Naturals: Roasted Turkey Breast, Organic Turkey Bacon, Organic Turkey Burgers, Natural Smoked Turkey Breast

Jennie-O: Turkey Burgers—all white meat, Maple Turkey Bacon, Split Turkey Breast, Turkey Breast Roast

TURKEY STOCK

Kitchen Basics: Original Turkey Cooking Stock

VANILLA

Adams Best Vanilla

McCormick Extract

VEGETABLE BROTH

Health Valley Fat Free Vegetable-flavored Broth

Pacific Organic Natural Vegetable Stock

Swanson Certified Organic Vegetable Broth

VEGETABLES, CANNED

Del Monte: All canned vegetables are gluten-free per the website

VEGETABLES, FROZEN

All plain frozen vegetables

VINEGAR

Bragg's Organic Apple Cider Vinegar

Heinz Apple Cider Vinegar, Red Wine Vinegar

Napa Valley Naturals: All products

Newman's Own Balsamic Vinegar

Regina: All vinegars

Suma Organic Balsamic Vinegar

NOTE: *Please be very careful to get "apple cider vinegar" and not the "apple cider flavored-vinegar." There is a difference. Make sure that the word "flavored" is not included in the name of the product. Generally, you can almost always have a white distilled vinegar.*

WORCESTERSHIRE SAUCE

French's

Heinz

Lea & Perrins

XANTHAN GUM

Bob's Red Mill

Ener G Xanthan Gum

YEAST

Bob's Red Mill Active Dry Yeast

Fleischmann's All-natural Active Dry Yeast

Red Star Active Dry Yeast: Red Star, SAF, and Bakipan

BOOZE AND YOUR BAR GUIDE

A WELL-STOCKED GLUTEN-FREE BAR

"No chord of music has yet been found to even equal that sweet sound which to my mind all else surpasses . . . the clink of ice in crystal glasses."   —Trader Vic Bergeron

What? Beer contains gluten? Yes. So do ale, lager, vodka—oh, yeah, many brands contain gluten. Here you have it . . . we tell you what brands we like that are gluten-free. For starters, potato vodkas, and unflavored rums and tequila are naturally gluten-free. Distilled whiskey, good brandies, and Cognac are also gluten-free. It is the added flavorings you need to watch out for. The list for gluten-free liquor continues to grow. We're going to tell you some of our favorites.

Typically red and white wines are safe; just stay away from the malted wine coolers. The smartest doctor we know says that you can have one to two drinks, provided you don't have another condition that makes consumption of alcohol unhealthy. Don't be pretentious about wines. Drink what you like. You can enjoy a good $10 or $20 bottle.

But if you are going to serve cocktails to others, make them with the best ingredients that you can afford. Don't be a chiseler. Guests will talk about you for years behind your back if you serve the cheap stuff, or heaven forbid, water down the booze because you are a skinflint.

We can't emphasize enough the importance of measuring the ingredients in cocktails: Professional bartenders measure their ingredients, and so should you. We urge you to buy a bartenders' drink guide. People like a good cocktail and, unless they are alcoholics, they don't like them overly strong.

BEER

Anheuser Busch Redbridge Beer

Bard's Gold Beer

Bard's Tale Dragon's Gold Beer

Green's All-Natural Gluten-Free Amber Ale

Lake Front Brewery New Grist Gluten-Free Beer

New Planet Tread Lightly Ale

O'Brien: Brown Ale, Natural Light and Pale Ale

Ramapo Valley Brewery: Honey Blonde Lager Beer and Passover Honey Beer

BOURBON

Maker's Mark Bourbon Whisky

BRANDY

Clear Creek Framboise (Raspberry) Brandy

Clear Creek Kirschwasser Brandy

Clear Creek Mirabelle Plum Brandy

Clear Creek Pear Brandy

COGNAC

Hine Vintage Cognac

Larsen Cognac

Maison Brillet Cognac

GIN

Gordon's Gin

Tanqueray Gin

GRAPPA

Clear Creek Grappa Moscato

Clear Creek Grappa Nebbiola

Clear Creek Grappa of Pinot Grigio

Clear Creek Grappa of Oregon Pinot Noir

Clear Creek Grappa Sangiovese

INGREDIENTS, OTHER

Cholula Hot Sauce

Granulated sugar

Sea salt

Oranges, limes and lemons

Mint leaves

Spice Islands Celery Salt

Tabasco sauce

Worcestershire sauce (see list of brands in Pantry List above)

LIQUEURS

Amaretto DiSaronno

Clear Creek: Blackberry, Cassis, Cherry, Loganberry

Clear Creek Eaux de Vie Kirschwasser (Cherry Brandy)

Drambuie

Drambuie Sylk Cream

Kahlua Coffee Liqueur

MIXERS

Club soda

Ginger ale

POM Wonderful pomegranate juice

7UP

Tonic water

Water, bottled

OUZO

Barbayanni Ouzo

Enom Ouzo

Giakarinis Ouzo

RUM

Bacardi Rum: 151, Gold, Limon, Select, Bacardi
    Superior

Captain Morgan Rum

Demerara El Dorado Rum

Malibu Island Spiced Rum

SCOTCH, BOURBON, WHISKEY/WHISKY BLENDS

Bulleit Bourbon

Crawford's Whisky

Crown Royal Whisky

George Dickel Whisky

Jack Daniel's Tennessee Whiskey

Johnnie Walker Scotch Whisky

Seagram's VO Whisky

TEQUILA

Bacardi Tequila Cazadores

Jose Cuervo: Silver, Gold

Pepe Lopez White Tequila

Sauza White Tequila

VERMOUTH

Martini & Rossi: Extra Dry, Rosso, Bianco

VODKA

Blue Ice Potato Vodka

Cold River Vodka

Gordon's Vodka

Grey Goose Vodka

Kamachatka Vodka

Teton Glacier Potato Vodka

Tito's Handmade Vodka

Zodiac Potato Vodka

INDEX